TOURISM AND TRANSPORT
ISSUES AND AGENDA FOR THE NEW MILLENNIUM

ADVANCES IN TOURISM RESEARCH

Series Editor: Professor Stephen J. Page
University of Stirling, U.K.
s.j.page@stir.ac.uk

Advances in Tourism Research series publishes monographs and edited volumes that comprise state-of-the-art research findings, written and edited by leading researchers working in the wider field of tourism studies. The series has been designed to provide a cutting edge focus for researchers interested in tourism, particularly the management issues now facing decision makers, policy analysts and the public sector. The audience is much wider than just academics and each book seeks to make a significant contribution to the literature in the field of study by not only reviewing the state of knowledge relating to each topic but also questioning some of the prevailing assumptions and research paradigms which currently exist in tourism research. The series also aims to provide a platform for further studies in each area by highlighting key research agendas which will stimulate further debate and interest in the expanding area of tourism research. The series is always willing to consider new ideas for innovative and scholarly books, inquiries should be made directly to the Series Editor.

Published:

THOMAS
Small Firms in Tourism: International Perspectives

KERR
Tourism Public Policy and the Strategic Management of Failure

WILKS & PAGE
Managing Tourist Health and Safety in the New Millennium

BAUM & LUNDTORP
Seasonality in Tourism

ASHWORTH & TUNBRIDGE
The Tourist-Historic City: Retrospect and Prospect of Managing the Heritage City

RYAN & PAGE
Tourism Management: Towards the New Millennium

SONG & WITT
Tourism Demand Modelling and Forecasting: Modern Econometric Approaches

TEO, CHANG & HO
Interconnected Worlds: Tourism in Southeast Asia

Related Elsevier Journals - sample copies available on request

Journal of Air Transport Management
Annals of Tourism Research
International Journal of Hospitality Management
International Journal of Intercultural Relations
Tourism Management
World Development

TOURISM AND TRANSPORT
ISSUES AND AGENDA FOR THE NEW MILLENNIUM

EDITED BY

LES LUMSDON

University of Central Lancashire, U.K.

STEPHEN J. PAGE

University of Stirling, U.K.

2004

ELSEVIER

Amsterdam – Boston – Heidelberg – London – New York – Oxford
Paris – San Diego – San Francisco – Singapore – Sydney – Tokyo

ELSEVIER B.V.
Sara Burgerhartstraat 25
P.O. Box 211,
1000 AE Amsterdam
The Netherlands

ELSEVIER Inc.
525 B Street, Suite 1900
San Diego,
CA 92101-4495
USA

ELSEVIER Ltd
The Boulevard, Langford
Lane Kidlington,
Oxford OX5 1GB
UK

ELSEVIER Ltd
84 Theobalds Road
London
WC1X 8RR
UK

First edition 2004

Library of Congress Cataloging in Publication Data
A catalog record is available from the Library of Congress.

British Library Cataloguing in Publication Data
A catalogue record is available from the British Library.

ISBN: 0-08-044172-6

⊗The paper used in this publication meets the requirements of ANSI/NISO Z39.48-1992 (Permanence of Paper). Printed in The Netherlands.

Contents

Contributors

William R. Black
Department of Geography, Indiana University, Bloomington, IN 47401, USA

David Briggs
Manchester Metropolitan University, Hollings Faculty, Manchester, UK

Paul Freathy
Department of Marketing, University of Stirling, Stirling, UK

Derek Hall
Scottish Agricultural College, Auchincruive, Ayr, UK

Les Lumsdon
Lancashire Business School, University of Central Lancashire, Preston, UK

Gianna Moscardo
James Cook University, Townsville, Queensland 4814, Australia

Aylin Orbaşlı
Oxford Brookes University, Oxford, UK

Elwyn Owen
University of Wales in Cardiff, UK

Stephen J. Page
Department of Marketing, University of Stirling, Stirling, UK

Philip L. Pearce
James Cook University, Townsville, Queensland 4814, Australia

Bruce Prideaux
University of Queensland, Ipswich Campus, Queensland, Australia

Steve Shaw
Centre for Tourism, University of North London, UK

Rodney Tolley
Staffordshire University, College Road, Stoke on Trent, Staffordshire, UK

Brian Turton
University of Keele, Staffordshire, UK

Robert E. Wood
Rutgers University, Camden, USA

List of Figures

List of Tables

Preface

Many researchers and reviewers will probably consider the contents of this book and ask themselves — why a research monograph covering transport and tourism, when a number of well established texts have emerged that address the transport-tourism interface in some detail with numerous case studies and examples for undergraduate students. But many of these studies do not develop the higher level research agendas which are needed if subject areas are to progress. With the proliferation of research outputs in the rapidly expanding field of tourism, these comments may be germane and in fact valid at a very superficial level when any search of the main journals will highlight a number of papers that seemingly address the area of transport and tourism. Indeed, *Elsevier Science* publishes many of the mainstream journals within the transport field, most notably the *Transportation Research A-F Series*, *Transport Policy* and the *Journal of Transport Geography*. It also publishes a well established and specialist *Journal of Air Transport Management* which has become the key source of research on the air transport sector, much of which has a direct or indirect bearing on the global growth and development of tourism.

Yet to assume that these journals and the interconnections they recognise with tourism are well worn areas of research is not borne out from a detailed analysis of the articles in these journals. In the case of the *Journal of Air Transport Management*, it published six articles between 1994 and 2003 with a direct reference to tourism in its abstracts and contents with a further 23 that referred to "travel," mainly in relation to air services. Similarly the journal *Transport Policy* makes no mention to tourism and some 52 articles it published have referred to travel, with some elements relevant to tourism but not explicitly discussed. In the Transportation Research collection of journals, only four articles are listed under "tourism" which appeared between 1981 and 2003 in *Transportation Research A*, while one in *Transportation Research D*. Similarly in the *Journal of Transport Geography* of the three articles listed under "tourism," only one of these actually addresses tourism issues explicitly. Whilst a wide range of associated terms may have widened the range of articles emerging, there is a general trend here: tourism is not pursued as a theme vigorously by transportation researchers. It is not their passion and not surprisingly, research funding from funding agencies (with the exception of the EU) have largely been concerned with non-leisure traffic.

Critics could rightly point to these journals not specifically being concerned with issues of tourism and that there are more specialist journals which should deal with these themes. However, that said, many of these transportation research journals are set within a wider social science framework which does indicate that wider analyses of transport and tourism are certainly respectable areas for research. But it would appear that this has not been the case with a few exceptions. Yet if one argues that it is to the tourism literature we must turn to gain these conceptual insights and developments in the interconnections and interface between tourism and transport, then we are equally disappointed by the lack of progress in this area. For example, a search of the journal *Tourism Management* using the term 'transport' yields 41 items, but only 20 of these are articles published between 1982 and 2003, less than one article for each year of publication. For a journal which publishes around 30–40 articles a year as full length research articles or research notes/case studies this will give some indication of the limited number of papers in this area. Similarly the journal *Annals of Tourism Research* lists 54 items under "transport" but only four can specifically be deemed to be full-length research articles.

Therefore, given this paucity of literature, it is no major surprise that within the tourism field, transport research remains substantially neglected despite its dynamic role in the creation of tourist movements at different geographical scales. Whilst a number of tourism researchers have legitimately published their research findings on transport topics in other journals, the field has still not substantially progressed in the last decade. Much of the research remains case-study driven in the business and management fields, while more systematic evaluations, often based on highly quantitative methods is derived from transportation researchers and a limited number of tourism researchers.

Perhaps transport and tourism are not the "hot" topics of the new millennium for tourism researchers as sustainability and ecotourism were in the 1990s. Perhaps the neglect is based on a somewhat pigeon-holed view of transport and tourism being two discrete areas that researchers should not cross as the research in transportation is dominated by transport economists. Equally, the language and terminology of these researchers is not the everyday language and approach which many tourism researchers adopt, dependent upon their own disciplinary bent. It is clear that transport economics is also a more defined area of study with a much longer history of development than the study of tourism per se, and so the tourism researchers probably have to stray into areas which have traditionally been the preserve of economists. The policy area also been dominated by many of the same researchers who have worked in transport economics with some notable exceptions and tourism has not been seen as a priority. Whatever explanations one adopts toward the existing state of knowledge on transport and tourism as a focus for research, it is undeniable that there are clear synergies.

Whatever the past development of research agendas may have been, it is clear that a greater degree of cooperation is now needed across disciplines and subject areas as has permeated mainstream transportation research, to cross-fertilise tourism research. Tourism is so heavily dependent upon transportation that to not study its interactions and significance in tourism is a massive oversight and neglect that will continuously hold back our understanding of the operation of tourism as a business and global phenomenon. Even perspectives from transport history, a somewhat distant area from tourism has many important perspectives to offer the tourism researcher. For example, with the current focus of tourism researchers on integration within the tourism industry and globalisation, they seem to think this is a new concept which the tourism industry has developed and utilised in the post-war period. In fact many examples of integration and nascent globalisation exist. For example, the development of global shipping routes by P&O in the Victorian and Edwardian period simply adopted business strategies that many airlines have developed in the post-war period in terms of route competition. Similarly, the strategies of tour operator

integration which the large European companies have pursued in the
be seen in other sectors as far back as the 1920s. For example, with
British railway companies in the 1920s to create the "Great Four"
and Southern), integration occurred through moving into bus operation
railway hotels to accommodate guests most notably in Scotland with Gleneagles
development of golf tourism, as well as the utilisation of modern marketing methods such
as the use of advertising. Here the iconography of the inter-war years railway advertising
and highlights the significance of applying interdisciplinary approaches to appreciate the
sophisticated messages which these companies sought to use to attract leisure travel.

Similarly, the use of sales and promotion techniques highlights the evolution of strategies
to develop modes of yield management in relation to tourist traffic and to segment markets
in much the same way as the airlines have done in the post-war years. Thus, what is important to stress is that tourism research needs to be informed and driven by interdisciplinary
perspectives and this is no where more evident than in the transport-tourism area. So what
can this book offer to developing this agenda?

The editors are realistic in accepting that this monograph will not address all the points
raised so far in this discussion. In fact it will not lead to a radical reconceptualisation of
the area. But what this book will do is re-evaluate some of the key issues which now face
this important area of research in the early years of the new millennium. It offers some
fresh insights into the way forward for transport and tourism research as a unified area of
study by questioning where research exists, what agendas might be necessary to advance
our understanding and where new developments are occurring. The contributors to this
book make significant contributions to further this end by examining tourism and transport
as a phenomenon which deserves a better research effort than is currently the case. The
editors also recognise that without raising the profile of this area of research, it will remain
neglected and distant from many of the existing researchers with transport and tourism
interests. At the same time, the contributors were asked to examine issues they felt were
important in the tourism-transport interface and consequently a broad interdisciplinary set
of contributions widens the scope for further research in these areas.

We hope you will find the contributions both illuminating and valuable in an area which
students, researchers and practitioners constantly criticise for failing to offer sufficient
research outputs and activity. Whilst many journals such as *Travel and Tourism Analyst* and
market research studies exist to provide up to date and accessible data on transport-related
themes, this monograph recognises that it is the conceptualisation of transport and tourism
which offers many future areas for development which can be informed by empirical
studies. Therefore, we hope the contributions in this book will be both timely and valuable
in taking the debate forward on transport and tourism.

Stephen J. Page and
Les Lumsdon
May 2003

Chapter 1

Progress in Transport and Tourism Research: Reformulating the Transport-Tourism Interface and Future Research Agendas

Les Lumsdon and Stephen J. Page

Introduction

The significance of transport as an integral component of the tourism system has been the subject of discussion in the tourism literature since the 1970s (Chew 1987; Lundgren 1973). The functional element of travel, and especially the transitory stage or flows between generating and receiving destinations has been modelled in a similar manner to gravity models in transport, although in reality these tend to simplify the complexity of trip making for tourism purposes (Hobson & Uysal 1992; Travis 1989). The nature of tourism flows is illustrated in Figure 1.1 This implies that although transport is clearly an essential element in the operation of tourism, the conceptualisation of the interface between transport and tourism requires further investigation (Laws 1991).

In a wider context, the development of a theoretical framework of analysis has focused on a systems approach. The tourism system is defined by McIntosh *et al.* (1995: 21) as a "set of inter-related groups co-ordinated to form a unified whole and organized to accomplish a set of goals." Mill & Morrison (1992), in explaining the tourism system highlight the exchange process between consumers and suppliers by way of four integrating components, the market, the travel element, the destination and the marketing mechanism. These elements are linked, in the first instance, by flows of information followed by visitors travelling between originating and receiving destinations. The processes, which enable this to happen, through for example, travel intermediaries and transport providers facilitate the tourism experience. A number of authors expand our knowledge about the nature of the tourism system, including Getz (1986), and Gunn (1994); they conclude that it comprises a mesh of interrelated, functional relationships which are interdependent, dynamic and embrace both supply and demand. The first section of this chapter seeks to explain the interface between transport and tourism with reference to the tourism and transport systems. In the second part the authors address some of the major challenges constraining tourism transport and how this might shape the agenda for future research.

Tourism and Transport: Issues and Agenda for the New Millennium
Copyright © 2004 Published by Elsevier Ltd.
ISBN: 0-08-044172-6

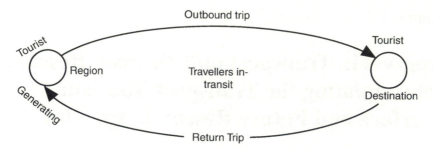

Figure 1.1: The tourism system. *Source:* Redrawn from Page 1994, 1999.

Whilst most authors analyse the tourism system in a holistic manner, it has also been readily divided into sub systems. For example, Leiper (1990) analysed the tourist attraction system and in relation to the transport element, Page (1999a) discussed the tourism transport system. Both authors reveal structures and processes which characterise these sub-systems and provide an explanation of how they fit within the wider tourism system. Page (1999a) defines the tourism transport system as a group of factors, which affect the entire tourism experience, from pre-travel planning to the last stage of the return journey. The approach is cognisant of a behavioural approach which explains why people travel and why they choose different forms of holiday, destination and transport (Oppermann 1997; Pizam & Mansfield 1999). For example, a number of studies have undertaken preliminary investigations into choice behaviour in relation to car-based tourism (Lew 1991). In Chapter 2, the nature of motivation and choice is extended by Pearce and Moscardo. In this contribution the authors draw a conceptual map to develop the connections between life cycle, tourist motivation and experiential consequences of transport using a case study of travellers in Northern Australia.

Developing the Transport-Tourism Interface: Key Conceptual Challenges

Despite the overlapping worlds of tourism and transport, there has only been limited progress evidenced in the literature. Page (1999a) points to the lack of coverage in the major transport text books and little can be sourced from the transport journal literature; this is despite the growing level of tourism trip generation within and between many regions of the world. Whilst analysis tends to be multi-disciplinary in transport as in tourism studies, the emphasis and direction of research has focused on the random utility theory which models choice of travel although this has been influenced more by human activity approach in recent years (Fox 1995). Thus, travel demand is modelled using a set of behavioural characteristics and assuming that the individual or household makes a rational choice based on the saving of time, for example. Despite its critics this approach still shapes conceptual frameworks, definitions and measurement of travel behaviour research (Hensher 2001). Thus, in transport studies, there is no conceptual difference in the approach to modelling trips for utility or leisure purposes.

There are a number of barriers which make comparisons between transport and tourism trips difficult or inoperable. For example, there is little co-ordination of data collection; transport and tourism data are inconsistent and definitional problems as to what is being measured are problematic. Indeed, some transport operators would argue that they do not actually carry tourists but only a homogenous group they label passengers. This dated perspective is losing ground with many larger operators applying marketing techniques to differentiate between market segments such as tourist and leisure travel. Thus, the definitions, which have been almost universally applied in transport studies, are not formulated similarly in tourism. In transport, for example, a trip involves a movement of a person between two places in order for activities to be undertaken. Places are usually referred to as originating and destination zones. In transport studies, a trip can be undertaken by using one mode of transport only or several modes. Furthermore, the trip can be divided into trip legs, each leg being a section of the overall trip made by one mode. The duration of the trip is the time between the start and finish of a journey. A tour refers to more than one trip from an originating zone to other places, but finally returning to the base destination zone. Tourism studies draw on a parallel framework but the conceptual base and definitions often differ. For example, the terms "trip" and "tour" are less clearly specified in tourism than in transport studies. Journey purpose is also defined differently in that transport trips can be made for work, leisure, and educational purposes whereas tourism trips include business, pleasure, visiting friends and relatives, health and religion. There are currently attempts to harmonise conceptual frameworks and data collection, mainly in relation to long distance travel, but they are still in gestation. For example, in the European Union the Methods for European Surveys of Travel Behaviour (MEST) and the DATELINE studies are seeking to co-ordinate survey design, procedures and sampling across EU member states. Within the tourism sector, there have also been several recent developments to align research and monitoring approaches which includes data on transport (Eurostat 1998; World Tourist Organization 2000).

In reality, the relationship between transport and tourism is asymmetrical. Transport is the facilitator without which tourism could not exist whereas the reverse is clearly not true. This being the case and given that the study of transport focuses on utility, such as journeys to work, school and other everyday personal business, tourism and recreational trips tend to be subsumed in a generalised modelling of transport systems. In a recent call for a widened research agenda in transport so as to integrate transport and wider socio-economic activity implicit references to were made to include leisure (Preston 2001). However, the current position is that transport analysis is based on core concepts such as derived demand in relation to trips which are made for *any* purpose. This begs the question as to whether tourism trips are sufficiently different to utility trips to warrant specific attention.

Are Tourism Trips Sufficiently Distinctive for Transportation Research?

The debate has focused on two key areas of discussion; the nature of trip characteristics and the volume of tourism trips. Firstly, there are several discernible differences in terms of trip characteristics. Most utility trips are made on a regular, and often habitual basis within the locality or a wider zone within which a person resides. In contrast, the tourism trip, by definition, involves journeys to places other than a resident's usual environment. As many tourism trips are not only infrequent, but are also first time or singular journeys, the visitor is often unfamiliar with the transport systems and available options. Thus, behavioural patterns are likely to be different; decisions as to where and how a visitor travels is partly determined by a chosen activity but is also more likely to be a coping strategy based on limited information. This applies not only to the transitory phase of travel but also at the destination. Thus, the choice of mode is likely to be affected by the level of information available, the choice of alternatives and ease of access to them.

Secondly, the volume of trips is an important factor within the pattern of overall demand. Tourism trips tend to be far longer on average than utility trips and have been growing at a faster rate than journeys for other purposes. Tourism has enjoyed continued growth for the past four decades. International tourist arrivals have risen from 60 million in 1960 to 692 million in 2001 (World Tourism Organization 2002). This figure excludes domestic tourism in each country which is estimated to inflate this aggregate figure tenfold (Cooper *et al.* 1998). There is, however, no overall estimation to indicate the percentage of tourism trips in relation to all cross-border trips at a global level. Almost all countries are both generators of tourism markets and receiving destinations. However, there is a major imbalance on an inter-regional and intra-regional basis. In developing countries outbound tourism is relatively small although even limited growth in an outward market can adversely affect the tourism balance of trade. In the North, countries such as Germany with a population of 80 million and the U.K. with a population of 58 million generate the highest proportion of outbound tourism trips per annum per capita. In the European Union, it is estimated that tourist travel accounts for 9% of all passenger kilometres and the average length of travel per capita is 1,800 km per annum (European Environmental Agency 2003). In terms of cross border travel, tourism accounts for approximately 75% of all international trips and 20–30% of all domestic trips (Artist 2000). Of the 75% of international trips these can be sub-categorised into 61% long staying holidays and 13% short breaks (European Tourism Monitor 1998). However, the trend is for people to take shorter holidays. For example, in France, it is estimated that between 1975 and 1994 the number of tourism trips per person increased from 3.1 to 4.8 per annum and that the average length of each holiday fell from 18 to 13 days (European Environmental Agency 2003). It is forecast that there will be far more short breaks in future years; stimulated by higher rates of disposable income, cheaper travel costs, more free time and life-style values which favour travel.

The lack of recognition of tourism as a major generator of trips in transport planning at the region, country and destination level remains the subject of discussion. However, there are issues which require further research, and at the outset there is a need for a clarity in definition. As a starting point, the following section draws upon Page's earlier work on tourist transport which encompasses the entire experience of travelling on a mode of transport. It is important, however, to distinguish between transport for tourism and the tourism transport experience. This offers a theoretical base on which to build a sound understanding of tourist travel behaviour. It is also important to consider the implications for destination development, a line of investigation progressed in Chapter 6 by Prideaux when he refers to the key transport factors which stimulate or inhibit the growth of tourism places. Turton in Chapter 5 also addresses the subject but referring to the difficulties experienced by developing countries, which seek to use airlines as a statement of national identity and at the same time compete in the market for long haul tourists (Raguraman 1997).

Transport for Tourism

Gunn (1994: 69) comments that "... transportation is not usually a goal; it is a necessary evil of tourist travel." Transport in this context is utilitarian and the degree of satisfaction or utility is a function of time which is a proxy for cost; it is construed as derived demand where the mode of travel adds little or no direct intrinsic value to the tourism trip. Thus, in terms of tourism economics, travel has been traditionally modelled as a cost rather than a benefit (Prideaux 2000). The visitor is confronted with a trade off. There is a choice between the time spent and cost of resources expended on a journey in relation to a willingness to travel a given distance in order to enjoy recreation at a destination. This is sometimes referred to as the travel distance decay model (Clawson & Knetsch 1966; Loomis & Walsh 1997). It has considerable implications for destinations or attractions seeking to attract visitors from longer distances.

Modes of travel from originating to destination zones include the bicycle, horse, car, coach, train, sea and air travel and all cases involve walking. Of these the car and air travel dominate in most parts of the world but this is not always the case. In the Pacific, sea travel is more important, and between capital and principal cities train and coach travel can be the dominant mode for tourism travel. Many tourism trips involve a degree of inter-modality. The package holiday, for example, might include a taxi trip to the airport, a walk trip through the air terminal, a flight, followed by a coach transfer to the hotel at the destination. In comparison, many independent domestic holidays might involve only one form of transport such as the car.

The modal choice factor is also important, not only for the visitor, but also in terms of externalities generated in the transitory and receiving destinations. In terms of international travel, air transport accounts for 43% of trips whilst road represents 42%. Rail travel accounts for only 8% of the total and sea transport 7% (World Tourist Organization 2000). Analysis of the data indicates that there has been a gradual increase in air travel over road surface transport. There are, however, regional differences. Air travel is more important in Latin America and South East Asia in comparison to Europe. This is a reflection of distances between the generating and receiving destinations as well as the lack of alternative modes of travel. In general, air travel dominates long haul but gives way to road, rail and sea for medium length trips (Tolley & Turton 1995). The car tends to dominate in the mass market for short distance trips within and between countries in Europe and North America.

Transport as Tourism

Within the tourism transport system, it is also appropriate to differentiate transport as a means to an end and transport which is integral to the tourism experience. The discussion about transport as the facilitator of tourism has, for the most part, overshadowed research into transport *as* tourism, a perspective which suggests that transport can be an integrative part of the tourism offering rather than simply providing access to the experience (Cooper *et al.* 1998; Page 1999a). The concept "tourism transport" explains how tourism and transport can come together as the tourism transport experience. In respect to the former element, transport still serves a purpose of moving visitors from place to place but in so doing it also provides an attraction in its own right, either by virtue of its location, heritage, degree of interest, novelty or health-related potential. This form of tourism transport is planned and designed to form an essential part of overall tourism experience. Thus, Orbaşlı and Shaw, Chapter 7, advocate the sensitive planning of transport in historic cities, not only as a circulatory mechanism to facilitate visitor access but also to enhance the public realm to conserve cities as places to enjoy a quality of life.

The extent to which a form of transport is purely utilitarian on the one hand or a moving visitor attraction on the other can be represented as a continuum. It is important to recognise that almost all forms of transport contribute to the overall tourism experience. However, transport for tourism tends to be characterised by its multi-purpose and market, functionality, directness, and speed. Clearly, tour operators and destinations seek to make transitory arrangements convenient but they also design to add value to an overall holiday by using the travel time to sell goods and services, interpretation and educational guidance to the visitor. Nevertheless, the design form concentrates on processing people as speedily as possible between generating and receiving zones. Alternatively, the tourism transport experience tends to be designed or in use mainly for the visitor market only, is often indirect as it seeks to offer a different perspective of a destination, and is rarely fast. The travel cost model does not apply in this context. The expenditure of time or duration of travel is the prime purpose of the trip and *is* the main benefit and therefore seemingly cannot be modelled as a cost. In this respect, it is important to determine the key factors and processes, which constitute the tourism transport experience. The nature of the tourism transport experience is defined either by a single mode or a combination of transport modes, it still involves movement from one location to another, and a degree of attraction or more precisely a satisfaction of wants associated with the actual process of travelling. The key distinction in transport for tourism tends to offer low intrinsic value within the overall experience and the tourism transport experience a higher intrinsic value. The continuum is represented in Figure 1.2 which shows that some forms of transport, such as the taxi or metro are designed to move people at speed between two points whereas at the other end of the scale, cruising or cycle tourism tend to be designed as the tourism experience.

Recent papers illustrate the concept of transport as tourism, including those featuring train travel (Dann 1994; Halsall 2001), cruises (Morrison *et al.* 1996; Travel & Tourism Analyst 1998), scenic car tours (Lew 1991) and thematic routes (Murray & Graham 1997). The continuum simplifies the reality. For example, one writer refers to a day trip excursion as "more properly a form of attraction than transport" (Bull 1991: 32). It would depend, of course, on the nature of travel used on a day excursion, and the degree to which it enhances (or detracts) from the tourism experience. This is an underlying principle of the tourism transport system, i.e. that all or some of the transport components have at least the potential to add directly to the value of the tourism experience. This theoretical proposition is in juxtaposition to utilitarian transport, which is purely functional and adds little or no intrinsic value to the tourism experience at a destination. As Page concludes:

Transport as utility   ————————————————————▶   Transport as tourism

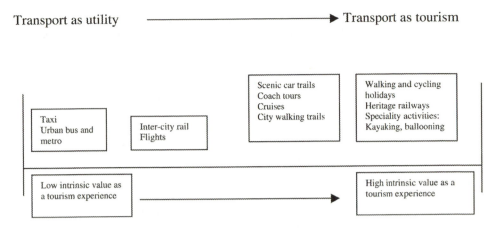

Figure 1.2: The tourism transport continuum.

> The mode of transport tourists choose can often form an integral part of their journeys and experience, a feature often neglected in the existing research on tourism
>
> (Page 1999b: 8).

In summary, tourism transport is a generic term which covers all trips within the tourism transport system. However, there is increasing recognition that transport is an attraction in its own right and therefore should be planned and marketed differently to transport for tourism. Thus, Wood provides a detailed debate of the cruise line sector as a classic form of the tourism transport experience and points to the driving forces which have seen this sector increase in size on a global scale during the past two decades. The issue is also discussed in another context by Lumsdon & Tolley (Chapter 11) in their appraisal of non-motorized transport. The authors draw on several case studies to illustrate the importance of walking and cycling as modes of transport at a destination but also in terms of the tourism transport experience.

Within the widening debate on transport as a crucial element of tourism, there are numerous issues that currently occupy a prominent position in the transport-tourism interface, to which our attention now turns.

Constraints on Tourist Travel

Whilst the global growth of travel has seen continued increases in volume and scale, such travel by tourists has not been unabated as different factors have also constrained its development. Among those which have been most prominent are terrorist attacks such as September 11th, 2001, conveniently labelled 9/11 which has affected tourist willingness to travel even after initial restrictions were lifted for travel to and from the USA (Goodrich 2002; Page 2002). Similarly natural disasters such as the Foot and Mouth epidemic in the U.K. led to dramatic changes in the geography of tourist travel, as rural travel was constrained by limited access in many areas further concentrating visits in gateway cities and regions within the urban hinterland (Page 2003a). These macro issues which have affected national, domestic and international travel patterns, are notable for their negative economic consequences for the transport sector. Given the capital-intensive nature of transport provision and costs of operation, any major swings in demand induced by such crises have major effects on the sector.

What is clear is that in the USA, these events contributed further to the financial problems facing major airline carriers such as United Airlines which are operating on the fringe of bankruptcy. This is also symptomatic of the profound changes now affecting the airline sector in both the nature of the traffic it handles (Doganis 2001) and the strategies it adopts in light of international restrictions and aviation policies (Chang & Williams 2002). Many of the larger carriers are still seeking to realign themselves to the realities of the new millennium as well as the greater diversity of market segments, each having their own particular idiosyncracies and specific needs.

In fact, little academic research has sought to model the state of the airline sector in relation to conditions of constrained markets. There is a notable absence in the research literature, particularly given the rapid growth of low cost carriers in Europe and elsewhere (with the exceptions of Calder 2002; Child 2000; Doganis 2001; Donne 2001; Gillen & Morrison 2003). The highly aggressive, adaptable and responsive managerial structures of these new genre of airline organisations in Europe have contributed to their continued suc-cess despite these unfavourable operating environments reported by larger carriers during the onset of macro economic constraints. A recent study by Mason *et al.* (2000) identified many of the factors which explained airline economic performance according to the stan-dardised operating costs (i.e. flying expenses, maintenance and aircraft depreciation) and indirect operating costs such as ground costs, passenger services, ticketing and sales and administration.

What is clear from the new reality of airline operation is that the low cost airlines have taken a more holistic approach to operation, using a wide range of both economic tools and business expertise in strategy and marketing. For this reason, it is useful to provide a brief discussion of this new phenomenon for tourist travel, given the impact on both the U.S. market on European markets and potential effects in Asia-Pacific, since it poses many significant policy issues for many countries (Page 1999a; Papatheodorou 2002).

The continued growth generated by low cost carriers has also been the subject of critical debate with regard to environmental impact. Forecasts of air travel highlight a sustained rate of growth across the world, albeit at a slower pace than in previous decades in some regions (Patterson & Perl 1999). In the U.K., low cost carriers have placed increased pressure on South East airports (Humphreys & Francis 2002), creating rapid growth at airports such as Stansted and Luton. Such growth also raises wider issues over airport policy and the wasteful duplication of resources with regional airports competing for business, thereby fragmenting the potential market and reducing the services which can be provided at a local level. Graham & Guyer's (2000) analysis of regional airports, and air services, in the U.K. highlighted three issues which create a conundrum for airport policy: the relationship of air transport to sustainable development; the integration of air transport with surface transport modes and the role of airport growth in relation to regional economic development. The low cost airline growth issue has certainly added a new set of policy implications in the U.K.

where the recent government consultation on airport policy (www.dftgov.uk) in June 2002 saw many of the current debates on airport development extensively documented through industry and non-industry submissions.

Even so, such policy debates focus on the internal contradictions in government policy towards the transport sector, where the airport consultation highlighted the need for more airport capacity. At the same time, there are conflicting interpretations from other research such as the Royal Commission on Environmental Pollution (2002) report on *The Environmental Effects of Civil Aircraft*. This recommended replacing short-distance flights with rail travel for environmental reasons. As Page (2003a) indicated, this report highlighted some of the implications of hidden subsidies such as aviation fuel, which is exempt from tax under international agreements. As a result, the full costs of pollution are not charged to the users and suppliers. It is estimated that this may subsidise the U.K. aviation industry by £7 billion a year and give it unfair advantages over and above other forms of tourist transport. Page (2003b) indicated that substituting air travel for rail is only successful where journey times are up to three hours in length. Yet despite these issues, low cost carriers are seemingly popular on short haul routes. Research on the new patterns of tourist travel in Eastern Europe indicate that some of this growth has been promoted by the advent of low cost carriers and lower production costs for tourism services in this region. This is likely to expand further with the growth of the new Member States to be added to the EU, known as the Central European candidate countries (CEC). It will also have an impact on the Trans European Networks (TENs) which are considered to be vital for encouragement of European travel.

The Low Cost Airlines: Development Amidst Adversity for the Global Carriers?

Much of the debate on low cost airlines emanates from the growth of SouthWest airlines in the USA since 1971. This company epitomises the traits of the low cost carrier and established many of the basic business principles of streamlined airline operations which many subsequent carriers have sought to emulate (see Table 1.1). A study by Reynolds-Feighan (2001) examined network concentration and the rise of new low cost airlines in the USA in the 1990s. It found that two types of operators could be discerned: the point to point operators such as SouthWest with relatively low levels of concentration in networks, with average non-stop flights of 500 miles or less; and those with high levels of concentration in the network with flight sectors of 750 miles or more with some connecting traffic. These organise their traffic flows and routes in a similar manner to traditional full-service carriers using small nodes or hubs.

What the low cost carriers have achieved based on the SouthWest model of airline provision and management is a cost structure well below its revenue. This means it can operate at a cost base, which is often 25–40% below that of its competitors where unrestricted fares are low. Further, many of its flight sectors are often short and so revenue per kilometre flown is relatively high, with a simple fare structure, high levels of punctuality and correspondingly high levels of customer satisfaction. What researchers have begun to focus on is the challenge of carriers such as SouthWest which have attracted business

Table 1.1: Key characteristics of low cost carriers which make them more competitive than other carriers.

- Some carriers have introduced single/one-way fares not requiring stopovers or saturday night stays to get advanced purchase (APEX) prices
- No complimentary in-flight service (no frills) which often reduce operating costs 6–7%
- One class cabins (in most cases)
- No pre-assigned seating (in most cases)
- Ticketless travel
- High frequency routes to compete with other airlines on popular destinations and up to three flights a day on low density routes
- Short turnarounds often less than half an hour, with higher aircraft rotations (i.e. the level of utilisation is higher than other airlines) and less time charged on the airport apron and runway
- The use of secondary airports where feasible (including the provision of public transport where none exists)
- Point to point flights
- Lower staffing costs, with fewer cabin crew as no complimentary in-flight service which also reduces turnaround times due to the lack of cleaning caused by food service
- Flexibility in staff rostering, a lack of overnight stays for staff at non-base locations and streamlined operations (e.g. on some airlines toilets on domestic flights are only emptied at cabin crew requests rather than at each turnaround to reduce costs)
- Many of the aircraft are leased, reducing the level of depreciation and standardising costs
- Many airline functions are outsourced, such as ground staff, check-in, minimising overheads reducing overhead costs by 11–15%
- Standardised aircraft types (i.e. Boeing 737s) to reduce maintenance costs and the range of spare parts which need to be held for repairs
- Limited office space at the airports
- Heavy emphasis on advertising, especially billboards to offset the declining use of travel agents as the main source of bookings
- Heavy dependence upon the internet and telephone for bookings
- Small administrative staff, with many sales-related staff on commission to improve performance (as well as pilots in some cases)

Source: Page (2003a).

and leisure travellers. This was a feature examined by Mason (2000) and the implications of marketing for the selection of low cost and full-service airlines in a subsequent study (Mason 2001). Research by Williams (2001), however, has ruled out the demise of charter airlines in Europe due to competition by low cost carriers, with long established charter carriers owned and run by vertically integrated tour operators. Charter airlines retain lower operating costs than low cost carriers where they are focused on core business — package holidays and a proportion of seat-only sales. Furthermore, with some low cost airlines being unprofitable, the charter market is likely to retain its cost advantage.

Therefore, these innovations in low cost flying have been translated into the low-cost revolution that has now affected the U.K. and mainland Europe, whilst other examples, which exist in Australasia and Asia, are following this pattern. The development of the low cost airline revolution in the USA means that up to 15% of all domestic air travel is on low cost carriers (Page 2003a). In Europe, this figure is much lower at 3%, although it is growing rapidly, especially in the U.K. Therefore it is certainly a notable development in a global aviation market characterised by constraints on development due to high entry barriers, vested interests and global interests represented through alliances.

Despite the success of low cost carriers, there are more underlying constraints on tourist travel which impact upon transport provision and the ability of the tourism sector to operate in a predictable environment independent of risk and crises. Some of these issues are now addressed since they add a useful context to the book.

Interdisciplinary Research Challenges in Tourism and Transport Research for the New Millennium

Health and Travel

Travel by its very nature leads to changes in the normal environment in which people live, and the move to an unfamiliar environment poses its own risks and challenges in terms of managing the health, safety and implications for tourism transport systems. The interdisciplinary nature of transport and tourism research means that there is an ever expanding body of knowledge emerging as new fruitful areas of inquiry develop through the synergies with other disciplines. It is interesting that within an emerging area of study the travel medicine literature (for example, the *Journal of Travel Medicine*), many of the studies of air travel note that over 60% of travellers are apprehensive or nervous about flying despite the global rise in the demand for air travel. The health issues which travellers encounter on tourism transport systems have assumed a significant profile for transport operators, with concerns about reducing the stress of travel through better design and ease of access to terminals. What is not so widely debated outside of the travel medicine literature are the consequences of such issues for tourist travel (see Wilks & Page 2003 for a review of this area). Travellers can be subject to a range of illnesses induced by travel on different forms of transport such as motion sickness although research is still unclear about the precise causes of this problem. Probably the most prominent issue of recent years which airlines have had to address through legal action is the recognition of *Deep Vein Thrombosis* (DVT), especially after long haul flights. Research in this area remains at an early stage and it will be some years before this is able to impact upon the ergonomic design and conditions which air travellers endure on long-haul flights. The current concern with DVT has somewhat paled into insignificance given the recent concerns associated with the spread of infections by air travellers, where close proximity to other passengers and re-circulated air poses increased risks such as Severe Acute Respiratory Syndrome (SARS).

SARS and Tourist Transport

SARS first emerged in China and Hong Kong in November 2002 and is a new virus (a corona type virus) producing flu-like symptoms which can be potentially fatal. The distribution of the virus by a number of super carriers meant that it was subsequently passed on to other travellers and then infected other areas such as Vietnam, Canada, Singapore and other regions of the world. The geographical distribution of the cases are shown in Figure 1.3 for the period from the initial outbreaks until the end of April 2003 which shows the rapid diffusion by air travellers from the initial source. This illustrates just how tourist travel can turn a regional problem into a global issue and have major repercussions for transport operators, through to crisis management measures at airports using thermal cameras to detect possible cases of fever in travellers.

The spread of cases of the virus from Gunagdong province in China to Hong Kong (Figure 1.3) occurred between February 1, 2003 and February 29, 2003 and was then spread across the globe after one infected super carrier in Hong Kong infected 12 other people who then travelled by air to: Canada, USA, Vietnam and Singapore. By April 21, 2003, there were 3,000 cases in 27 countries. Some of the effects accompanying the global media hype and publicity of the problem resulted in Cathay Pacific seeing passenger numbers drop by two thirds and losses of US$3 million a day, cutting its services by 45% (i.e. 218 flights a week). Hotel occupancy rates in Hong Kong's buoyant tourism sector slumped from 85% to 10–20% in some cases. Within Hong Kong public transport services, operated by Stagecoach, have also seen massive drops in usage which have brought about substantial financial losses. In the U.K., travel insurers in late April withdrew cover for travel to SARS-affected areas whilst airlines continued to reduce capacity. What is also interesting to observe is the response by government agencies in different countries to restricting global travel and tourism, through visa restrictions, official travel advice and the intervention of the World Health Organisation issuing travel advice regarding infected regions. It is also evident that poor crisis management in a number of destinations compounded by media activity combined to create panic, severe responses and a sudden drop in tourist travel.

Yet SARS needs to be viewed in the context of Hong Kong with a resident population of 6.8 million people. The SARS-induced panic has put between 50,000 and 100,000 jobs at risk in the tourism and associated service sector. Outbound tourism from Hong Kong has dropped 80% during the SARS outbreak while inbound has dropped by a similar proportion, especially as business travel has been cancelled. Estimates from local media in Hong Kong have reported some of the following effects on tourism:

- Drops in hotel occupancy down to single digits;
- Hotels for sale and forecasts of receiverships;
- 40% of flights to and from Hong Kong have been cancelled;
- the loss of Easter weekend business and China Golden Week in early May (two weeks trade) will lead to a loss of around US$250 million in revenue;
- up to 5,000 restaurants could close;
- 300 travel agents could be forced to close;
- economic growth in Hong Kong may only be 0.5% compared to forecasts of 3%;
    Source: McKercher (2003).

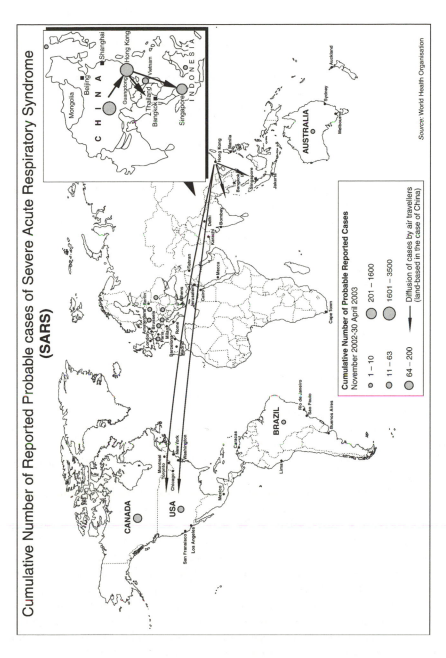

Figure 1.3: The geographical distribution of SARS cases November 2002 to April 30, 2003. *Source:* Developed from World Health Organisation disease surveillance data.

In Singapore similar problems have been posed by SARS, with visitor arrivals down 61%. This illustrates the fickle nature of tourism and the sudden impact of crises which can have devastating impacts on the transport sector when the visitors stop travelling although tourism does have the potential to recover quickly.

In addition to illnesses induced by travel, the quality of the conditions in which people travel on-board certain forms of tourist transport, particularly the quality of air, has been a great cause for concern among consumer groups in recent years. Air quality has been a major cause of concern, since many airline companies only provide re-circulated air for its passengers and fresh air to the cockpit. As Page (2002) observed, the main areas of concern are:

- *Pressurisation*, since cabin pressure is low and may impact upon those with breathing difficulties;
- *Ventilation*, where cabins have low rates of ventilation and are ideal environments for the transmission of disease pathogens. Until the 1980s, cabins were ventilated by outside air, but in the 1990s the practice of mixing fresh and recycled air in a 50:50 proportion which add to feelings of fatigue and jet-lag, were withdrawn. The reintroduction of air flow nozzles on older aircraft are being re-evaluated for wider reintroduction to address such concerns;
- *Ozone pollution* on board aircraft;
- *The use of pesticides* to disinfect aircraft.

These health-related issues also highlight the growing concern among consumers about security and quality management issues.

Service Quality and Security

The SARS outbreak has highlighted the concern travellers have for their well-being when in transit on different forms of transport, which underlines a more general trend within the transport sector for security as a key factor within an overall desire for improved service quality. In the EU, for example, recent policy changes with the White Paper on transport highlight the need to reverse the decline in public transport and to make such travel options more attractive. This has important implications for the tourism sector, especially in the surface transport sector where the EU is prioritising major quality improvements in both rail and bus/coach travel (Page 2003b, c). To stem the decline of rail and bus use, an internal EU study — the QUATTRO study — examined the Public Transport Quality Matrix (European Commission 2000), to explain which factors impact upon passenger perception of quality. This is shown in Table 1.2 and highlights a wide range of issues which transport operators and the public sector funders of transport systems need to grapple with in addressing the erosion of public transport usage, primarily due to the impact of the car. In tourism terms, this matrix has an even greater significance where visitors use public transport services because it forms an image of the destination and its ability to meet vital mobility needs to travel to and between attractions in urban and rural areas.

In terms of security and creation of a more ambient environment for travel, The EU Study Guide — Urban Interchanges — A Good Practice Guide (2000) illustrated how important

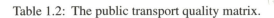

Table 1.2: The public transport quality matrix.

Quality

1. Availability
    1.1. Network
    1.2. Timetable

2. Accessibility
    2.1. External interface
    2.2. Internal interface
    2.3. Ticketing

3. Information
    3.1. General information
    3.2. Travel information — normal conditions
    3.3. Travel information — abnormal conditions

4. Time
    4.1. Journey time
    4.2. Punctuality and reliability

5. Customer care
    5.1. Commitment
    5.2. Customer interface
    5.3. Staff
    5.4. Physical assistance
    5.5. Ticketing options

6. Comfort
    6.1. Ambient conditions
    6.2. Facilities
    6.3. Ergonomics
    6.4. Ride comfort

7. Security
    7.1. Safety from crime
    7.2. Safety from accident
    7.3. Perception of security

8. Environment
    8.1. Pollution
    8.2. Natural resources
    8.3. Infrastructure

Source: Common work Quattro/CEN TC320 WG5.

good interchange facilities are for travellers to achieve seamless travel where travel routes converge. The interchange needs to offer both access and a transfer function and requires more strategic public transport network planning to be balanced with a customer-focused information strategy to set out all public transport options. One of the greatest innovations here is the development of Real Time Information systems so that travellers have up-to-date travel information. In the U.K. one notable development has been the introduction of the Traveline project (see Lyons & Harman 2002) to unify multiple sources of travel information. Many of the European bus operators and rail operators (see Page 2003c) report passenger and staff security as major challenges for attracting business, with many resorting to CCTV, security staff and a greater police presence in urban areas which are most prone to assaults on staff and passengers. Similarly, the rise in air rage incidents reported by the Civil Aviation Authority in the U.K. comprising disruptive behaviour by passengers, has seen a gradual increase in recent years Although not a major problem, it is symptomatic of some of the operational issues now facing transport operators carrying passengers. For example, 1,055 incidents were reported in the U.K. in the year ended March 31, 2002; violence occurred in 10% of cases, with alcohol involved in a further 45% of cases and smoking (which is banned on most European flights) mainly in toilets. The Civil Aviation Authority acknowledge that the majority of such offences are committed by males in 77% of cases, largely aged 20–40 years of age, with only 5% of cases occurring in first or business class. Problems faced by airline staff are disruptive passengers, using verbal abuse and being unruly although serious offences are still rare.

Marketing Surface Transport

Transport operators have seen a new wave of interest in marketing to develop positive images of public transport, around stronger brand identities for land-based transport for tourists. In 2003, the National Express company in the U.K. re-branded all of its operations under a new logo and identity. This replaced a familiar icon of express coach travel from the early 1980s and the *National Express* nationalised bus company logo. This is seen as critical as a way to translate corporate values into passenger growth through for example offering passengers an opportunity to support the planting of trees to balance the CO_2 emissions of their coach fleet. In this case it is evident that the company is seeking to communicate the brand through naming, design, advertising and promotions whilst unifying a diverse range of products under one banner.

Across the transport sector, the pursuit of the competitive tourist spending is now seeing advertising and the wider philosophy of marketing applied routinely to corporate business strategy. There appears to be a gradual realisation by many transport operators, especially the larger transnational groups, such as Arriva or Stagecoach; they are moving from a traditional operational focus to a more marketing-orientated strategy to maintain existing customer bases and to develop new markets.

The Future of Tourist Transport

It is evident that the new millennium has led to the realisation, that traditional operational approaches to the provision of tourism transport are having to adapt to consumer tastes.

One of the most pervasive developments for transport businesses, which have substantial tourism interests, is the vertical integration with tour operators (for example, airlines) and horizontal integration by purchasing the competition (for example, Ryanair's purchase of Buzz and Easyjet's purchase of GO). At the same time, the traditional land transport sectors of rail and bus/coach travel, which have hitherto not been integrated, are now firmly transnational groups (Page 2003b). There are also trends towards globalisation, most notably with Stagecoach's operation of bus/coach operations in Canada, USA (Coach USA), Australia, New Zealand, China, Hong Kong and the U.K. Large transport groups such as Stagecoach recognise that investment is critical to attracting additional passenger growth after years of neglect in the public transport arena where operator margins have been reduced by unregulated competition and an inability to provide state of the art vehicles, passenger comfort and a high quality travel experience. After safety, these are the key factors required by visitors.

The major challenge in the aviation sector remains the impact of deregulation in many markets previously protected by state regulation, and similar policy decisions have been applied in the airport sector where state governments have privatised operations to attract much needed investment for expansion and development (Hooper 2002). Oum & Zhang (2001) point to the interaction between privatised airlines and airports and their importance in hub and spoke operations. Where a hub is selected it is evident that the airline makes a substantial investment in the location as a vital stakeholder. At a global level, research has identified how airports have sought to compete to become international hubs, as in the case of South East Asia (Page 2001). Furthermore, this has brought about major changes in the development and positioning of airports. In Chapter 8 Freathy analyses the current trends in airport development and the move towards terminals also becoming centres of retailing.

This is complemented by a growing realisation that airlines need to work in partnership through the concept of strategic alliances although the level of involvement and motivation for alliance involvement is complex. Indeed, the types of alliance range considerably from the tactical level as code shares on selected routes, through to linking of routes which requires a more embedded approach to collaboration. Yet for many global airlines, the pressures of operating remain an ever-present challenge with revenue per passenger dropping as seat prices fall (Doganis 2001). Briggs, in Chapter 9, argues that the future of airline development will feature not only the increasing collaboration of regional companies toward global alliances but will be driven increasingly by technical and operational imperatives within the next decade.

Doganis (2001) outlined a number of key challenges for this sector in the new millennium as the most heavily capitalised and probably the transport provider most vulnerable to economic changes with its dependence upon business travel for its profitability (excluding the low cost and charter market). Among the principal challenges it faces according to Doganis (2001) are: competition between alliances and their hubs as change and uncertainty remain the two hallmarks for the new millennium in the air transport sector. The challenge of adapting to continuous change means that airlines have to evaluate which markets they wish to operate in (global vs. niche) and the identification of appropriate strategies to achieve these corporate goals. Other key pressures will remain in terms of cost reduction, the need to improve yields, increased adoption of marketing and an ability to constantly reassess the objectives of the airline's core business.

Another major challenge is the way in which suppliers of transport are having to develop potential synergies between travel, telecommunications and information technology (Golob 2001). The advances in internet, mobile telephone, and personal digital assistance have been embraced in tourism and transport provision but increasingly rapid technological change is likely to bring widespread benefits which are not yet applied. This also includes satellite navigation and positioning systems which bring many commercial gains for businesses, for example, in terms of tracking progress of vehicles en route. The technological benefit is well developed in North America and will be strengthened in Europe through the EU-sponsored Galileo project.

The advent of the internet has changed the nature in which transport suppliers offer their services to other businesses but also the relationship with consumers who have access to far more information than ever before. As the market for personal and household internet appliances broadens across all countries this is likely to have a lasting effect on patterns of transport. For example, shopping from home is forecast to become more important and travel intermediaries will change even more to meet this change or perish. Low cost airline carriers have demonstrated how fast the fusion of customer culture can be. The use of IT to improve advance and real time travel information will remove some of the uncertainty about travel and hand-held equipment such as the mobile' phone will enable visitors to access current information about local public transport or congestion at resorts. Smart card technology at a destinations will also help to afford access to facilities including public transport and parking places. Whilst, it is unlikely that increased access to telecommunications will lead to a reduction in travel it will change patterns of travel (Lyons *et al*. 2002).

Sustainable Development

The issue of sustainable development (meeting the needs of the present but not at the expense of future generations) and the current negative contribution of transport has been the subject of extensive discussion in recent years (Banister *et al*. 2000; Hayashi *et al*. 1999). There has been a detailed evaluation of the likely effects of an increase in tourism related transport: energy consumption, pollution and other impacts consequent on growth of air transport and the motorised vehicle (Adams 1997; Burns & Holden 1995; Gillingwater 2003; Greene 1997; Janic 1999). A number of studies have also focused on related socio-economic barriers to sustainable development and questions of equity in the process (Black 2000; Hall 1999). The distinction becomes more poignant in low income countries where subsistence-based communities live in a walking world and tourists speed by in four-wheel drives on newly built roads (Porter 2002). Hall takes this discussion forward in Chapter 3 when he questions the extent to which current transport systems deliver tourism in an equitable manner.

The pivotal role of the car in relation to the change of urban structure has been the subject of critical analysis in transport analysis. The phenomenal growth of car ownership in earlier decades in developed countries is well documented (Nijkamp *et al*. 1990). The emphasis is not surprising; society has witnessed a tenfold global increase from 53 million vehicles registered in 1950 to 500 million recorded in 1992 and with a continuing increase of approximately 3 million cars per annum in Europe per year being reported (Forward 2000). The benefits of personal convenience which the car offers is set against the negative effects such as safety issues, congestion and pollution (Sartre 1997; Wilks *et al.* 1999). Furthermore, the issue of global warming, the consumption of finite energy resources and globalisation are driving forces, which are likely to shape the future of transport systems, and hence tourism transport (Newman & Kenworthy 1999; Tolley 2003; Topp 2002).

The question of land use planning and surface transport for tourism is another area where research has been limited. In reality, the relationship between transport and tourism tends not to be integrated into an overall policy process for sustainable development and hence is not analysed in any detail (Giannakodakis 1994; Gunn 1994; Lamb & Davidson 1996). There is often recognition of a relationship between tourism and transport in the planning documentation, but for the most part the implementation of policy is afforded by different organisations and there is a variance between professional values, methods and approaches (Goodwin *et al.* 1995). This imbalance has resulted in a negative trade-off for other modes than the car, which make up the overall transport system (Hallsworth & Whitelegg 1997; Whitelegg 1993). There has, in recent years, however, been a renewed interest in visitor attractions having formal travel plans which encourage modal transfer from the car to more sustainable modes of travel. This signals a change in the way the tourism sector is responding to transport (English Tourist Council 2001). However, few academic studies have evaluated the development of tourism transport systems, particularly those designed to provide sustainable transport and or a tourism experience (Lumsdon 2000).

What is certain in the wider context of tourist transport is the continued growth of car-based recreation and tourism at the expense of other modes, although comparatively little research is directed towards this area (Høyer 2000). The problem is particularly pressing in countries with high car ownership and energy consumption levels such as the USA and the European Union (see Table 1.3). The car has seen unprecedented growth since the 1960s, for example, at many destinations which have many sensitive environmental areas such as the Alpine areas of central Europe. For example, in 1991, 103 million visits were made to National Parks in the U.K. (Countryside Commission 1992; Cullinane 1997), the most popular being the Lake District and Peak District Parks, i.e. over 90% of visitors arrive by car. In terms of car usage, car traffic was estimated to grow by 267% by the year 2025 from the levels current in 1992. The greatest pressures of rising car usage have coincided with the decline in public transport usage for tourist and recreational trips. Yet many National Parks seem unlikely to be able to cope with the levels of usage predicted to the year 2025, given their urban catchments and the relative accessibility by motorway and main roads in the U.K. Eaton & Holding (1996) reviewed the absence of effective policies to meet the practical problems of congestion facing many sites in the countryside in Britain, a feature further investigated in their analysis of strategies designed to reduce car dependence in resort areas (Holding 2001).

One interesting explanation of the wide acceptance of the car which seems set to continue to grow, aside from its flexibility, is its ability to be more appealing than public transport (Cohen & Harris 1998). In destinations with vast areas to explore, the car and road travel has been seen as a way of exploring areas more flexibly and in establishing individual itineraries (Taplin & McGinley 2000; Taplin & Min 1997). There is also some evidence to suggest that visitors will pay a road toll to gain access (Steiner & Bristow 2000). In most cases, attitudes of visitors to public transport options, especially in National Parks illustrate the continued problems of demand management and of providing inducements to switch to attractive

Table 1.3: Performance of EU passenger transport by mode 1970–2000 (1,000 mn passenger Kms).

Year	Mode of Transport					Total
	Passenger Car	Bus and Coach	Tram and Metro	Railway	Air	
1970	1,582	269	39	219	33	2,142
1980	2,295	348	41	248	74	3,006
1990	3,199	369	48	268	157	4,041
1991	3,257	378	48	276	166	4,126
1995	3,506	382	47	274	202	4,410
1996	3,558	391	48	282	209	4,488
1997	3,622	393	49	285	222	4,571
1998	3,702	402	50	287	241	4,682
1999	3,788	406	51	295	260	4,801
2000	3,789	413	52	303	281	4,839
% Change 1991–2000	+16%	+9%	+10%	+10%	+70%	+17%

Source: European Commission, Directorate-General for Energy and Transport, EU Energy and Transport in figures 2002.

forms of public transport. In some areas such as the North Yorkshire Moors in the U.K., this may also be integrated into plans for increasing greater levels of social inclusion by making scenic areas more accessible to non-car users in the local population. However, whatever the future of the car remains in relation to tourism and recreational travel, de-marketing of the car (Wright & Egan 2000) must be a germane area for future research. For many tourism destinations, managing the car, its environmental impact and flexibility remain portent forces for individual localities at a time when the car is widely viewed as a lifestyle enhancing factor (Goodwin 1997; Mintel 2003). Owen & Lumsdon (Chapter 12) outline the problems facing tourism planners in attempting to introduce schemes to enhance sustainable modes of travel at the expense of the car. They discuss mechanisms for consultation and how this can be problematic in light of resistance from traders at the destination. In another study, Shailes *et al.* (2001) observed the manner in which car-based tourists adjust their travel behaviour in response to congestion rather than switch to other modes of transport.

Conversely the bus and coach sector has fared badly in relation to the car and attempts to revive its fortunes in different countries are being promoted by the public sector. This action is not only for environmental and sustainability reasons, but also to reduce the costs of congestion and road building to accommodate not only commuters, but also leisure and tourism trips as experienced in many re-emerging city destinations. Both road-based public transport and rail-based options are seen by many consumers as outdated and outmoded forms of transport from another age (i.e. the 1960s and 1970s). Yet ironically in many destinations, the use of public transport to see the attractions and sights in a destination are proving very popular. This is especially in relation to the use of vehicles that add nostalgia and a heritage experience (i.e. trams and cable cars in destinations such as Lisbon and San Francisco). While many such services still need public subsidies to operate they provide attractive services for visitors which have become tourism transport experiences in their own right. The role of destination tour buses and their impact on tourist patronage of attractions and sites along their routes remain poorly understood at the micro level even though they are familiar element in many destinations.

The activities of the transnational and global operators have also attracted comparatively little attention in terms of their leadership role in developing new strategies to make tourist use of land transport more attractive rather than the car. It is clear that future research will need to take these agents of change into account as new approaches to tourism transport are formulated in many larger cities. Similarly, the role of bus and coach travel still remains weakly developed within the transport studies literature and particularly in relation to tourism. Although a number of studies have examined the industry structure of coach businesses (e.g. Gauf & Hughes 1998; Mintel 2002), there has only been few theoretical insights into the nature of the coach tourist (Downward & Lumsdon 1999; Seaton 2002) and the significance of the coach as a form of tourist travel. There is a paucity of studies which investigate other forms of public transport such as transit minibuses and taxis (Waryszak & King 2000).

Rail-based tourist travel has been similarly absent from many of the conventional tourism journals although by its very nature tourist travel is subsumed within all forms of rail travel despite its significance, a feature reiterated in numerous studies (Page 1994, 1999a, 2003a). Much of the existing research has been policy-based (Shaw *et al.* 2003) making little distinction of the role it plays in tourism despite the significance for VFR travel, leisure trips and scenic travel (Prideaux 1999). Many railway companies have acknowledged the importance of tourism and leisure market segments as significant contributors to revenue, especially in relation to new product development. This is also the case as privatisation of railways in developing countries where concessionaire companies are segmenting their markets more effectively such as in Brazil and Mexico (Campos 2001). It is clear that further research on the role of tourist rail travel and its responsiveness to increased marketing, tactical promotional campaigns and its price sensitivity vs. the low cost airlines remains an important and under-explored area (Milan 1997). Modal competition has attracted highly quantitative and theoretical research by modelling travel behaviour. Yet the explicit tourism and leisure dimension remains a virgin area for research to understand the relationship between the potential for modal switching for pleasure travel rather than the prevailing focus of many transport studies on commuting. With a new policy focus in the EU towards making rail transport a more attractive option for cross-border travel, the significance of country-based and EU-wide initiatives that may see rail become competitive with investment in high-speed infrastructure, is certainly important for future patterns of tourist travel.

Likewise, the importance of European and global trends in the ferry market and cruise ship market have attracted a great deal of industry-based market intelligence studies but few academics have developed more sophisticated models of the characteristics of cruise tourists and the relationship to other forms of tourism they engage in. In other words we do not fully understand cruise tourists in relation to what Pearce (1993) described as the travel career ladder and how travellers develop their tourism experiences. Simply adopting marketing classifications to describe types of tourists does not acknowledge the dynamic nature of the travellers through time and how a one-time cruise tourist might equally be an ecotourist or fervent package holiday maker. More sophisticated analyses of tourists and their use of transport and underlying travel preferences through time would help transport providers to recognise the nature of travellers over and beyond simple marketing classifications. What is apparent from current market intelligence studies such as those published in *Travel and Tourism Analyst* is that the market has become more highly developed to the extent that certain itineraries have become saturated by cruise ships (see Miller & Grazier 2002). In addition, consolidation in the industry has followed trends in the wider transport sector in terms of control and investment in new plant. Wood explores the nature of the cruise sector and its considerable growth; he provides several insights into the segmentation of the cruise market in Chapter 10.

Finally, the importance of non-motorized transport has been totally understated in the discussion of visitors at destinations. Whilst this is not the world of large scale projects it is in reality the most common form of transport available to visitors and the management of walking trips is often crucial to the retail sector in tourism destinations and large scale attractions. Cycling is also important for short trips in many countries. Whilst destinations continue to build highways and parking in central zones, walk and cycle trips will decline except for the small enclave areas reserved for retailing. However, there is growing interest in developing non-motorized transport not only to ease congestion and reduce energy consumption but also to enhance the destination as a tourism experience; again the sector has been undervalued. These elements are worthy of detailed research.

So What of the Future for Tourist Transport Provision?

The tourism sector is far from static. It is constantly evolving as new trends, economic conditions, visitor preferences and product development combine with innovation to create one thing that is certain: nothing is and can be certain — change is the overwhelming element (Page 2003a). There are also major changes forecast in terms of the energy use and externalities of transport for tourism. These will, alongside rapid development of telecommunications, substantially change the nature of tourism supply (Hanson 1998).

For the transport sector, this is particularly challenging given the massive investment in capital intensive plant and equipment that cannot easily be disposed of or changed if trends and tastes change suddenly or rapidly. Therefore, two vital elements for the transport sector dependent on tourism markets are:

(a) The need for innovation, marketing and supply leadership so that demand can be more effectively managed (i.e. the consumer becomes more central in the process). This requires better communication with the consumer, a greater understanding of their needs, wants and tastes and how these can be met through aligning the provision to best fit their requirements.
(b) The need to address the principles of sustainable development by encouragement of energy reduction, and minimisation of externalities as envisaged in Agenda 21 (World Travel & Tourism Council *et al.* 1995).

Many of the chapters within this book contribute to this need for greater reflectivity in tourism and transport research to see the synergies between the two sectors: the tourism and transport sector have mutual interests in fulfilling customer demand. Recognising changing trends and tastes is critical, but so is a more holistic approach to the inter-relationships between both sectors. The chapters in this book seek to explore some of these issues while others offer analyses focused on themes which now play a key role in the tourist transport interface. Any such book will necessarily be selective in the range of contributions it provides but we hope these will seek to push the research agenda forward, making more explicit the tourist transport interface and the need for more provocative and synergistic studies.

References

Adams, J. (1997). Can technology save us? *World Transport Policy and Practice*, 2(3), 4–17.

Artist (2000). *Agenda for research on tourism by integration of statistics/strategies*. Brussels: European Commission.

Banister, D., Stead, D., Steen, P., Akerman, K., Dreborg, P., Nijkamp, P., & Scleiser-Tappeser, R. (2000). *European transport policy and sustainable mobility*. London: Spon.

Black, W. R. (2000). Socio-economic barriers to sustainable transport. *Journal of Transport Geography*, 8, 141–147.

Bull, A. (1991). *The economics of travel and tourism* (p. 32). Melbourne: Longman.

Burns, P., & Holden, A. (1995). *Tourism a new perspective* (pp. 158–160). New Jersey: Prentice-Hall.

Calder, S. (2002). *The truth behind the low cost revolution in the skies*. London: Virgin.

Campos, J. (2001). Lessons from railway reforms in Brazil and Mexico. *Transport Policy*, 8, 85–95.

Chang, Y.-C., & Williams, G. (2002). European airlines' strategic reactions to the Third Package. *Tourism Policy*, 9, 129–142.

Chew, J. (1987). Transport and tourism in the year 2000. *Tourism Management*, 8(2), 83–85.

Child, D. (2000). TTI Tourism Award: The emergence of no-frills airlines in Europe: An example of successful marketing strategy. *Travel and Tourism Analyst*, 1, 87–121.

Clawson, M., & Knetsch, J. (1966). *Economics of outdoor recreation*. Baltimore: John Hopkins University Press.

Cohen, A., & Harris, G. (1998). Mode choice for VFR journeys. *Journal of Transport Geography*, 6(1), 43–51.

Cooper, C., Fletcher, J., Gilbert, D., & Wanhill, S. (1998). *Tourism principles and practice?*

Countryside Commission (1992). *Trends in transport and the countryside*. Cheltenham: Countryside Commission.

Cullinane, S. (1997). Traffic management in Britain's national parks. *Transport Reviews*, 17(3), 267–279.

Dann, G. M. S. (1994). Travel by train: Keeping nostalgia on the track. In: A. V. Seaton (Ed.), *Tourism — A State of the Art* (pp. 775–783). Chichester: Wiley.

Doganis, R. (2001). *The airline business in the twenty-first century*. London: Routledge.

Donne, M. (2001). The growth and long term potential of low-cost airlines. *Travel and Tourism Analyst*, 4, 1–15.

Downward, P. M., & Lumsdon, L. (1999). The determinants of day excursion coach travel: A qualitative market analysis. *Services Industries Journal*, 19(4), 158–168.

Eaton, B., & Holding, D. (1996). The evaluation of public transport alternatives to the car in British national parks. *Journal of Transport Geography*, 4(1), 55–65.

English Tourism Council (2001). *Tourism and transport, the issues and solutions*. London: English Tourism Council.

European Commission (2000). *Quality in transportation (QUATTRO) study*. Brussels: European Commission.

European Environment Agency (2003). *Tourism travel by transport modes [2001]* http://themes. eea.eu.int/Sectors_and_activities/tourism/indicators/modes/index_html Accessed May 3, 2003.

European Travel Monitor (1998). *European travel monitor*. Luxembourg: European Community.

European Union Study Guide (2000). *Urban interchanges — A good practice guide*. Brussels: European Commission.

Eurostat (1998). *Community methodology on tourism statistics*. Luxembourg: European Community.

Forward, S. (2000). Walking at the beginning of the 21st century, attitudes and motivations. *Walk 21 taking walking forwards in the 21st century*. London, 21–22 February.

Fox, M. (1995). Transport planning and the human activity approach. *Journal of Transport Geography*, *3*(2), 105–116.

Gauf, D., & Hughes, H. (1998). Diversification and tour operators: The case of TUI and coach tourism. *Tourism Economics*, *4*(4), 325–337.

Getz, D. (1986). Models in tourism planning. *Tourism Management*, *7*, 21–32.

Giannakodakis, G. (1994). Transport Planning: A holistic systems approach. *Road Transport Research*, *3*(3), 4–21.

Gillen, D., & Morrison, W. (2003). Bundling, integration and the delivered price of air travel: Are low cost carriers full service competitors? *Journal of Air Transport Management*, *9*(1), 15–23.

Gillingwater, D. (Ed.) (2003). Special issue: Airports and sustainability. *Journal of Air Transport Management*, *9* (3), 139–200.

Golob, T. F. (2001). Travelbehaviour.com: Activity approaches to modeling the effects of information technology on personal travel behaviour. In: D. Hensher (Ed.), *Travel Behaviour Research, the Leading Edge* (pp. 145–183). Oxford: Elsevier Science Ltd.

Goodrich, J. N. (2002). September 11, 2001 attack on America: A record of the immediate impacts and reactions in the USA travel and tourism industry. *Tourism Management*, *23*, 573–580.

Goodwin, P. (1997). Mobility and car dependence. In: T. Rothegatter, & V. E. Carbonell (Eds), *Traffic and Transport Psychology*. Amsterdam: Pergamon.

Graham, B., & Guyer, C. (2000). The role of regional airports and air services in the United Kingdom. *Journal of Transport Geography*, *8*, 249–262.

Greene, D. L. (1997). Environmental impacts. *Journal of Transport Geography*, *5*(1), 28–29.

Gunn, C. A. (1994). *Tourism planning*. London: Taylor and Francis.

Hall, D. R. (1999). Conceptualising tourism transport: Inequality and externality issues. *Journal of Transport Geography*, *7*, 181–188.

Hallsworth, A., & Whitelegg, J. (1997). Summary and conclusions, looking around and looking ahead. In: R. Tolley (Ed.), *The Greening of Urban Transport* (pp. 453–461). Chichester: Wiley.

Halsall, D. A. (2001). Railway heritage and the tourist gaze: Stoomtram Hoorn-Medemblik. *Journal of Transport Geography*, *9*, 151–160.

Hanson, S. (1998). Off the road? Reflections on transportation geography in the information age. *Journal of Transport Geography*, *6*(4), 241–249.

Hayashi, Y., Button, K., & Nijkamp, P. (Eds) (1999). *The environment and transport*. Cheltenham: Edward Edgar Publishing.

Hensher, D. (Ed.) (2001). *Travel behaviour and research, the leading edge*. Oxford: Elsevier Science Ltd.

Hobson, J. S. P., & Uysal, M. (1992). Infrastructure: The silent crisis facing the future of transport. *Hospitality Research Journal*, *17*(1), 209–215.

Holding, D. (2001). The Sanfte Mobilitaet project: Achieving reduced car-dependence in European resort areas. *Tourism Management*, *22*(4), 411–417.

Hooper, P. (2002). Privatisation of airports in Asia. *Journal of Air Transport Management*, *8*(5), 289–300.

Høyer, K. G. (2000). Sustainable tourism or sustainable mobility? The Norwegian case. *Journal of Sustainable Tourism*, *8*(2), 147–160.

Humphreys, I., & Francis, G. (2002). Policy issues and planning of U.K. regional airports. *Journal of Transport Geography*, *10*, 249–258.

Janic, M. (1999). Aviation and externalities: The accomplishments and problems. *Transportation Research Part D*, *4*, 159–180.

Lamb, B., & Davidson, S. (1996). Tourism and Transportation in Ontario, Canada. In: L. Harrison, & W. Husbands (Eds), *Practising Responsible Tourism: International Case Studies in Tourism Planning, Policy and Development*. Chichester: Wiley.

Laws, E. (1991). *Tourism marketing: Service quality and management perspectives*. Cheltenham: Stanley Thornes.

Leiper, N. (1990). Tourist attractions systems. *Annals of Tourism*, *17*, 384–387.

Lew, A. (1991). Scenic roads and rural development in the U.S. *Tourism Recreation Research*, *16*(2), 23–30.

Loomis, J. B., & Walsh, R. G. (1997). *Recreation economic decisions: Comparing benefits and costs* (2nd ed.). State College, PA: Venture Publishing.

Lumsdon, L. (2000). Transport and tourism: A sustainable tourism development model. *Journal of Sustainable Tourism*, *8*(4), 1–17.

Lundgren, J. O. (1973). The development of the tourist travel system. *The Tourist Review*, January 2–14.

Lyons, G., Chatterjee, K., Beecroft, M., & Marsden, G. (2002). Determinants of travel demand — exploring the future of society and lifestyles in the U.K. *Transport Policy*, *9*, 17–27.

Lyons, G., & Harman, R. (2002). The U.K. public transport industry and provision of multi-modal traveller information. *International Journal of Transport Management*, *1*, 1–13.

Mason, K. (2000). The propensity of business travellers to use low cost airlines. *Journal of Transport Geography*, *8*, 107–119.

Mason, K. (2001). Marketing low-cost airline services to business travellers. *Journal of Air Transport Management*, *7*, 103–109.

Mason, K., Whelan, C., & Williams, G. (2000). Europe's low cost airlines: An analysis of the economics and operating characteristics of Europe's charter and low cost scheduled carriers. *Air Transport Group Research Report*, *7*. Cranfield: Cranfield University College of Aeronautics.

McIntosh, R. W., Goeldner, C. R., & Ritchie, J. R. B. (1995). *Tourism, principles, practices, philosophies* (pp. 17–21). Toronto: Wiley.

McKercher, B. (2003). SARS and SIPs. *Trinet Communication*, 28.4.2003 by email.

Milan, J. (1997). Comparison of the quality of rail and air networks in West Central and Eastern Europe. *Transport Policy*, *4*(2), 85–93.

Mill, R. C., & Morrison, A. (1992). *The tourism system: An introductory text*. New Jersey: Prentice-Hall.

Miller, A., & Grazier, W. (2002). The North American cruise market and Australian tourism. *Journal of Vacation Marketing*, *8*(3), 221–234.

Mintel (2002). *Coach holidays, leisure intelligence*. London: Mintel.

Mintel (2003). *British lifestyles study*. London: Mintel.

Morrison, A., Yang, C., Cai, L., Nadnarni, N., & O'Leary, J. (1996). Comparative profiles of travellers on cruises and land-based resort vacations. *Journal of Tourism Studies*, *7*(2), 54–64.

Murray, M., & Graham, B. (1997). Exploring the dialectics of route-based tourism: The Camino de Santiago. *Tourism Management*, *18*(8), 513–524.

Newman, P. W. G., & Kenworthy, J. R. (1999). *Sustainability and cities: Overcoming automobile dependence*. Washington, DC: Island Press.

Nijkamp, P., Reichman, S., & Wegener, M. (Eds) (1990). *Euromobile: Transport, communications and mobility in Europe — a cross-national comparative overview*. Aldershot: Avebury.

Oppermann, M. (1997). Predicting destination choice — A discussion of destination loyalty. *Journal of Vacation Marketing*, *5*(1), 51–65.

Oum, T., & Zhang, Y. (2001). Recent studies on some key issues in international air transport. *Transport Policy*, *8*, 167–169.

Page, S. J. (1994). European bus and coach travel. *Travel and Tourism Analyst*, *1*, 19–39.

Page, S. J. (1999a). *Transport for tourism*. Harlow: Addison Wesley and Longman.

Page, S. J. (1999b). *Transport for tourism* (p. 8). London: Routledge.

Page, S. J. (2001). Gateways, hubs and transport interconnections in South East Asia: Implications for tourism development in the twenty-first century. In: P. Teo, T. Chang, & K. Ho (Eds), *Interconnected Worlds: Tourism in South East Asia* (pp. 84–102). Oxford: Pergamon.

Page, S. J. (2002). Tourist health and safety. *Travel and Tourism Analyst*.

Page, S. J. (2003a). *Tourism management: Managing for change*. Oxford: Butterworth Heinemann.

Page, S. J. (2003b). European rail travel: Special report. *Travel and Tourism Analyst*.

Page, S. J. (2003c). European bus and coach travel. *Travel and Tourism Analyst*.

Papatheodorou, A. (2002). Civil aviation regimes and leisure tourism in Europe. *Journal of Air Transport Management*, *8*, 381–388.

Patterson, J., & Perl, A. (1999). The TGV Effect: A potential opportunity for reconciling sustainability with aviation. *World Transport Policy and Practice*, *5*(1), 39–46.

Pearce, P. (1993). Fundamentals of tourist motivation. In: D. G. Pearce, & R. Butler (Eds), *Tourism Research: Critiques and Challenges* (pp. 113–34). London: Routledge.

Pizam, A., & Mansfield, Y. (Eds) (1999). *Consumer behaviour in travel and tourism*. New York: Haworth Press.

Porter, G. (2002). Living in the walking world: Rural mobility and social equity issues in sub-Saharan Africa. *World Development*, *30*(2), 285–300.

Preston, J. (2001). Integrating transport with socio-economic activity — a research agenda for the new millennium. *Journal of Transport Geography*, *9*, 13–24.

Prideaux, B. (1999). Tracks to tourism: Queensland rail joins the tourism industry. *International Journal of Tourism Research*, *1*(2), 73–86.

Prideaux, B. (2000). The role of transport in destination development. *Tourism Management*, *21*, 53–63.

Raguraman, K. (1997). Airlines as instruments for nation building and national identity: Case study of Malaysia and Singapore. *Journal of Transport Geography*, *5*(4), 239–256.

Reynolds-Feighan, A. (2001). Traffic distribution in low-cost and full-service carrier networks in the U.S. air transportation market. *Journal of Air Transport Management*, *7*, 265–275.

Royal Commission on Environmental Pollution (2002). *The environmental effects of civil aircraft in flight: Special report*. London: Royal Commission on Environmental Pollution.

Sartre, (1997). *Social attitudes to road risk in Europe*. European Commission.

Seaton, A. (2002). Observing conducted tours: The ethnographic context in tourist research. *Journal of Vacation Marketing*, *8*(4), 309–319.

Shailes, A., Senior, M., & Barry, P. (2001). Tourists' travel behaviour in response to congestion: The case of car trips to Cornwall, United Kingdom. *Journal of Transport Geography*, *9*(1), 49–60.

Shaw, J., Walton, W., & Farrington, J. (2003). Assessing the potential for a "railway renaissance" in Great Britain. *Geoforum*, *34*, 141–156.

Steiner, T. J., & Brisstow, A. L. (2000). Road pricing in National Parks: A case study in the Yorkshire Dales National Park. *Transport Policy, 7*, 93–103.

Taplin, J. H. E., & McGinley, C. (2000). A linear program to model daily car touring choices. *Annals of Tourism Research, 27*(2), 431–467.

Taplin, J., & Min, Q. (1997). *Annals of Tourism Research, 24* (3), 624–637.

Tolley, R. S. (Ed.) (2003). *Creating sustainable transport; planning for walking and cycling.* Cambridge: Woodhead.

Tolley, R. S., & Turton, B. (1995). *Transport systems, policy and planning: A geographical approach.* Harlow: Longman.

Topp, H. (2002). Traffic 2042 — mosaic of a vision. *Transport Policy, 9*, 1–7.

Travel & Tourism Intelligence (1998). The North American cruise market. *Travel & Tourism Analyst, 4* (pp. 1–23). London: Travel & Tourism Intelligence.

Travis, A. (1989). Tourism destination area development (from theory to practice). In: S. Witt, & L. Moutinho (Eds), *Tourism Marketing and Management Handbook* (pp. 487–498). Hemel Hempstead: Prentice-Hall.

Waryszak, R., & King, B. (2000). Tourist and taxis: An examination of the tourism transport interface. *Journal of Vacation Marketing, 6*(4), 318–328.

Whitelegg, J. (1993). *Transport for a sustainable future: The case for Europe.* London: Belhaven.

Wilks, J., & Page, S. J. (Eds) (2003). *Managing tourist health and safety.* Oxford: Pergamon.

Wilks, J., Watson, B., & Faulks, I. J. (1999). International tourists and road safety in Australia: Developing a national research and management programme. *Tourism Management, 20*, 645–654.

Williams, G. (2001). Will Europe's charter airlines be replaced by "no frills" scheduled airlines? *Journal of Air Transport Management, 7*, 277–286.

World Tourism Organization (2000). *Data collection & analysis for tourism management.* Madrid: World Tourism Organization.

World Tourism Organization (2002). *Tourism highlights 2002.* Madrid: World Tourism Organization.

World Travel & Tourism Council (WTTC), World Tourism Organisation, Earth Council (1995). *Agenda 21 for the travel & tourism industry: Towards environmentally sustainable development.* London, WTTC. WTTC.

Wright, C., & Egan, J. (2000). De-marketing the car. *Transport Policy, 7*(4), 287–294.

Chapter 2

Life Cycle, Tourist Motivation and Transport: Some Consequences for the Tourist Experience

Gianna Moscardo and Philip L. Pearce

Introduction

In the pioneering days of tourism study, Wahab (1975) argued that the area of tourist motivation is basic and indispensable in tourism analysis and fundamental to tourism development itself. Motivation is commonly seen as the driving force behind human actions (Crompton 1979; Fodness 1994; Iso-Ahola 1982). It is therefore a starting point for studying tourist behaviour and beyond that for understanding systems of tourism including the use of transport modes and their meaning (Gunn 1988; Mill & Morrison 1985; Pearce *et al.* 1998). This chapter will bring together an analysis of tourist motivation and the multiple roles of transport in the tourist experience. This analysis will proceed by briefly exploring some of the existing work pertaining to tourist behaviour, tourist motivation and transport. As an extension of the existing work a conceptual map developing the connections between life cycle, tourist motivation and the roles and experiential consequences of transport choice will be constructed.

The presentation of this conceptual map of the proposed links between tourist motivation and transport use and the consequences of other linkages will be followed by a case study of road travellers in Northern Australia. The material to be reported includes survey data from both international and domestic visitors to the Northern Queensland region. The case study provides empirical evidence pertaining to the links proposed in the conceptual map. A consideration of the rich and varied possibilities for research in this area will form a concluding part of this review.

Background

There are at least two dominant approaches linking tourists, their transport use and their experiences. The first category of work typically measures the relationship between the choice of a transport style and economic variables — notably price and income. Such work is often done to compare transport options (Johnson & Thomas 1992). In this kind of

Tourism and Transport: Issues and Agenda for the New Millennium
Copyright © 2004 Published by Elsevier Ltd.
ISBN: 0-08-044172-6

mathematical and modelling-oriented analysis, consumer tastes are fixed and the attitudes towards the individual business operations or transport companies are either seen as irrelevant or subservient to cost structures. Sometimes effort and distance rather than cost become the measuring tools in the choice modelling work, as exemplified by Burton (1994), who suggests, that for Europeans 1,000 kilometres from home base to the destination is an important figure in determining whether a private vehicle or air transport will be the dominant mode of travel.

Economic choice and modelling studies are not confined to between transport choices for tourists. Studies of route choice and recreation participation have also been approached with efforts to generate algorithms to explain car travel (Fesenmaier 1988; Taplin & Qiu 1997). There is also a considerable body of work in the transport rather than the tourism literature which emphasises models of tourist flow and transport dependency (Bannister 1995; Erlander & Stewart 1990; Sen & Smith 1995; Wood & Johnson 1993).

Johnson & Thomas (1992) in commenting on this stream of work observe that some powerful insights have been developed through economic models but a "more complete understanding of consumers' behaviour requires attention to the formation of tastes and preferences" (p. 3). It is this second kind of work on tourists and transport which occupies the stage in this analysis.

An experiential and motivational approach to travel behaviour and transport use diverges from the complementary economic appraisals in three ways. First, it tends to focus on particular contexts and situations, that is travellers from certain markets with particular profiles who have made actual choices. Second, while it is concerned with both traveller choices between and within transport options, it can be noted that in a number of remote and rural tourist contexts there are in fact no choices among transport modes and the hardy traveller may have to endure whatever is available in that setting. A third point of difference lies in the scattered and yet to be organised nature of the studies in the motivational and experiential reporting of tourist-transport material. Unlike the economic modelling and mathematical work, the second category of analysis does not have a systematic, conceptually well established theory to guide its development. In a small way, it is hoped that the concept map developed in this chapter may be an initial guide to serve this larger purpose of integrating and directing studies.

There are, as indicated already, several diverse kinds of studies within the experiential category of tourist-transport analysis. There exist a number of studies where customer satisfaction towards transport services has been assessed (Noe 1999). This work, much of which is not available for academic consideration because of business confidentiality issues, falls broadly into a framework of either employing confirmation-disconfirmation models based on measuring expected service and actual service quality, or using a benchmarking approach, that is comparing service providers (Kandampully *et al.* 2001; Noe 1999). Some of the recent writing in this area argues that the benchmarking approach will become the major approach in future practice and the comparison of satisfaction data will be needed (Kozac 2001). As the study of tourist-transport relationships continue, it might be worth considering more industry-academic partnerships to collect, organise and interpret some of this transport satisfaction material.

A second line of work represented by Oliver (2001) lies in continuing to explore how tourists travel through landscapes, principally but not exclusively, by private vehicle.

The work uses a technique labelled "route maps"; which is essentially a methodology of collating detailed sketches and notes on the travellers' experiences (Pearce 1981, 1999; Pearce & Fagence 1996; Walmsley & Jenkins 1992; Young 1999). Oliver reports that this field is extremely fertile in developing methods to elicit both recall and/or recognition of environments and could be used as a major approach to investigate differences between the experiences of private car travellers, coach tourists, and individual vs. package tours within a transport mode.

A third line of work encompasses trip planning, travellers' use of information and travel patterns. This work appears as a mix of tourist research and geographical studies and considers such topics as how scenic byways affect route choice in the United States and how trip patterns are anticipated, modified and realised in tourism regions (Elby & Molnar 2002; Lue *et al.* 1993; Opperman 1997; Parolin 2001).

In both the route map-based work and the travel pattern analysis, there is not a very direct focus on the transport medium itself. Rather, the emphasis is on the experience which results from the transport use. A more exacting and detailed linkage of the attitudes towards the transport and how it serves to inhibit, modify or embrace the traveller's experience still awaits exploration.

One set of studies pertaining to senior travellers in North America and Australia approaches the topic of the transport-tourist experience linkage a little more closely. Black and Rutledge (1995), Black and Clark (1998), McHugh and Mings (1992) and Wallis (1990) all explore the travel behaviour of retired or senior travellers on long distance journeys. While the work done by Black and colleagues is based in Australia and the remaining work is North American, the studies share the findings and observations that it is the travelling itself in the senior travellers' own carefully designed and packed vehicles which is integral to the holiday experience. It is a marriage of the pleasure and control associated with driving and touring which defines this kind of holiday experience as transport centred, and it has been suggested that few other major transport modes are so involved in the total holiday design and experience. This view may be overstated since cruise tourism, group coach travel and specialist tour options such as trail rides, canoe trips and bicycle tours could be seen as having a close nexus between the transport style and the experience.

A consideration of the existing literature establishes the need to present a conceptual map or overview of the tourism transport possibilities. A necessary additional topic to be reviewed prior to presenting an organising concept map is the central theme of motivation. The importance of the topic has been frequently acknowledged and it can be noted that motivation should be distinguished from the frequently measured purpose of travel (e.g. for "business" or for "pleasure"). Motivation reflects an individual's needs and wants rather than being an overt statement of trip purpose (Gee *et al.* 1989).

There are several existing theories of tourist motivation, all of which are in states of revision and development (Lee & Pearce 2002; Ryan 1998). Reviews of travel motivation approaches exist in a variety of other publications (McIntosh *et al.* 1995; WTO 1999) but it is worth observing that a good theory of tourist motivation will be clear and comprehensible and will integrate and stimulate other research. In addition, a sound theory should cover a diverse set of motives, provide a multi-motive assessment of complex behaviour, be measurable, and deal well with change both in the individual and the society's values (Pearce 1993).

Accompanying motivation, there is another set of forces which shape the tourist-transport linkages and these forces can be broadly summarised with the label life-cycle. The term is an integrative one, combining the person's age, family status, income, health and well being (Jafari 2000). It is used frequently to suggest categories of activity preferences (Mill & Morrison 1995). Life-cycle factors and other psychographic approaches can be seen as forces which intersect with and are expressed in the motivation of travellers. While motivation remains the basic and initial driving force for tourist behaviour, the actual motives individuals express are strongly shaped by life cycle forces. It is argued here that life cycle stages (e.g. young pre-marriage adults, older travellers without children) are loose descriptions and motivation provides a more exacting account of activity preferences and choices than do broad demographic factors (Moscardo *et al.* 1996a).

The links between traveller motivation, life cycle, the role of transport and the experiences from these links are presented in Figure 2.1. A consideration of Figure 2.1 raises some core issues in the development of the motivation-transport-experiences interface. Initially, it needs to be emphasised that the listing of motives should not be taken as

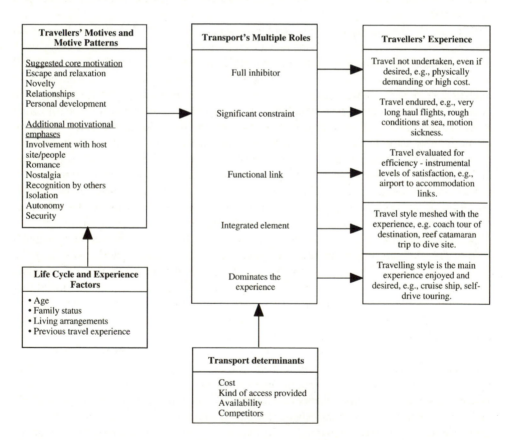

Figure 2.1: A conceptual map of the links between motivation, life cycle, transport roles and the travellers' experience.

presenting a view that travellers have one motive. Instead, it is argued that travellers will all have the core motives with slightly different individual emphases for each motive. Further, travellers may have a strong additional motivational profile supplied from the set of auxiliary motives.

An example will establish the way in which this motivational pattern emphasis can be seen to work in the transport-travel experience context. Studies of travellers who choose cruise ships as their holiday experience are clearly opting for a product where the transport role can be described as dominating the travellers' experience. Once aboard, the cruise ship passenger's holiday is defined by the routes, facilities, timelines, space restrictions and leisure possibilities uniquely inherent to this transport style. It is perhaps not surprising that one might argue that this kind of travel choice and experience is driven by a distinctive motivational profile and life cycle. Research studies in the area of cruise tourism suggest there are distinctive motivational and life cycle profiles associated with this industry sector. Moscardo *et al.* (1996b) assert that in addition to the kinds of core travel motivation factors described in Figure 2.1, a detailed study of tourist perspectives on cruising from large scale survey work (over 12,000 person sample), identified a significant additional motivational emphasis. For cruise ship holidays when compared to other holiday options the expressions and motives of "excellent food," "romance" and "exciting" were distinctive factors. A number of cruise ship studies also consider the life cycle and experience factors featured in Figure 2.1. On this occasion the studies tend to warn the reader not to assume that all cruise ship passengers are an older, retired group as new operations now provide for multiple market segments and life cycle categories (Bull 1996; Douglas & Douglas 1996).

The example of the importance of "romance," in particular, for the cruise ship passengers as a significant motivation in the pattern of motives can be reinforced by suggesting another motivational pattern for the self-drive touring traveller. On this occasion the pattern of motives can be described as featuring "autonomy" and "involvement with host site/people" as two auxiliary motives. This suggestion is reflected in the research on the United States "snowbirds" — travellers travelling to warmer southern states during the winter months — and the long distance senior Australian car touring market conducted by McHugh and Mings (1992) and Black and Clark (1998).

The central section of Figure 2.1 provides a classification of the multiple roles of transport. The range is considerable. The transport may be so daunting to the traveller, such as a long cruise to Antarctica, that despite motivation to visit the great wilderness of ice, for many the transport inhibiting factor is too great. At other times transport may be a significant constraint on the traveller's experience, and a range of examples from the mundane, such as long haul air flights, to the more exotic, such as llama backpacking in South America, serve to illustrate factors of stress, endurance and physical fitness needed to survive the process of "getting there." For many travellers transport is simply a functional part of the tourist system (Gunn 1994) and the efficiency of transport is the main issue in their assessment of its contribution to their holiday experience. The instrumental value of transport as a part of tourism is analogous to the work on the instrumental value of certain national park facilities in the environmental tourism field (Noe 1999). Examples in this category include internal transport within a large resort, airport to accommodation linkages and taxi, bus and subway services in cities. A less well known example is supplied by Soemanto (1995) who notes that tourists value the experience of the becak drivers in Indonesia, and here usefulness and the novelty value of the experience are combined.

Transport as an integrated element of the tourist experience has many expressions and is driven by a rich pattern of diverse motive profiles. In Figure 2.1, the illustrations of this kind of linkage are provided by a coach tour of a destination. The packaged coach tours of single or multiple countries in Europe can be seen as transport-tourism examples where novelty, escape and relaxation are potentially core motives of particular importance with the additional motive of security featuring strongly in the traveller's profile.

The final role of transport, where it can be seen as dominating the travellers, is illustrated by examples such as cruise tourism and touring by automobile. Other notable examples include bicycle tours, hot air ballooning and thrill rides. Attention will now be directed to a case study from this particular transport role category — automobile touring as a globally relevant activity, one which is sometimes quite lengthy in duration.

Case Study: The Travellers' Experience and Automobile Tourism

The location of this study is northern Queensland, Australia. More specifically, the study is based around the coastal city of Cairns which has a population of 120,000 residents and a total tourist visitor profile estimated at over one million domestic and international tourists annually (Queensland Government 2001). It is a location which provides access to sections of two World Heritage Areas — the Great Barrier Reef and the Wet Tropics. Analyses of the visitor market segments to this region have been conducted in a number of previous studies (Morrison *et al.* 1995). Broadly, these analyses can be summarised as revealing that there are a substantial number of domestic visitors varying in age as well as a sizeable international visitor market who tend to be either in the 18–35 age group or alternatively in a later life cycle phase (Pearce *et al.* 1996). The international visitors are predominantly from U.K./Europe, New Zealand, North America and Japan with rising numbers from other Asian countries.

The data for the present case study is drawn from a specific survey of 1,513 visitors conducted from April to June 1999. The surveys were distributed throughout the region and included locations in the main city of Cairns as well as accessing visitors in a number of smaller towns in the region (Figure 2.2). In each of the locations surveys were given out at transport hubs, shopping centres and precincts. The response rate for the survey was 71%. Participants were screened to ensure that those responding were tourists, that is they were staying away from their usual place of residence or work for at least one night and were involved in pleasure or holiday travel. The principal questions in the survey which help illustrate the tourist motivation and travel mode connections lie in the items used to identify the motives for visiting the area. Additionally the life cycle and demographic information collected in the study enables this case study to explore how motivation, life cycle and demographic factors combine.

The presentation of the results of this study proceeds in three steps. Initially some fundamental contrasts in motivation between those who choose the self-drive transport and those who do not are made. A second level of analysis considers the demographic

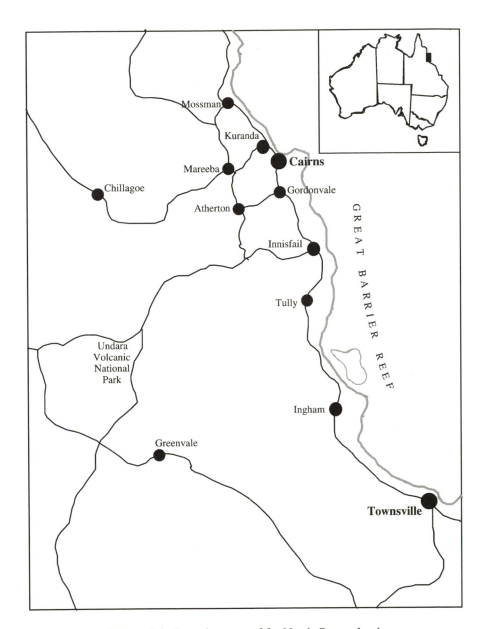

Figure 2.2: Location map of far North Queensland.

and life-cycle characteristics of sub-groups within the self-drive market. The motivational profile of these sub-groups is then compared.

There are six motive and destination feature items in Table 2.1 which are significantly different for the self-drive and non-self-drive tourism markets. Those individuals who elect to drive themselves are significantly more interested in activities for the whole family,

Table 2.1: The motivational responses of self-drive and non-self-drive markets to the North Queensland region.

Motivation and Destination Attribute Factors	Self-Drive Market (*N* = 751)	Non-Self-Drive Market (*N* = 762)
Warm sunny weather	46.9	44.0
Outstanding scenery	46.4	43.7
Chance to visit the Great Barrier Reef[a]	43.2	54.8
Opportunities to visit rainforest	39.9	47.6
Chance to escape a busy life	37.4	35.4
Access to wilderness/undisturbed nature	36.1	31.5
Chances to see wildlife not normally seen	34.0	33.5
Wide variety of things to do	33.2	36.8
Pleasant rural scenery[a]	30.8	22.4
Outdoor adventure activities	28.1	32.3
A place I can talk of when I get home	26.7	28.2
A place providing value for money	26.1	26.8
Friendly local people	26.1	23.4
Beaches for sunbathing, swimming	24.8	26.4
Opportunities to increase knowledge	19.5	23.3
Budget accommodation	19.0	26.2
Interesting small towns/villages[a]	18.5	11.2
Opportunities to visit family/friends	17.6	9.9
Activities for the whole family[a]	14.7	8.1
Inexpensive food	13.6	15.8
Shopping	10.5	18.4
A familiar well known place	10.4	9.6
First class accommodation	9.7	8.8
Resort areas	9.5	7.8
Experience indigenous culture[a]	8.7	14.9
Good nightlife entertainment[a]	7.9	12.1
High quality restaurants	6.7	6.5
A fashionable place to go	2.8	3.8

[a] Significant between group differences based on *t* tests for comparing means of the full item scale (1 = not at all important, 4 = very important).

pleasant rural scenery and interesting small towns and villages. The remaining items where differences were found are more important to the non-self-drive market. These motivational and attribute factors were the chance to visit the Great Barrier Reef, good nightlife and entertainment and the opportunity to experience indigenous culture.

An explanation of these differences in motivational attributes can be linked to the life-cycle and demographic variables defining these two groups. The non-self-drive market consists of two sub-sections, young budget accommodation international visitors, commonly referred to as backpackers (Murphy 1997), and resort/hotel and apartment guests from both domestic and international sources. They are predominantly first time visitors to the region. The total self-drive market consists of the combined responses from international self-drive tourists and domestic travellers both with and without children. The accommodation preferences for the self-drive group overall include more caravan parks and motels.

These differences in demographics and life-cycle factors can be linked effectively with the motivational statements reported in Table 2.2. A self-drive orientation, particularly where children are involved, is likely to lead to a relatively greater emphasis on activities and interesting towns and locations for exploration. Pleasant rural scenery is integral to the quality of the driving experience and not surprisingly is particularly emphasised by the self-drive group. Those travellers who elect not to drive themselves are presumably less mobile, a perspective consistent with the view that as a younger life cycle group of backpackers they are seeking nightlife and novel accessible opportunities to travel to the Great Barrier Reef and experience indigenous culture.

The motivational profiles and contrasts offered in Table 2.1, it can be argued, may mask differences within the self-drive group. As noted in some of the introductory remarks to this chapter, the experience based studies of tourists and transport need to focus on particular contexts, situations and sub-markets. The reason for this specificity of focus becomes more apparent as any case study is pursued. In the present case, the efforts of the researchers to provide a contrast between self-drive visitors and those who choose other means still does not provide a very detailed or revealing picture of the visitor diversity in the area. The context and sub-group studies are required to understand any of these transport experiences and styles in any complexity. The danger in this localised kind of work is that research efforts in this field become discrete, isolated reports of tourism transport. It is important therefore to establish how the more detailed analyses of this can strictly relate to the conceptual map of Figure 2.1. In brief, the following presentation of data represents an attempt to compare tourist motivational profiles when they are informed by life-cycle differences in the transport role labelled "Dominates the experience." It is to be hoped that by locating the present analyses in this conceptual map, future researchers will be provided with a point of organisation and reference to interpret both this work and their own studies.

The self-drive sub-groups identified in the North Queensland study can be summarised as follows.

International Self-Drive Market

The information pertaining to this group is drawn from 292 respondents. Predominantly from the United Kingdom/Ireland (35%) and Europe (33%), this group consists of a large number of couples (66%) with the balance of the party composition type being families and friends. The group is not exactly typical of all international visitors to the region since the two largest age groups are 21–30 (45%) and 31–60 (40%). The older age group of senior travellers, who are apparent in the broader demographics of the region's visitors (Tourism Queensland 2002) are under-represented in this self-drive market. The most common amount of time spent in the region is two weeks. The mean satisfaction for this

Table 2.2: The motivational responses of three self-drive markets to North Queensland region.

Motivation and Destination Attribute Factors	Self-Drive Market Sub-Group		
	International (N = 292)	Domestic — No Children (N = 388)	Domestic with Children (N = 71)
Opportunities to visit rainforest	51.2	48.9	44.3
Chance to escape a busy life	36.1	41.6	43.5
Activities for the whole family	10.9	14.5	42.9[a]
Chance to visit the Great Barrier Reef	61.5[a]	34.1	36.3
Outstanding scenery	49.1[a]	50.4[a]	34.3
Warm sunny weather	49.5[a]	49.9[a]	31.4
Wide variety of things to do	33.7	36.2	31.4
A place I can talk of when I get home	26.2	29.4	30.0
Access to wilderness/undisturbed nature	38.7	38.6	30.0
Outdoor adventure activities	36.4[a]	24.7	29.0
Chances to see wildlife not normally seen	42.3[a]	31.8	28.6
Beaches for sunbathing/swimming	29.5	23.0	27.5
A place providing value for money	23.0	32.1	22.9
Pleasant rural scenery	32.0	34.5	22.9
Interesting small towns/villages	13.6	23.8[a]	21.4[a]
Budget accommodation	22.6	18.4	20.0
A familiar well known place	7.5	12.7[a]	17.1[a]
Opportunities to increase knowledge	22.6	19.8	15.7
Resort areas	9.1	10.5	13.2
Inexpensive food	15.6	13.9	12.9
Shopping	7.8	13.6	11.4
Opportunities to visit family/friends	16.1	22.3[a]	11.4
Friendly local people	29.6[a]	28.6[a]	11.4
First class accommodation	7.2	13.2	10.2
High quality restaurants	6.1	7.9	7.2
Good nightlife/entertainment	11.6	6.3	7.2
Experience indigenous culture	15.5[a]	4.5	7.1
A fashionable place to go	2.5	3.5	2.9

[a] Significant between group differences based on analysis of variance tests.

group is 7.89 on a 0–10 scale. The locational information indicates that 11 sites are visited by at least 25% of these visitors — a statistic which indicates a modest reach in their travel behaviour compared to the other self-drive sub-groups.

Domestic Self-Drive Market — Without Children

The information pertaining to this group is drawn from 388 respondents. Predominantly from the Eastern states of Australia, this group is also characterised by people travelling with their partner (65%) but other family and friends are also common companions. The group is most likely to be over 51 years of age with 52% being in their 50s and 60s. For many of these visitors, unlike the international visitors, they are often on a second or third visit to the region. They tend to spend a little less time in the region than the international visitors (just less than two weeks) and are highly likely to stay in a caravan (54%) or a motel/hotel (20%). The locational information indicates that 22 sites are visited by at least 25% of these visitors and while this indicates a considerable effort and achievement it may be confounded by previous visit recollections. The mean satisfaction for this group is 8.32 on a 0–10 scale, a figure which is statistically significant in terms of being the highest satisfaction score recorded for the sub-groups.

Domestic Self-Drive — With Children

The information pertaining to this group is drawn from 71 respondents. Predominantly from the state of Queensland itself (49%) as well as the Eastern states of Australia, the adults are most often accompanied by either one or just two children (32%). Like the other domestic visitors they have visited the region on multiple previous occasions but their length of stay is typically seven days rather than the fourteen days or more of the other groups. Like the other domestic travellers, staying in a caravan (46%) or hotel/motel (20%) are important accommodation options. There is some accommodation with friends and relatives for this group. The locational information indicates a visit to 17 locations by at least 25% of the sample. A distinctive feature of this group is the amount of planning for the holiday with 69% of these travellers having planned five months in advance of their travel — the corresponding figure for the other two self-drive segments are 50% for the international travellers and 57% for the domestic self-drive without children group. The mean satisfaction for this group lies between the scores of the other two segments — on this occasion the mean satisfaction with their visit to the North Queensland region was 8.01 on the 0–10 satisfaction scale.

This broad demographic, trip planning, localised and satisfaction information on these three self-drive market sub-groups can be expanded by considering the motivational profile responses for the three groups. This material is presented in Table 2.2. The material presented in Table 2.2 reinforces several points made in this chapter. As with the material presented on the differences between self-drive and non-self-drive tourists, the motivation and destination attribute features can be seen as a pattern of responses. The data presented represent the percentage of people who consider this attribute to be very important, so that even a low percentage still indicates that some people think it is very important and further, it is highly likely, that a large number of people think it is somewhat important. This finding and presentation of the data corresponds to one of the attributes of a good approach to motivational studies noted in the introductory sections of this chapter. Specifically, the presentation of findings on motivation, it was argued, should reflect a multi-motive view of human behaviour. Further, this notion was effectively incorporated in the conceptual map of Figure 2.1 where a range of core motives common and important to many tourist situations was outlined but was supplemented by a further set of motives likely to be highly important in some situations.

An inspection of the numerical information in Table 2.2 confirms these patterned responses of fluctuating levels of importance of the motives and destination attribute information in this specific context where the transport dominates the tourist experience. For example, the domestic self-drive group with children consider a number of motives/features to be very important but they are distinctive in clearly identifying activities for the whole family, interesting small towns and villages and a familiar well known place as relatively more important than do the other groups. The effects of life-cycle factors, in this case the presence of usually one or two children as a part of the travel party, expresses itself in the greater importance given to these motivational statements. Similarly the domestic travellers with children place relatively less importance, although these features are not unimportant, in opportunities to visit family and friends, outstanding scenery, friendly local people and experiencing indigenous culture.

A consideration of the traveller motivation, life-cycle and demographic links manifested in the self-drive transport choices can be developed in a similar way for the domestic — no children travellers. This group places a relatively greater importance on outstanding scenery and warm sunny weather, interesting small towns and villages, opportunities to visit family/friends and friendly local people.

The international travellers are distinctive in relation to the other two self-drive groups with defining and contrasting items being the importance of having the chance to visit the Great Barrier Reef, outstanding scenery, warm sunny weather, outdoor adventure activities and chances to see wildlife not normally seen. Friendly local people and the chance to experience indigenous culture are also relatively more important for the international self-drive group.

In many of the contrasts presented in Table 2.2 it needs to be stated that the items identified as different from those of other groups are not the most important item or items in the entire motivation/destination features list. For example, five items are considered very important by all groups; these are opportunities to visit rainforest, chance to escape a busy life, activities for the whole family, wide variety of things to do, a place I can talk of when I get home, and access to wilderness and undisturbed nature. Again the importance of the current pattern-based approach to motivational research can be stressed since the profiles being explored here represent some divergences from a common base rather than markedly different independent results.

Broader Issues and Research Directions

The findings of this case study illustrate, even within one style of transport, that there are motivational differences amongst similar traveller types. Further, the study illustrated that these motivational differences and the satisfaction visitors received from their holiday experiences were linked to life-cycle and demographic sub-group differences.

There are numerous opportunities for additional studies extending our understanding of transport and its role in the tourist experience. Confining attention to road travel and the self-drive market, there is already active research effort collecting demographic material on road-related accidents and injuries (Wilks *et al.* 2000). The response of visitors to warning signs and information about hazardous conditions could be developed as a part of a preventive program to support this kind of travel (Peach & Bath 1999).

Another area for development lies in greater consideration of the tourist's travelling partners. An important issue identified in the present study is whether or not the travel was conducted with other people, especially with children, and travel party composition was linked to such motivational needs as activities for the whole group. There are other ways in which this travel party composition could be explored and linked to transport choice. For example, experiences of single independent travellers could be compared for various kinds of transport. Similarly travel party composition linked to life-cycle stages such as couples travelling without children, family travel, seniors travelling together, and affinity groups on tour could all be compared.

A further approach offering possibilities for linking motivational profiles and transport use would be to assess how the use of a particular transport style varies with the travellers' previous experiences and confidence. This set of studies could include retrospective accounts recalling the use of different transport styles in the travel career of participants. Additionally, the issue of how travel is used on arrival in a new setting and how the use changes with time could be explored.

A further possibility for research effort in this field would be to tie studies to the concept map outlined in this paper. In particular, the kinds of work described in this chapter could be repeated for the transport roles defined as integrated, functional and significant constraint. It can be readily predicted that a variety of patterns will emerge according to the contexts and market segments analysed. It is to be hoped, however, that active research attention to motivation and the transport role categories outlined here may, in future, develop some cumulative power.

Acknowledgments

The authors would like to acknowledge the efforts of Anne Norris in assisting with the statistical analyses. This work was partly funded by the Rainforest CRC.

References

Bannister, D. (Ed.) (1995). *Transport and urban development*. London: E. & F. N. Spon.

Black, N., & Clark, A. (1998). *Tourism in North West Queensland: 1996. Tourist characteristics, numbers and travel flows*. Townsville, Australia: Tropical Savannas CRC.

Black, N., & Rutledge, J. (1995). *The Outback: The authentic Australian adventure*. Townsville, Australia: James Cook University Press.

Bull, A. (1996). The economics of cruising: An application to the short ocean cruise market. *Journal of Tourism Studies*, 7(2), 28–35.

Burton, R. J. C. (1994). Geographic patterns of tourism in Europe. In: C. P. Cooper, & A. Lockwood (Eds), *Progress in Tourism, Recreation and Hospitality Management* (pp. 3–25). Chichester: Wiley.

Crompton, J. (1979). Motivations for pleasure vacation. *Annals of Tourism Research, 6,* 408–424.

Douglas, N., & Douglas, N. (1996). P&O's Pacific. *Journal of Tourism Studies, 7*(2), 2–14.

Elby, D. W., & Molnar, L. J. (2002). Importance of scenic byways in route choice: A survey of driving tourists in the United States. *Transportation Research Part A, 36,* 95–106.

Erlander, S., & Stewart, N. F. (1990). *The gravity model in transportation analysis: Theory and extensions.* Utrecht: VSP.

Fesenmaier, D. (1988). Integrating activity patterns into destination choice models. *Journal of Leisure Research, 20*(3), 175–191.

Fodness, D. (1994). Measuring tourist motivation. *Annals of Tourism Research, 21*(3), 555–581.

Gee, C. Y., Makens, J. C., & Choy, D. J. L. (1989). *The travel industry* (2nd ed.). New York: Van Nostrand Reinhold.

Gunn, C. A. (1994). *Tourism planning* (3rd ed.). New York: Taylor and Francis.

Gunn, C. (1988). *Tourism planning* (2nd ed.). New York: Taylor & Francis.

Iso-Ahola, S. (1982). Toward a social psychological theory of tourism motivation: A rejoinder. *Annals of Tourism Research, 9*(2), 256–262.

Jafari, J. (Ed.) (2000). *The encyclopedia of tourism.* Oxford: Pergamon.

Johnson, P., & Thomas, B. (Eds) (1992). *Choice and demand in tourism.* London: Mansell.

Kandampully, J., Mok, C., & Sparks, B. (2001). *Service quality management in hospitality, tourism, and leisure.* USA: Haworth Press.

Kozac, M. (2001). A critical review of approaches to measure satisfaction with tourist destinations. In: J. Mazanec, G. Crouch, J. R. Brent Ritchie, & A. Woodside (Eds), *Consumer Psychology of Tourism Hospitality and Leisure* (Vol. 2, pp. 303–320). Wallingford, Oxon: CABI Publishing.

Lee, U.-I., & Pearce, P. (2002). Travel motivation and travel career patterns. In: *Proceedings of First Asia Pacific Forum for Graduate Students Research in Tourism, 22 May 2002, Macao* (pp. 17–35). Hong Kong: Hong Kong Polytechnic University.

Lue, C., Crompton, J., & Fesemaier, D. (1993). Conceptualisation of multi-destination pleasure trips. *Annals of Tourism Research, 20*(2), 289–301.

McHugh, K., & Mings, R. C. (1992). Canadian snowbirds in Arizona. *Journal of Applied Recreation Research, 17,* 255–277.

McIntosh, R., Goeldner, C. R., & Ritchie, J. R. B. (1995). *Tourism principles, practices, philosophies.* New York: Wiley.

Mill, R. C., & Morrison, A. M. (1995). *The tourism system: An introductory text.* New Jersey: Prentice-Hall.

Morrison, A. M., Hsieh, S., & O'Leary, J. T. (1995). Segmenting the visiting friends and relatives market by holiday activity participation. *Journal of Tourism Studies, 6*(1), 48–63.

Moscardo, G., Morrison, A. M., Pearce, P. L., Lang, C.-T., & O'Leary, J. T. (1996a). Understanding destination vacation choice through travel motivation and activities. *Journal of Vacation Marketing, 2*(2), 109–122.

Moscardo, G., Morrison, A., Cai, L., Nadkarni, N., & O'Leary, J. (1996b). Tourist perspectives on cruising: Multidimensional scaling analyses of cruising and other holiday types. *Journal of Tourism Studies, 7*(2), 54–63.

Murphy, L. (1997). *Young budget travellers: A marketing and decision-making analysis.* Unpublished doctoral dissertation, James Cook University, Townsville, Australia.

Noe, F. P. (1999). *Tourism service satisfaction.* Champaign, IL: Sagamore.

Oliver, T. (2001). The consumption of tour routes in cultural landscapes. In: J. A. Mazanec, G. I. Crouch, J. Brent Ritchie, & A. G. Woodside (Eds), *Consumer Psychology of Tourism, Hospitality and Leisure* (pp. 273–284). Wallingford, Oxon: CABI.

Opperman, M. (1997). First-time and repeat visitors to New Zealand. *Tourism Management, 18*(3), 177–181.

Parolin, B. P. (2001). Structure of day trips in the Illawarra tourism region of New South Wales. *Journal of Tourism Studies, 12*(1), 11–27.

Peach, H., & Bath, N. (1999). Visitors without health and safety information in North Queensland: Extent of the problem. *Journal of Tourism Studies, 10*(2), 62–69.

Pearce, P. L. (1981). Route maps: A study of travellers' perception of a section of countryside. *Journal of Environmental Psychology, 1*, 141–155.

Pearce, P. L. (1993). Fundamentals of tourist motivation. In: D. Pearce, & R. Butler (Eds), *Tourism Research: Critiques and Challenges* (pp. 85–105). London: Rutledge and Kegan Paul.

Pearce, P. L. (1999). Touring for pleasure: Studies of the senior self-drive travel market. *Tourism Recreation Research, 24*(1), 35–42.

Pearce, P. L., & Fagence, M. (1996). The legacy of Kevin Lynch: Research implications. *Annals of Tourism Research, 23*, 576–598.

Pearce, P., Morrison, A., & Rutledge, J. (1998). *Tourism: Bridges across continents*. Sydney: McGraw-Hill.

Pearce, P. L., Morrison, A., Scott, N., O'Leary, J., Nadkarni, N., & Moscardo, G. (1996). The holiday market in Queensland. Building an understanding of visitors staying in commercial accommodation. In: G. Prosser (Ed.), *Tourism and Hospitality Research* (pp. 427–442). Canberra: Bureau of Tourism Research.

Queensland Government (2001). *2000–2001 Annual Report*. Brisbane: Tourism Queensland.

Ryan, C. (1998). The travel career ladder: An appraisal. *Annals of Tourism Research, 25*(4), 936–957.

Sen, A., & Smith, T. E. (1995). *Gravity models of spatial interaction behaviour*. Berlin: Springer.

Soemanto, R. B. (1995). Low cost transportation and tourism. A profile of the becak's role in tourism development in Surakarta, Central Java. In: T. Sofield, & Sri Samiati Tarjana (Eds), *A Profile of Javanese Culture* (pp. 33–36). Townsville: James Cook University.

Taplin, J. H. E., & Qiu, M. (1997). Car trip attraction and route choice in Australia. *Annals of Tourism Research, 24*(3), 624–637.

Tourism Queensland (2002, September). *Tourism Queensland News*, Issue 10. Tourism Research. Brisbane: Tourism Queensland.

Wahab, S. E. (1975). *Tourism management*. London: Tourism International Press.

Wallis, M. (1990). *Route 66: The mother road*. New York: St. Martin's Press.

Walmsley, D. J., & Jenkins, J. M. (1992). Tourism cognitive mapping of unfamiliar environments. *Annals of Tourism Research, 19*, 268–286.

Wilks, J., Watson, B., & Hansen, J. (2000). International drivers and road safety in Queensland, Australia. *Journal of Tourism Studies, 11*(2), 36–43.

Wood, D. F., & Johnson, J. C. (1993). *Contemporary transport*. New York: MacMillan.

World Tourism Organization (WTO) (1999). *International tourism*. Madrid, Spain: WTO.

Young, M. (1999). Cognitive maps of nature-based tourists. *Annals of Tourism Research, 26*, 817–839.

Chapter 3

Transport and Tourism: Equity and Sustainability Issues

Derek Hall

Introduction

This chapter seeks to explore issues of equity and sustainability relating to tourism transport. Although issues of "sustainability" have been in the forefront of academic, and to some extent public, discussion, in both the transport and tourism policy arenas, little synergy or complementarity has been achieved between the transport and tourism debates on the impacts of transport externality costs borne by host populations and environments in tourism destination areas. Issues of social, economic and spatial equity represent important elements of such debates (e.g. Lyons *et al*. 2002), yet they are rarely addressed systematically and holistically at the tourism/transport interface (Hall 1999; Page 1999: 4).

Framework

Within tourism destination areas, transport demand can be conceptualised in terms of three ideal categories of transport users, all potentially competing with each other for transport and transport space in terms of public transport access and road space, including parking, cycling and pedestrian space:

- the host community: residents of the destination area who are not directly involved in the tourism industry but who find themselves competing with both tourists and tourism industry employees;
- employees of the tourism industry — who may be drawn from the host community or may be incomers from other parts of the region or country, or from another country — and who may have particular transport needs because of the demands of tourism's unconventional working hours; and
- tourists: who may or may not use specialised, differentiated transport.

While oversimplifying the complex range of relationships between, and relative identities, of "host" and "guest" (e.g. Kohn 1997), as a framework for addressing competition for access to transport and transport space, this categorisation provides a potentially useful conceptual framework within which to explore the equity and sustainability of guest-host relations through transport access and use.

One obvious constraint on the development of a literature in this area is the ability or otherwise of identifying tourism transport as a discrete functional entity for analytical and policy purposes (Halsall 1992; Page 1994, 1999: 2). This reflects the obvious logistical problems that:

(a) tourism transport embraces a diverse range of modes, functions, spatial relationships, and ownership patterns;
(b) transport forms may be employed for tourism purposes exclusively (charter aircraft, tour coaches, cruise liners, "heritage" transport), partly (scheduled air services, express buses, taxis, hire cars, long distance trains, ferries), occasionally (private cars, local public transport in a seasonal tourism destination), or rarely (private and public commuter transport); and
(c) transport forms also may be employed for tourism purposes explicitly (charter company aircraft, touring coaches, cruise ships), or anonymously (hire cars, private cars).

Recognition of these analytical and conceptual issues helps to set the context within which to identify the way in which transport may amplify and articulate equity and sustainability questions in international tourism. The conceptualisation of such relationships may be severely limited by the cultural context. Notable in this respect is the dichotomy between less developed societies where tourism transport may be seen as an instrument and/or symbol of differentiation and inequality (e.g. Simon 1996), and economically more developed societies where the very lack of differentiation between transport of host and guest, commuter and recreationalist, may pose practical administrative and planning problems for addressing ways of tackling the external costs of different transport functions (Oberholzer-Gee & Weck-Hannemann 2002). In this chapter, this dichotomy will be employed to articulate equity and sustainability issues, respectively.

Equity Issues

In less developed societies, the role of transport as the potential regulator to culture contact, constraining or encouraging host-tourist interaction, may be implicit rather than explicit. Policies on itineraries, transport mode and regularity may impose significant economic, social and environmental benefits or dis-benefits on the host population. Income and life-style differences between tourists and the "host" population may be expressed in the contrast between, for example, air-conditioned tourist transport and local para-transit modes, or between a modern concrete and glass international airport and impenetrable, densely populated spontaneous settlements of poor migrants thrown up just beyond its perimeter. In such ways, tourism transport may act as a symbol reinforcing notions of inequality, unattainability, relative deprivation and/or demonstration effects (e.g. see Seaton 1997, in the context of Cuba).

Tourism's role in reinforcing explicit inequity may be exacerbated and "institutionalised" where charter operators and multinational chains promote their own transport and excursions. They may do this by employing operatives from outside of the host region, who may be encouraged to provide minimal or even mis-information about locally-owned transport modes for their clients, perhaps out of genuine (albeit encouraged) personal ignorance, in order to retain their custom (e.g. see Kalisch 1997). This may be accompanied by dark warnings not to visit certain places or areas, perhaps again for reasons of commercial competition. The resulting reinforcement of host-guest segregation by (Western) multinational tour organisations might be viewed as an outcome of a "corporate authoritarian" stance.

In countries whose governments have followed "state authoritarian" ideologies, the deliberate separation of tourists from the host population may be institutionalised in an attempt to forestall any ideological, cultural or financial contagion passing from foreigners to locals. Under such circumstances, tourism transport may be seen as an instrument of policy and a symbol of underlying political philosophy, which may be expressed in a process of mutual exclusion. For example, under neo-Stalinist ideological circumstances, formerly in Albania, and still in North Korea, foreign tourists are barred from using public transport unescorted. Instead, they are almost hermetically sealed within state-owned tourist transport which is rendered very explicitly exclusive and inaccessible to the "host" population by virtue of a range of largely administrative constraints (Hall 1990). In "revolutionary" Cuba, from the 1960s to the 1990s locals were legally prohibited from owning or undertaking transactions in foreign currency. This effectively excluded them from international tourist facilities (which, somewhat ironically, undertook transactions exclusively in U.S. dollars), including tourist taxis and buses (Hall 1992, 2001; Seaton 1997). Of course, in the context of any such formal proscription, "black market" activity and the role of the grey economy is stimulated, albeit largely unchronicled. For example, spare parts intended for tourist transport may be trickled down and diffused through the local informal economy.

It has long been recognised that tourism can perform a prestige and propaganda role by attempting to present a region or country's "good face" to the rest of the world. The roles that transport may have in this respect include:

(a) the provision of high quality facilities of which transport is a part, and
(b) by prescribing tourists' itineraries which can be carefully managed by the host authorities in such a way as to exclude, or at least minimise, the possibility of foreign visitors being confronted by negative images of the host society and environment.

In response, the very physical nature of the transport employed as an instrument of such policy may act as a source of pride for the local population, or may emerge as both a source of envy and object of hatred in its symbolism of host-guest inequalities and of the suppressive and hypocritical nature of the host country's political regime.

Offshore, the globalised nature of ocean cruise tourism (Wood 2000) raises a number of equity issues. First, cruise liners' very size symbolises high concentrations of multinational capital. They spend much of their time in non-territorial waters, only briefly visiting favoured ports of call. where cost savings can be made by taking advantage of destinations which have cheap or low-tax fuel bunkering (Bull 1996). Second, cruise ship crews may represent highly diverse labour forces originating from up to 50 countries on a single ship. Such globally-recruited labour is usually stratified into three groups — officers, staff and crew — who have separate living quarters, segregated dining areas, and different rules of engagement concerning interaction with passengers. They also enjoy vastly different pay levels, with usually a clear ethnic distinctiveness attached to the hierarchical divisions. Third, Avoidance of national or international regulations is a major characteristic of cruise lines (Wood 2000). The use of flags of convenience (FOCs) circumvent home country employment laws, taxes and maritime regulations. Indeed, cruise development has been assisted by the climate of deregulation and availability of pools of flexible and cheap migrant labour. FOC ship crews are subject to the laws of the country in which the ship is flagged, and in most FOC countries employment laws protecting the rights of workers are virtually non-existent. Although dominated by the American market, not a single cruise ship plying the Caribbean flies the U.S. flag. For example, Royal Caribbean Cruise Lines, although based in Florida, is registered as a Liberian corporation and is estimated to save around US$30 million annually in U.S. taxes by registering its ships under FOCs (Frantz 1999).

Sustainability Issues

In developed countries, the substantial tourism impacts literature has only occasionally addressed political and social dimensions of leisure transport's external costs. In debates on road tolls, congestion pricing, carbon taxes and other mechanisms seeking the repayment and/or reduction of road transport externalities, the differentiation of tourists and non-tourists competing for road space is rarely addressed, largely because of the potential difficulties of implementing any discriminatory policy (e.g. see Fietelson 2002). Similarly, the competition between tourists and hosts for public transport use has rarely attracted critical analysis (e.g. Robbins 1997).

In many parts of the world, urban areas bear much of the burden of increasing tourism pressures, as coastal resorts, capital cities or heritage sites. Many suffer traffic congestion and pollution and most lack adequate policies to cope with these challenges which both exert adverse economic effects and diminish the quality of life for many residents and travellers. In the EU, more than 90% of external costs of transport derive from road transport: motor cars, the main form of tourist transport, accounting for around 60% (Rothengatter & Mauch 1994).

Although the sustainability of tourism activity is a much discussed and contested concept, the substantial tourism impacts literature has only rarely addressed the externalities and inequalities arising from transport, and then often at a global level in terms of air transport impacts (Schipper *et al.* 2001).

The contradiction of the motor car literally providing the vehicle for more and different recreation and tourism activities while causing likely irrevocable local and global damage in the process, is articulated in the fact that:

(a) road transport and specifically the motor car is the least suitable form of transport in terms of its impact on the environment and society; it represents one of the greatest threats to the physical and socio-cultural well-being, particularly in more popular rural destinations; yet

(b) for the individual traveller the car is one of the cheapest and most convenient and flexible forms of motorised transport; and

(c) for many governments, particularly during the 1970s–1990s, provision of adequate road capacity for predicted levels of traffic was pursued to ensure maximum mobility in the economy (Docherty 1999).

There are several management approaches which can be taken to combat problems of motor car use, the first two of which at least are not sustainable:

- *Do nothing*: allowing congestion to act as its own deterrent is the simplest and most negative approach. Of course the wider environmental implications of such an approach are considerable, and while congestion is often localised and seasonal, it may act as a major repellent to potential repeat visiting tourists and tour transport companies.
- *Predict and provide*: improving the road network and car park provision. But building new roads, upgrading existing ones and providing more parking may improve accessibility in the short term and appears attractive to visitors, and as such tends to generate even more traffic in a self-perpetuating spiral (although see Prakash *et al.* 2001).

Of the more positive policy instruments available to restrain motor transport use, there are restrictive policies, economic incentives/disincentives, policies to influence attitudinal change, integrated land use planning, priority for public transport, support for "green" modes, and application of technological innovation (Hall 1998). The first three will be briefly considered in relation to the externalities of tourism pressures and questions of differentiation between leisure- and non-leisure-related transport use.

Restrictive Policies

Conventional wisdom suggests that any restrictive policy needs to embrace wide ranging objectives likely to receive public support. However, in tourist destination areas, components of that public — the host community and visitors — may hold very different aspirations and vested interests. For example, traffic restrictions in central Athens and in Italian cities such as Florence pursued for explicit environmental reasons (Jones 1991) tend to affect indiscriminately both leisure- and non-leisure traffic in these explicitly tourist cities. With the substantial global growth of urban tourism and the post-industrial prospect of us all becoming either tourists and/or the objects of tourism, areas of encroachment and conflict are increasing. This is not simply between transport users, as exemplified when the residents of the historic town of Bath in the U.K. opposed the noise and inconvenience of an open-top double-decker sightseeing bus service with running commentary passing through their crescent with tourist "gazers" at bedroom height.

The designation of traffic-free zones — essential for tourism access to, and appreciation of, city centres where a significant proportion of an urban area's cultural heritage attractions may be found (Monheim 2000) has often met initial opposition from retailers. They assume that a lack of motorised access to their premises will result in a loss of custom (as well as creating potential difficulties for deliveries). Yet, support for restraint schemes usually increases after their introduction, as drivers and retailers come to recognise their benefits (Hass-Klau 1993). Further, substantial potential for the development of street-based recreation is opened with traffic-free spaces. Conventional street recreation such as socialising, play and window shopping are enhanced, while the removal of traffic and its emissions reduces health threats, encourages the external cleaning and refurbishment of buildings. Furthermore, the provision of street furniture such as seats to assist heavily laden shoppers, older and less physically mobile people, and the planting of flowers and other vegetation (Williams 1995).

Indeed, the freeing up of space for the extension of urban green areas can provide an important stage for the recreational interaction of visitors and locals. Ironically, the success of such schemes may result in tourist pressures and congestion becoming so great that even in pedestrianised areas constraints on access may need to be imposed to acknowledge carrying capacities, as, for example, suggested for the congested Charles Bridge in Prague (e.g. Simpson 1997; Stevenson 1997).

The debate on traffic access to, and congestion problems at, rural honeypots such as national parks has a long history. In the U.K., over half of road traffic growth in rural areas in the 1990s was leisure-related (Cullinane & Stokes 1998), with over 90% of visitors to national parks in England and Wales arriving by car (Countryside Commission 1996). The transport implications of new forms of rural — particularly activity — tourism have been at least three-fold:

(1) the additional greater reliance upon private motor transport because of the need to convey such bulky items as golf or ski equipment, surfboards, dinghies and hang gliders (Charlton 1998),
(2) penetration of traffic to more remote rural locations, which are more likely to be isolated from public transport routes,
(3) the likelihood of increased congestion, particularly at peak holiday periods, causing greater inconvenience for both rural dwellers and visitors.

This has implications: (a) for negative environmental impacts, in generating atmospheric pollution (notably carbon dioxide) and potential traffic accidents (Sharples & Fletcher 2001); and (b) for social exclusion processes, whereby those who cannot afford or who do not have access to personal motorised transport are virtually excluded from these recreational activities.

National park traffic management policies (e.g. Coleman 1997; Steiner & Bristow 2000), tend to be of the "carrot" variety (Cullinane & Cullinane 1999), such as providing park-and-ride facilities and car exclusion zones. For example, provision of the North York Moors national park Moorsbus service is claimed to have saved over 100,000 miles of recreational car journeys annually. In the Derwent Valley of the Peak District national park, roads have been closed to motorised traffic and visitors have been encouraged to explore the region on bicycles. In the USA, the use of private cars is now banned in Yosemite national park and visitors are required to use the provided transport system. But generally, such schemes are only viable in managed areas where access may be restricted, and often appear to be unpopular with sufficient proportions of electorates to inhibit support from politicians. As a result, relatively little influence appears to have been exerted on modal choice (Eaton & Holding 1996), although several German authors are more optimistic (e.g. Geissler 1998; Wöhler 1998).

Economic Incentives/Disincentives

The imposition of taxation and/or economic disincentive measures aims to increase the relative costs of motor travel in order to move towards representing its true external cost to society. It should also aim to encourage changes in land use policy which influence both recreational and non-recreational travel patterns (Jackson 2001). But policy implementation has been patchy: one relatively isolated example being a carbon-related tax introduced in Sweden in 1990 which was revised upwards in 1994 (Maddison *et al.* 1996; Sterner 1994). Urban road pricing and congestion charging is much discussed (e.g. Ahlstrand 2001; Harrington *et al.* 2001; Viegas 2001), and has become something of a political football in such major tourist cities as Edinburgh and London (e.g. Crawford 2000; Jeffery 2002).

In theory, open access to road networks can be rationed through area licensing systems or by employing electronic distance charging. Differential rates can be charged according to the time of day and congestion conditions. Precedents for differential charging exist within the experience of yield management on public transport, particularly in attempts to dissuade discretionary travel during peak periods. Much tourist road transport, for example, could potentially be charged out of peak traffic times, given the usually discretionary nature of leisure travel. Charges for road damage could be related to the distance a vehicle travels, its weight and number of axles: this could equally apply to tourist coaches, motor homes and towed caravans as to heavy goods vehicles. Evidence from Norway at least, suggests that as people become conditioned to them, toll systems become easier to deploy both to restrain traffic and to stimulate congestion pricing (Larsen & Østmoe 2001; Odeck & Brathen 1997).

An ideal set of policy instruments would be able to differentiate charges between vehicles with respect to emission profiles, congestion factors and such variables as trip function, including whether they were being used formally for tourism purposes. This latter dimension poses logistical problems of implementation: if targeting hire cars, for example, how can their purpose of use be distinguished? For privately-owned vehicles the task is even more difficult: few drivers would admit to pursuing a higher charge activity if they could get away with paying a lower charge. Information technology development has rendered such policies technically possible, but addressing their political, social, cultural and psychological components requires imagination and strength of purpose. With electronic road congestion pricing and a vehicle quota system, Singapore is often cited as representing one of the best examples of what can be done with strong political will (Chu 2002; Seik 1998, 2000). However, it is usually assumed that in "Western democracies" attitude and behaviour change should be brought about by education and information rather than by imposition, particularly in the face of significant political interest groups such as the roads lobby.

Attitudinal and Behavioural Change

Policies to reduce the negative externalities of transport use need to be aimed at changing attitudes at a number of levels of both public and political awareness. Educational campaigns, through targeted information, publicity and community programmes should emphasise the full external effects of travel behaviour to encourage acceptance and understanding of the need for change, and to change attitudes towards the use of non-car modes — public transport, cycling and walking — by promoting their positive aspects (Stradling *et al.* 2001; Wright & Egan 2001). This embraces common cause with the pursuit of sustainable tourism which calls for tourists to be educated in terms of the sensitivity of their cultural and environmental behaviour — to the point of developing codes of conduct — and for tourism companies and the global travel industry to adopt philosophies and practices embracing sustainability ideals (e.g. Orams 1997). However, implicit in both but rarely explicitly expressed, and never by the tourism industry, is the environmentally beneficial effect that less travel would bring. In an era of increasing leisure time and longer-distance travel, when freedom to travel is equated with democracy and human rights, restrictions on travel, as current urban congestion debates indicate, are politically difficult to enact.

Yet with clear global impacts of transport emissions, and notably from aircraft (Olsthoorn 2001; Schipper *et al.* 2001), ever-increasing mobility may require some future global rationing and allocation process other than that of the free market. Potential alternatives — virtual reality travel and tourism, space tourism or sub-marine tourism — would all appear to have severely constraining limitations.

Through the expansion and diffusion of information technology, it has become conventional wisdom that many jobs traditionally carried out in city-centres could be accomplished as effectively at home, thereby reducing the need to travel to work (Graham 1991; but see also Grimes 2001; Hjorthol 2002). As a service industry, however, much tourism employment is based on face-to-face activity. If tourism centres and leisure complexes can be seen as the factories of the twenty-first century, tourism employers need to pursue more tangible and immediate ways to influence travel behaviour. This might be through the adoption of integrated plans for their employees, a direction in which the U.K. transport white papers have pointed (DETR 1998; Scottish Office 1998), although they have not been followed through in policy application in the face of powerful private motoring lobbies. But tourism tends to be characterised by large numbers of small enterprises for whom "green" transport plans are more difficult to manage and monitor (e.g. Coleman 2000).

Conclusions

This chapter has raised several analytical questions concerning the actual and symbolic representations of equity expressed in leisure and tourism mobility and the sustainability implications of the externalities arising from such mobility. Such issues have significance for members of host communities, transport and land-use planning in host areas, tourists and the tourism industry. Within this framework, the chapter has explored two sets of questions which appear to have been neglected at the interface of the literature on transport and tourism.

In terms of equity, transport has the potential to act as a gatekeeper to culture contact, constraining or encouraging host-tourist interaction and explicitly exacerbating inequity. As seen in the case of cruise tourism, it can very explicitly act to exploit the globalisation of labour and capital for recruitment to the tourism industry. In terms of sustainability, transport exerts substantial externality effects, as witnessed by growing alarm over the growth and impact of international air travel at a global level. But while there has long been concern over the local impacts of tourism development processes, the role of tourist mobility at a local level has tended not to be placed in a prominent position in debates on externality effects. In addressing pricing mechanisms for road transport's externalities, the differentiation of tourists and non-tourists is problematic but not insurmountable.

Sustainability is a key strategy concept in both transport and tourism policies, and acts as an area of practical implementation binding the two functions and areas of government policy together such as recreation-related strategies within local transport plans. But its attainment continues to be constrained by:

(a) our relatively poor knowledge and understanding of the complex patterns of tourism-related activity,
(b) the almost universal separation of transport and tourism responsibilities between different (and often competing) government ministries, and
(c) the fragmented nature of the industry into myriad private, public and voluntary bodies involved in implementation.

References

Ahlstrand, I. (2001). The politics of transport investment and pricing in Stockholm. *Journal of Transport Economics and Policy*, 35(3), 473–490.

Bull, A. O. (1996). The economics of cruising: An application to the short ocean cruise market. *Journal of Tourism Studies*, 7(2), 28–35.

Charlton, C. (1998). Public Transport and sustainable tourism: The case of the Devon and Cornwall rail partnership. In: C. M. Hall & A. A. Lew (Eds), *Sustainable Tourism: A Geographical Perspective* (pp. 132–145). Harlow: Longman.

Chu, S. (2002). Auctioning rights to vehicle ownership: Singapore's experience with sealed-bid tenders. *Transportation Research Part A: Policy and Practice*, 36(6), 555–561.

Coleman, C. (1997). Tourist traffic in English national parks — an innovative approach to management. *Journal of Tourism Studies*, 8, 2–15.

Coleman, C. (2000). Green commuter plans and the small employer: An investigation into the attitudes and policy of the small employer towards staff travel and green commuter plans. *Transport Policy*, 7(2), 139–148.

Countryside Commission (1996). *Peace in the parks — but too many cars, survey reveals*. Countryside Commission press release (http://www.coi.gov.uk/depts/GCM/coi4029c.ok).

Crawford, I. A. (2000). *The distributional effects of the proposed London congestion charging scheme*. London: Institute for Fiscal Studies, Briefing Note No. 11 (http://www.ifs.org.uk).

Cullinane, S., & Cullinane, E. (1999). Attitudes towards traffic problems and public transport in the Dartmoor and Lake District National Parks. *Journal of Transport Geography*, 7(1), 79–87.

Cullinane, S., & Stokes, G. (1998). *Rural transport policy*. Oxford: Pergamon.

DETR (Department of the Environment, Transport and the Regions) (1998). *A new deal for transport*. London: The Stationery Office.

Docherty, I. (1999). *Making tracks: The politics of local rail transport*. Aldershot: Ashgate.

Eaton, B., & Holding, D. (1996). The evaluation of public transport alternatives to the car in British National Parks. *Journal of Transport Geography*, *4*(1), 55–65.

Fietelson, E. (2002). Introducing environmental equity dimensions into the sustainable transport discourse: Issues and pitfalls. *Transportation Research Part D: Transport and Environment*, *7*(2), 99–118.

Frantz, D. (1999). Gaps in sea laws shield pollution by cruise lines. *New York Times*, January 3.

Geissler, H. (1998). Verkehrsverlagerungen in verkehrlich hoch belasteten Fremdenverkehrsregionen. Möglichkeiten der Bahn im Freizeitverkehr. *Informationen zur Raumentwicklung*, *6*, 415–420.

Graham, S. (1991). Telecommunications and the local economy: Some emerging policy issues. *Local Economy*, *6*, 116–136.

Grimes, S. (2001). Extending the information society beyond urban locations: Prospects and reality. In: L. Roberts & D. Hall (Eds), *Rural Tourism and Recreation: Principles to Practice* (pp. 106–110). Wallingford: CAB International.

Hall, D. R. (1990). Stalinism and tourism: A study of Albania and North Korea. *Annals of Tourism Research*, *17*(1), 36–54.

Hall, D. R. (1992). Tourism development in Cuba. In: D. Harrison (Ed.), *Tourism and the Less Developed Countries* (pp. 102–120). London: Belhaven.

Hall, D. R. (1998). Urban transport, environmental pressures and policy options. In: D. A. Pinder (Ed.), *The New Europe: Society and Environment* (pp. 435–454). Chichester and New York: Wiley.

Hall, D. (1999). Conceptualising tourism transport: Inequality and externality issues. *Journal of Transport Geography*, *7*(4), 181–188.

Hall, D. (2001). Tourism and development in communist and post-communist societies. In: D. Harrison (Ed.), *Tourism and the Less Developed World* (pp. 91–107). Wallingford: CAB International.

Halsall, D. A. (1992). Transport for tourism and recreation. In: B. S. Hoyle & R. D. Knowles (Eds), *Modern Transport Geography* (pp. 155–177). London: Belhaven Press.

Harrington, W., Krupnick, A. J., & Alberini, A. (2001). Overcoming public aversion to congestion pricing. *Transportation Research Part A: Policy and Practice*, *35*(2), 93–111.

Hass-Klau, C. (1993). Impact of pedestrianization and traffic calming on retailing. A review of the evidence from Germany and the U.K. *Transport Policy*, *1*(1), 21–31.

Hjorthol, R. J. (2002). The relation between daily travel and use of the home computer. *Transportation Research Part A: Policy and Practice*, *36*(5), 437–452.

Jackson, T. (2001). Environmental taxation: A new tool for local planning. *Regional Studies*, *35*(1), 80–86.

Jeffery, S. (2002). What will motorists have to pay to drive in central London? *The Guardian*, February 26 (http://www.guardian.co.uk/transport/Story/0,2763,519544,00.html).

Jones, P. (1991). *Devising new options for tackling traffic congestion in city centres*. Oxford: University of Oxford Transport Studies Unit.

Kalisch, A. (1997). Boom or bust for Kerala's taxi drivers. *In Focus*, *25*, 12.

Kohn, T. (1997). Island involvement and the evolving tourist. In: S. Abram, J. Waldren & D. V. L. Macleod (Eds), *Tourists and Tourism: Identifying with People and Places* (pp. 13–28). Oxford: Berg.

Larsen, O. I., & Østmoe (2001). The experience of urban toll cordons in Norway: Lessons for the future. *Journal of Transport Economics and Policy*, *35*(3), 473–490.

Lyons, G., Chatterjee, K., Beecroift, M., & Marsedn, G. (2002). Determinants of travel demand: Exploring the future society and lifestyles in the U.K. *Transport Policy*, *9*(1), 17–27.

Maddison, D., Pearce, D., Johansson, O., Calthrop, E., Litman, T., & Verhoef, E. (1996). *Blueprint 5: The true costs of road transport*. London: Earthscan.

Monheim, R. (2000). Fussgängerbereiche in Deutschen innenstädten. *Geographische Rundschau, 52*(7–8), 40–47.

Oberholzer-Gee, F., & Weck-Hannemann, H. (2002). Pricing road use: Political-economic and fairness considerations. *Transportation Research Part D: Transport and Environment, 7*(5), 357–371.

Odeck, J., & Brathen, S. (1997). On public attitudes towards implementation of toll roads — the case of Oslo Toll-Ring. *Transport Policy, 4*(2), 77–83.

Olsthoorn, X. (2001). Carbon dioxide emissions from international aviation: 1950–2050. *Journal of Air Transport Management, 7*(2), 87–93.

Orams, M. B. (1997). The effectiveness of environmental education: Can we turn tourists into 'greenies'? *Progress in Tourism and Hospitality Research, 3*, 295–306.

Page, S. J. (1994). *Transport for tourism*. London: Routledge.

Page, S. J. (1999). *Transport and tourism*. Harlow: Longman.

Prakash, A. B., Oliver, E. D. D. A., & Balcombe, K. (2001). Does building new roads really create extra traffic? Some new evidence. *Applied Economics, 33*(12), 1579–1586.

Robbins, D. (1997). *The relationship between scheduled transport operations and the development of tourism markets to peripheral island destinations*. Paper, International Tourism Research Conference: Peripheral Area Tourism, Research Centre of Bornholm, Nexø.

Rothengatter, W., & Mauch, S. (1994). *External effects of transport*. Paris: Union Internationale des Chemin de Fers.

Schipper, Y., Rietveld, P., & Nijkamp, P. (2001). Environmental externalities in air transport markets. *Journal of Air Transport Management, 7*(3), 169–179.

Scottish Office, The (1998). *Travel choices for Scotland*. Edinburgh: The Stationery Office.

Seaton, A. V. (1997). Demonstration effects or relative deprivation? The counter-revolutionary pressures of tourism in Cuba. *Progress in Tourism and Hospitality Research, 3*(4), 307–320.

Seik, F. T. (1998). A unique demand management instrument in urban transport: The vehicle quota system in Singapore. *Cities, 15*(1), 27–39.

Seik, F. T. (2000). An advanced demand management instrument in urban transport: Electronic road pricing in Singapore. *Cities, 17*(1), 33–45.

Sharples, J. M., & Fletcher, J. P. (2001). *Tourist road accidents in rural Scotland*. Edinburgh Central Research Unit: Scottish Executive.

Simon, D. (1996). *Transport and development in the Third World*. London: Routledge.

Simpson, F. R. (1997). *Planning, conservation and tourism: A comparison of capacity analysis in Edinburgh and Prague*. Unpublished Ph.D. thesis, Heriot-Watt University, Edinburgh.

Steiner, T. J., & Bristow, A. L. (2000). Road pricing in national parks: A case study in the Yorkshire Dales National Park. *Transport Policy, 7*(2), 93–103.

Sterner, T. (1994). Environmental tax reform: The Swedish experience. *European Environment, 4*(6), 20–25.

Stevenson, G. (1997). The good, the bad and the ugly: Post-communism tourism in the Czech Republic. *Tourism, 92*, 12–13.

Stradling, S. G., Meadows, M. L., & Beatty, S. (2001). Helping drivers out of their cars: Integrating transport policy and social psychology for sustainable change. *Transport Policy, 7*(3), 207–215.

Viegas, J. M. (2001). Making urban road pricing acceptable and effective: Searching for quality and equity in urban mobility. *Transport Policy, 8*(4), 289–294.

Williams, S. (1995). *Outdoor recreation and the urban environment*. London: Routledge.

Wöhler, K. (1998). Determinanten der Busnutzungsbereitschaft — eine empirische Studie zur Verlagerung des sekundären Ausflugsverkehrs von PKW auf den Bus. *Zeitschrift für Verkehrswissenschaft, 69*(3), 176–197.

Wood, R. E. (2000). Caribbean cruise tourism: Globalization at sea. *Annals of Tourism Research, 27*(2), 345–370.

Wright, C., & Egan, J. (2001). De-marketing the car. *Transport Policy, 7*(4), 287–294.

Chapter 4

Sustainable Mobility and Its Implications for Tourism

William R. Black

Introduction

Current high levels of tourism in the world are attributable in large part to the transport systems developed over the past several decades. All forms of tourism, whether it is a day of biking in the Black Forest of Germany or an automobile trip to the Rocky Mountains, or a flight to Scotland for a golfing holiday, involves the use of these or other transportation systems. During the past decade researchers have begun to question whether these same transport systems are sustainable given the externalities generated by their existence. If these transport systems are non-sustainable then one would expect that the tourism that depends upon them must also be non-sustainable, but is that the correct inference?

The purpose of this chapter is to explore the nature of sustainable mobility as it relates to tourism. We begin with a discussion of the nature of current transport systems and what it is that makes these non-sustainable. This is followed by an examination of the way in which transport and tourism interact. The economic nature of tourism must also be examined since it may generate benefits that exceed the negative externalities from the transport sector. An index of sustainable mobility is discussed and is used to examine the interaction of sustainability and mobility. We will conclude with an examination of whether tourism is sustainable based on its dependence on transport.

Sustainable Mobility

The term sustainable mobility is a phrase used primarily in Europe, but it is virtually identical to the North American notion of sustainable transport. The origins of the latter phrase go back to the 1987 Brundtland Report on sustainable development (World Commission on Environment and Development 1987). Although that report dealt only with sustainable development, which it defined as "development that meets the needs of the present without compromising the ability of future generations to meet their own needs," it has served as a springboard for definitions of sustainable agriculture, sustainable forestry, sustainable manufacturing, sustainable mobility or transport and others. In the transport case, *sustainable mobility* may be viewed as *satisfying current transport and mobility needs without compromising the ability of future generations to meet these needs* (Black 1996).

Future generations will find it difficult to use our current systems if we virtually deplete world stocks of the principal transport fuel: petroleum. They will also find it difficult to continue using these same fuels in view of the damage that their emissions do to the global atmosphere and local air quality. Finally, the excessive number of fatalities and injuries created by these systems will make it difficult for future generations to accept them, unless significant steps are taken to improve this situation. Let us examine each of these in a little more detail.

Petroleum Depletion

The transportation systems of the world are fueled primarily by petroleum, which due to its finite nature is not sustainable. This fossil fuel is the stock from which we manufacture diesel fuel, propane, jet fuel, gasoline (petrol), and reformulated gasoline. Estimates vary as to what reserves of crude petroleum remain, but it is unlikely that these will be sufficient to fuel our transport systems beyond the middle of the century.

Using 2000 data, it is evident that the world is using about 76.7 million (76.7×10^6) barrels of petroleum each day, or 28 thousand million (28×10^9) barrels a year (International Energy Agency 2001). We do not know the total reserves, but estimates are that these are in the vicinity of 1,058 thousand million ($1,058 \times 10^9$) barrels. If we assume that consumption grows at the current growth rate for energy consumption, there will be a 2.3% annual growth in petroleum consumption. This would result in the depletion of global reserves by the year 2027. If reserves prove to be greater than the current estimate of slightly more than one million million (1×10^{12}) barrels, then fuel supplies will go a little further. Even if we assume reserves are more in the range of 1.8 million million (1.8×10^{12}) barrels to 2.6 million million (2.6×10^{12}) barrels, MacKenzie (1995) demonstrated that global consumption will peak in 2018 or 2025 and then begin its inevitable decline. Assuming that all of the 2.6 million million barrels are found and recovered, and the same rate of growth (2.3%) in consumption continues, then the world will run out of petroleum by the year 2050. Similar concerns regarding petroleum reserves and petroleum use are raised by Hatfield (1997) and Deffeyes (2001), although they are not as optimistic as the above. Economists on the other hand argue that we will never run out of petroleum since the price system will tend to ration petroleum stocks as they become scarce. Whether the fuel ceases to exist, or whether it becomes unaffordable, amounts to the same thing. It can no longer be used as a transportation fuel.

Deteriorating Air Quality and Atmospheric Changes

A second area of concern is atmospheric quality. The use of petroleum-based transport fuels is in part responsible for acid deposition, global warming, metropolitan ozone and urban air pollution. Automobile air conditioners contribute to the thinning of stratospheric ozone levels or what are commonly called "holes in ozone layer."

Acid Deposition   Acid deposition is essentially due to sulfur dioxide and nitrogen oxides entering the upper atmosphere and being transported usually long distances by winds. They then may fall out of the atmosphere as acid precipitation or as dry acid deposition. This may result in negative impacts on trees, marine life in streams and lakes, and structures. Some of the sulfur dioxide and nitrogen oxides come from the transport sector. Many of these are released at ground level and find their way into the upper atmosphere through convectional activity. Nitrogen oxides may also be released at higher elevations by jet aircraft. It is conceivable that we will eliminate the problem of acid deposition in the next several years in the United States as provisions of the 1990 Clean Air Act calling for reductions in oxides of nitrogen and sulfur oxide emissions become active. However, the international nature of acid deposition elsewhere in the world (e.g. Scandinavia or Korea) suggests a longer solution time will be necessary for these areas.

Urban Air Pollution   Emissions from transport vehicles burning fossil fuels include carbon monoxide, nitrogen oxides, sulfur oxides, hydrocarbons, particulate matter, and lead. Carbon monoxide can create problems for the circulatory system and in high concentrations it may lead to death due to asphyxiation. Nitrogen oxides can combine with hydrocarbons in the presence of sunlight to create urban ozone. We want these pollutants removed from the air primarily because they create medical problems for the citizenry. Most of these create problems for the human respiratory system; breathing difficulties from urban ozone and the oxides of nitrogen and sulfur to cancers resulting from some particulates and hydrocarbons. Lead can result in blood disorders and developmental problems for children. Failure to remove any one of these from the air would be a negligent act if we have the technology to do so. While significant progress has been made in the U.S. in reducing these emissions, the growth of personal transport vehicles result in most of these emissions continuing to be a problem.

Stratospheric Ozone Depletion   The ozone layer or ozone shield occurs at a distance of 12–50 km (7–30 miles) above the Earth's surface, where it reduces the amount of ultraviolet (UV) radiation that would otherwise hit the surface of this planet. Reductions in the amount of ozone in this layer will increase the amount of UV radiation reaching the surface and this will lead to increases in skin cancer, cataracts, and retinal damage for humans. It also has the potential of creating vision problems for animals and impacting phytoplankton populations of the oceans. The latter could significantly interfere with the food chain of the oceans.

The exact reason for the holes in the ozone layer and reductions elsewhere appear to be attributable to chlorofluorocarbons (CFCs), better known as Freon 11 and Freon 12. These man-made chemical compounds have found many uses, including as refrigerants in automotive air conditioners. Although the Montreal Protocol as amended terminated production of CFCs at the end of 1995, the atmospheric chain reaction they initiated continues today. In addition, there are a large number of vehicles still operating that contain CFCs as their air conditioning refrigerant. In the case of automobiles, the CFC refrigerants have been replaced by HFC-134a, which is less harmful to the environment, but not harmless. It is also to be phased out by 2030, or sooner if the Kyoto Protocol is ratified.

Global Warming This planet has another group of gases surrounding it; these produce what is often called the "greenhouse effect." This effect allows incoming short wave solar radiation to pass through the greenhouse gases in the atmosphere and reach the surface, warming it. The resulting long wave heat radiation rises from the surface and might very well leave our atmosphere except for the fact that the greenhouse gases absorb or re-radiate most of this back to the surface and some to outer space. If we did not have the greenhouse gases, Earth would be too cold for human life. So the effect of the greenhouse gases is beneficial.

The gases that produce this greenhouse effect include water vapor, carbon dioxide, methane, and several other lesser gases. If we increase significantly the amount of one or more of these gases, could we actually make the greenhouse layer of gases more con-centrated and would this lead to a "forcing" of the greenhouse effect, or a warming of the planet? The belief among nearly all scientists is that it would lead to a warming. There is also no dispute that the greenhouse effect exists. Everyone knowledgeable in the field believes this. There are some arguments about whether the planet is releasing enough additional greenhouse gases to create this forcing, and whether the Earth has already begun to warm.

A warming of the planet could result in a series of transport impacts. Ocean levels would rise due to thermal expansion of the oceans, melting of polar ice caps and mid-latitude glaciers. Storms would increase due to more water in the atmosphere (due to more evapora-tion on a warmer planet), and highways and railroads, as well as urban subway systems in coastal areas could be hit quite hard by sea surges during storm events. Existing transport networks may find they are in the wrong place in terms of new agricultural production. Port facilities around the world would have to have major investments and so forth (see Black 1990, for a more complete discussion of these impacts).

The transport sector is a major source of anthropogenic carbon dioxide emissions, a greenhouse gas. The use of gasoline derived from petroleum as a power source for our motor vehicles is responsible for a significant amount of the carbon dioxide and methane emitted today.

A solution to the global warming problem is quite distant and may be unreachable since world policy makers will be locked into adaptation by the time they receive a clear signal that global warming has begun. We do not want to dismiss the actions taken by some countries to return to 1990 carbon dioxide emission levels, although few of these appear to be having much success. The most recent trend in warming had already begun by 1990. Returning to those levels will accomplish very little in terms of the long-run problem. We will have to move away from fossil fuels if we are to prevent global warming from continuing beyond the next century.

Highway Crashes and Fatalities

During the 20th century more than three million individuals were killed in motor vehicle accidents in the United States. Records have not been kept on the number injured in crashes, but recent data place these in excess of three million a year. These numbers are significantly influenced by traffic volumes and if we remove the influence of traffic volumes and examine the number of fatalities per 100 million vehicle kilometers traveled (VKT), we find that the U.S. runs a little under one fatality per 100 million VKT. Since traffic volumes peak during the summer months of June through mid-September, it is reasonable to infer that many of the accidents are tourism related. While the other modes also have fatalities, these are minor in comparison to those on the highway systems of the world.

Downey (1995) has given global estimates that there are currently 250,000 fatalities and 10 million persons injured annually in motor vehicle crashes. Forecasts of a million fatalities and 40–50 million injuries a year by 2020 may actually be on the conservative side.

What About Congestion?

Some might argue that congestion is in the process of making our transport systems tend toward gridlock, and as a result this is also one of those factors that may prevent our transport systems from being sustainable (MIT and Charles River Associates 2001; ECMT 1995; Mazza & Rydin 1997). Although one might not think so, congestion is probably not that important. It may result in drivers and passengers being delayed, and there is also some concern about the increased fuel used in slow traffic and the increases in emissions that result from such slow movement. To some extent several of these variables are incorporated in our earlier discussion and are already considered in the overall notion of sustainable mobility.

The Nature of Tourism

While there are a number of formal definitions of tourism, the spectrum or the relationship between tourism, recreation and leisure is not comprehensively defined. We could fall back on a standard dictionary definition and say that it is "the practice of traveling for pleasure." Anyone who has flown a seven to nine hour transatlantic flight in economy class would hardly say they were traveling for pleasure. The definition also does not include what we believe tourism to be in a popular sense and it does not satisfy the academic use of the term. The former believes the term says something about going to a location at a distance from one's home for pleasure, while the latter wants to include everything we do in the form of leisure activity as tourism (see for example, Anable 2002). This is not the place to resolve this, but the author would lean more toward the popular view of tourism than the academic view.

We have seen phenomenal growth in tourism in the latter part of the twentieth century. The World Travel and Tourism Council (2002) estimates that worldwide tourism consumption in 2001 was $US3.0 trillion a year with investment in the sector being about $US623 billion. They anticipate these numbers will double by 2012.

The growth in the tourism sector appears to be due to a number of different factors including: (1) a general increase in the level of prosperity and disposable income;

of motorization; (3) decreases in working time and a commensurate increase in
me; and (4) the general growth of urbanization, which creates monotony in one's
e (Krippendorf 1984). Since these four factor continue to increase it is reasonable
to conclude that tourism will continue to grow.

The Interaction of Tourism and Transportation

It should be obvious that tourism could not exist without transportation (Page 1994). Every form of tourism requires transport in one form or another, whether we are hiking along the Appalachian Trail from Georgia to Maine or staying aboard the space shuttle for six weeks. The tourism between these two extremes makes use of ships, air transport, motor coaches, trains, and increasingly the motor vehicle/highway system. The type of tourism that we are talking about may vary from day or local tours involving use of a motor vehicle (Capineri & Spinelli 2002) to overnight trips to metropolitan areas, countries, islands, or environmentally sensitive areas usually involving aviation today.

To this point we have only addressed the transport portion of "getting there," but there is a transport role once one arrives at the destination as well. Some people fly to a foreign city for a holiday and once there they need to have some form of transport to get around. Some will rent a car, others will use a taxicab, others may try a subway, rail transit, bus or trolley, or a bicycle. Most Americans will go for the taxicab, being unfamiliar with the street system they will hesitate to rent a car, and in most cases they will be unfamiliar with the other modes. If the other modal systems are easy to use and this is pointed out to those arriving in the foreign city, then they may very well use them. International travelers used to car transfers will use public transport facilities such as the Gatwick Express from Gatwick Airport into London, and bus connections from airports to the central part of several European cities if they are attractive and easy to use. Once in the central city they may very well revert to the use of taxicabs again.

Returning to the question of whether these travel behaviors are sustainable we would have to say that for most travel the use of the motor vehicle is non-sustainable, but that is simplistic. Nearly all transport modes use petroleum, pollute local and global environments, and result in fatalities and injuries. In addition, none of the transport modes recover fees for the externalities they generate, so that none of them can be called sustainable. We do tend to favor certain mass transport modes if they carry many travelers and reduce these externalities to a relatively low level on a per capita basis.

Sustainability is only part of our concern. Recall that our definition also included mobility, i.e. satisfying current transport and mobility needs without compromising the ability of future generations to meet these needs. We must recognize the mobility dimension of our question because although the most primitive societies are sustainable based on the criteria identified earlier, they have little or no mobility. The developing world needs mobility if it is to succeed economically in the world.

It is possible for nations of the developing world to increase their level of mobility without doing much harm to the level of transport sustainability. In fact it is almost imperative that they do so if they are going to develop successfully. Therefore what is sought is a situation where the level of transport approaches sustainability and the level of mobility is reasonably high and improving.

Measuring Sustainable Mobility

Beginning in the 1990s numerous researchers began trying to identify exactly what it was that made transport systems sustainable or non-sustainable. That research led to an encyclopedic list of indicators based on the work of EPA (1996), Litman (1998), and others. It is one thing to suggest the many variables that might be related to sustainability and quite another thing to use these in some type of index that could be used for measurement purposes.

Beginning at about the same time the author suggested an approach to measuring sustainability that incorporated several different variables believed to reflect sustainability or the lack of it (Black 1998). The index developed identified a couple of important points. The first point is that no matter how good of an index is developed, there will always be some that question the manner in which different variables (indicators) are weighted in the index. There will always be situations where the certain variables are important and others are less so, and these will not be constant over space. So any index developed that meets the interests of one country will not be likely to meet the interests of other nations. In a similar vein the consumer price index (CPI) is not particularly relevant to you if you don't purchase the goods on which it is based. However, this does not stop it from being a reasonably good index of consumer prices over geographic space. The second point is that if we rely solely on those variables that make an area sustainable in terms of transport, then sustainability will be most obviously present in areas that have the least of all these variables. This means that the countries that are the most sustainable are those that: (1) have minimal pollution; (2) do not use much petroleum; and (3) have very few motor vehicle fatalities or injuries. While such nations do exist, it should be apparent that they are extremely underdeveloped and may border on primitive. This is not quite a reasonable or desirable target for other nations. What was obviously missing from this approach was some measure of mobility or potential mobility. If we want to measure sustainable mobility we need to have indicators not only of transport sustainability, but also of potential mobility.

In order to handle the weighting problem a set of variables that included carbon dioxide emissions, carbon monoxide emissions, nitrogen oxide emissions, emissions of volatile organic compounds, motor vehicle crash fatalities, motor vehicle crash injuries, gasoline sales, motor vehicle registrations, and vehicle kilometers of travel was subjected to a principal component analysis to collapse these different variables down to a single dimension (Black 2000). The variable most closely related to this single component was vehicle kilometers of travel (VKT). This is actually a very interesting variable from a sustainability point of view in that it will increase as an area becomes more and more dependent on automobiles for personal transportation. On the other hand if an area has good rail passenger service or urban transit in its various forms, this will tend to decrease an area's VKT. In addition, as indicated by the component analysis it is highly related to emissions, injuries and fatalities, and fuel use.

On the other hand if some areas tend to have smaller vehicles that use less fuel (e.g. most of Western Europe), or if they tend to be switching over to an alternate fuel source (e.g. California), then VKT may overstate the non-sustainability of the system in place. Therefore, it does seem prudent to incorporate a variable indicative of the amount of fuel being used. Since most of the negative externalities associated with fuel use tend to be related to gasoline (petrol) and diesel fuel, this variable was set aside for inclusion in the index to be developed.

Potential Mobility

The sustainability side of the index is taken care of, but we must address the mobility side of our sustainable mobility index. Mobility seems to have slipped into European transportation research on sustainability because of that area's recognition that concern for the environment must always be balanced with concern for the economy. If you make transport completely sustainable you may destroy the economy, so discussions there have tended to have this balanced approach. On the other hand, U.S. policy makers seem to view such balance as impossible and they appear to believe that any move toward a sustainable transport system will destroy the economy.

Mobility is the existence of a host of transport stocks ranging from highways to runways to airports, as well as other modal stocks. Owen (1964) viewed transport stocks of this nature as indicative of a nation's mobility. Our concern is not so much with whether these stocks exist, but rather if they have the potential to exist and what that potential mobility might be. One indicator of mobility that captures all of the differences between modes is a nation's gross domestic product (GDP), the value of all goods and services produced.

Creating the Index

The next step was to combine these measures of travel and transport (VKT), fuel use and potential mobility into a single index value that will measure sustainable transport and potential mobility. To do so, we first divide all of these values by the area's population. This is necessary since we do not want to measure purely size effects. We next change the sign on the VKT and fuel variables, so that larger values (i.e. lower fuel use and travel) represent more sustainable situations. We then place all three measures in the same units (see Black 2002, 2003). This yields the index of sustainable transport and potential mobility, or more simply the sustainable mobility index (SMI) below:

$$\text{SMI} = \text{GDP} - \frac{\text{VKT} + \text{FUEL}}{2}$$

Once again one should bear in mind that all of these variables were converted to per capita figures and standardized. Each has a mean of 50 and a standard deviation of 10, except for SMI.

If an area has an average value of 50 for each of the variables, the value obtained for the index will be 0. This is a desirable value that indicates the level of potential mobility is relatively the same as travel and fuel use. For most states of the U.S. the potential mobility level is high, while their sustainability component is low and this results in a positive value for the SMI. These areas have the economic potential to provide good mass transit services, fuel efficient vehicles, and so forth, but they opt to rely on personal transport modes that use high levels of fuel. Developing countries will frequently be unable to provide high levels of mobility to their population (low potential mobility). At the same time they do have higher, sustainable levels of transport through using mass transit, walking, biking, and so forth. Their SMI values will tend to be negative.

A few real examples may clarify some of these ideas. Let us look at three different areas noted for their tourism types of activities: Florida, France, and Kenya. Substituting values for the U.S. recreational tourism state of Florida in the above equation we get:

$$SMI = 55.36 - \frac{42.61 + 44.76}{2} = 11.67$$

This reflects a relatively wealthy state with excessive use of personal transport vehicles (as indicated by a standardized low VKT value) and excessive per capita fuel use (a low standardized FUEL value).

Substituting values for France, Europe's "prime international destination," in the above equation we get:

$$SMI = 52.31 - \frac{52.35 + 53.40}{2} = -0.565$$

This is a desirable value in that it is near zero implying that the country has a desirable level of sustainable transport and potential mobility.

For the eco-tourism nation of Kenya the figures are:

$$SMI = 33.76 - \frac{63.52 + 64.71}{2} = -30.36$$

While Kenya has attractive sustainability values, it is apparent that this is due to a low level of mobility, which is also undesirable.

Countries of the developing world tend to have low negative values (less than -10) reflecting low levels of potential mobility in the presence of what would ordinarily be viewed as sustainable travel and transport. This is an undesirable situation and these nations should attempt to attain lower values (more travel) on their VKT measure as GDP increases in the future.

Developed countries of the OECD and Europe have scores that fall for the most part between $+10$ and -10. This is a desirable range indicating average levels of mobility (as reflected by average per capita GDP) along with average levels of fuel use per capita and VKT per capita.

The states of the United States tend to have high positive values (greater than $+10$), which indicates sufficient wealth to provide high mobility stocks, but an excessive use of personal vehicles and high per capita fuel use as reflected in the Florida example above.

Further Use of the Index in Tourism Situations

Aside from the index giving an area some indication of its standing relative to other areas in the world, the index can also be used to assess the impacts of increasing or decreasing tourism on different areas, states and nations. To illustrate this usage, let us return to the Florida case where the index value obtained was 11.67. Approximately 12.6% of the GDP of Florida is attributable to tourism. If that state were to manage a 10% increase in GDP from an increase in tourism resulting in a net growth of 10% to GDP, VKT and fuel use, then the SMI index becomes much worse increasing to 16.07. One could argue that the 10% increase in GDP might not bring with it a 10% increase in VKT and fuel use, but the level of automobile dependence in the state of Florida is high. If the 10% growth in GDP was accompanied by some transport investment that resulted in a 20% drop in VKT and fuel use, then the SMI would drop to 9.78. In effect, growth in the tourism sector with a contribution to the state's GDP without some investment in transport that allows VKT and fuel use to decrease will only make the state worse off than it was before in terms of sustainable mobility.

The index appears to be sluggish in the case of Florida, but it should be. The population in most of the states of the U.S. has become far too dependent on the automobile. It is not a situation that will change quickly in reality or by minor changes in the components of the index. If we do something to reduce the fuel variable, this will result in reductions in emissions of global and local air pollutants. If we do nothing to the fuel variable, then these will continue. If whatever we do results in no change in VKT, then highway crash injuries and fatalities won't increase or decrease. Similarly, if VKT remains at the same level there will be no impact on congestion. In effect, the index doesn't improve a lot unless the VKT and fuel variables decrease.

Governmental tourism agencies could improve the sustainable mobility of areas if they could increase the use of alternate modes (public transit and passenger rail transport) in tourist areas. Once again, it would appear that these modes and their use is included in the index, albeit indirectly. As use of different mass transit modes increase, overall vehicle kilometers of travel decrease, as does fuel use. It would be possible to measure the use of these modes directly with a modified index, but then we would end up double-counting their influence since their use decreases VKT and fuel use, assuming its new users are former automobile users.

The only logical way in which the SMI values for countries of the developing world will change is through increasing per capita GDP, perhaps through tourism. Although a less sustainable transport system would also make the index values rise toward zero, this is unlikely to happen with the low levels of GDP observed. The solution is to increase GDP along with transport infrastructure without allowing rapid motorization to occur.

Conclusion

What the SMI index seems to suggest is that tourism that makes excessive use of highway/motor vehicle transport systems will be detrimental from a sustainable mobility point of view. For those areas with good levels of sustainable mobility, the growth of urban tourism does not seem to offer much of a threat. Finally, for less developed economies on islands or similar remote areas, it would seem that tourism may actually improve their overall level of sustainable mobility.

References

Anable, J. (2002). Picnics, pets, and pleasant places: The distinguishing characteristics of leisure travel demand. In: W. R. Black, & P. Nijkamp (Eds), *Social Change and Sustainable Transport* (pp. 181–190). Bloomington, IN: Indiana University Press.

Black, W. R. (1990). Global warming: Impacts on the transportation infrastructure. *TR (Transportation Research News)*, *150*(2–8), 34.

Black, W. R. (1996). Sustainable transportation: A U.S. perspective. *Journal of Transport Geography*, *4*, 151–159.

Black, W. R. (1998). Sustainable transportation. In: R. D. Knowles, & B. S. Hoyle (Eds), *Modern Transport Geography* (2nd ed., pp. 337–351). New York: Wiley.

Black, W. R. (2000). Toward a measure of transport sustainability. *Transportation Research Board Meeting 2000, Conference Preprints CD*. Washington, DC: Transportation Research Board.

Black, W. R. (2002). Sustainable transport and potential mobility. A paper presented at STELLA Focus Group 4, Helsinki, Finland, May 3, and forthcoming in *European Transport and Infrastructure Research*.

Black, W. R. (2003). *Transportation: A geographical analysis*. New York: Guilford Press.

Capineri, C., & Spinelli, G. (2002). The impact of day tourism on the environment and sustainability: The Northwestern Mediterranean Arc. In: W. R. Black, & P. Nijkamp (Eds), *Social Change and Sustainable Transport* (pp. 191–199). Bloomington, IN: Indiana University Press.

Deffeyes, K. S. (2001). *Hubbert's peak: The impending world oil shortage*. Princeton, NJ: Princeton University Press.

Downey, M. J. (1995). Transportation trends. A paper presented at the Symposium on Challenges and Opportunities for Global Transportation in the 21st Century, John A. Volpe Transportation Systems Center, Cambridge, MA, USA.

ECMT (European Conference of Ministers of Transport) (1995). *Urban travel and sustainable development*. Paris: Organisation for Economic Co-operation and Development.

EPA (U.S. Environmental Protection Agency) (1996). *Indicators of the environmental impacts of transportation*. Washington, DC: EPA, Report EPA 230-R-96–009.

Hatfield, C. B. (1997). Oil back on the global agenda (Commentary). *Nature*, *387*, 121.

International Energy Agency (2001). *World Energy Outlook 2001*. Paris: IEA.

Krippendorf, J. (1984). Die Ferienmenschen. Für ein neues Verständnis von Frezeit und Reisen. Orell Füssli Verlag, Zürich and Schwäbisch Hall. Cited by H. Knoflacher (2000), "Austria," in ECMT. *Transport and Leisure, Roundtable 111*. Paris: OECD.

Litman, T. (1998). *Sustainable transportation indicators*. www.islandnet.com/~litman/sti.htm

MacKenzie, J. J. (1995). Alternative fuels to reduce petroleum consumption, global warming and urban air pollution. A paper presented at the Symposium on Challenges and Opportunities for Global Transportation in the 21st Century, John A. Volpe Transportation Systems Center, Cambridge, MA, USA.

Mazza, L., & Rydin, Y. (Eds) (1997). Urban sustainability: Discourses, networks and policy tools. *Progress in Planning*, *47*(1).

MIT (Massachusetts Institute of Technology) & Charles Rivers Associates (2001). *Mobility 2001: World Mobility at the End of the Twentieth Century and Its Sustainability*. Geneva, Switzerland: World Business Council for Sustainable Development. Also at www.wbcsdmobility.org

Owen, W. (1964). *Strategy for mobility*. The Transport Research Program. Washington, DC: Brookings Institution.

Page, S. (1994). *Transport for tourism*. New York: Routledge.

World Commission on Environment and Development (1987). *Our common future*. Oxford: Oxford University Press.

World Travel and Tourism Council (2002). The impact of travel & tourism on jobs and the economy — 2002. London: WTTC.

Chapter 5

Airlines and Tourism Development: The Case of Zimbabwe

Brian Turton

Introduction

Tourism has been recognised by many developing countries as a means of generating essential foreign currency and of providing employment in the service sector (Cooper & Wanhill 1997). The rapid growth of cheap, long haul air transport and the rise of tourism operators has also enabled those developing states located thousands of miles from the main tourist generating areas in North America and Western Europe to enter the international tourism market (Page 1994; Pearce 1987). The extent to which tourism can benefit the economies of less developed states has been the subject of much research and the problems associated with the impact of mass tourism upon local communities and societies have been also been widely assessed. (Britton 1992; De Kadt 1979).

This chapter reviews the relationship between tourism and airline development in one southern African state, Zimbabwe, since its independence in 1980. During recent decades Zimbabwe has attempted to attract tourists to its natural attractions; the chapter assesses the significance of long haul and domestic air transport services in contributing to the growth of its tourism sector. In particular, the part played by the national airline, Air Zimbabwe, in this growth is examined in terms of its ability to compete in the international passenger market for long haul tourist traffic. Zimbabwe, in common with several other independent African states in the period after 1960, followed a policy of supporting its national airline financially as a means of promoting a national identity, improving internal links between towns where surface transport was often unsatisfactory and maintaining international connections within the world-wide network of air routes (Hilling 1996).

Tourism in Southern Africa

Although several African countries consider that tourism should be a vital part of their economies the continent as a whole only generates less than 4% of global tourism. African-owned airlines carry less than 3% of all air passengers on their scheduled flights

Tourism and Transport: Issues and Agenda for the New Millennium
Copyright © 2004 by Elsevier Ltd.
All rights of reproduction in any form reserved.
ISBN: 0-08-044172-6

and no African city is currently included in the leading 25 city-pair connections based upon air traffic (Graham 1995; Simon 1996). Zimbabwe itself is not a leading destination within the continent, lagging behind states such as South Africa, Kenya, Tanzania and Tunisia. The latter four states have several advantages; they can offer a combination of inland and coastal-based tourism packages. Zimbabwe is wholly land locked and whilst offering a combination of wilderness, wildlife and culture, it has not been able to position itself in a similar manner to Kenya or Tanzania. It relies upon a principal attraction of the Victoria Falls, the largest waterfalls in the world which are spectacular in their own right. There are also several lesser destination such as Lake Kariba, the Eastern Highlands (particularly the Nyanga National Park) and the Great Zimbabwe ruins, the largest collection of ancient monuments in Africa south of the Egyptian Pyramids (see Figure 5.1).

The key tourist destinations in southern Africa are served by the major airlines of western Europe and southeast Asia but the relative importance of gateway airports such as Johannesburg, Capetown and Harare has changed in recent years. In 2000 arrivals into Zimbabwe from Europe accounted for 58% of all non-African tourists in 2000–2001, with the United States and Canada acting as the second largest market. Tourist arrivals into Zimbabwe in 2000 from all sources outside Africa totalled about 464,000 compared with 1.4 million from other African countries (see Table 5.1). This latter total however includes 812,000 from South Africa and Botswana and a large proportion of these are short stay travellers who are visiting friends and relatives rather than longer staying visitors paying for accommodation in the main resorts. Both the South African, Botswana and Zambian frontiers are also the scene of regular crossings by informal traders and when these are included in the official tourist counts they distort the overall pattern (Turton & Mutambirwa 1996; Zinyama 1989).

The Development of Tourism Policy in Zimbabwe

Both the First and Second National Development Plans developed by the Zimbabwe government recognised the potential of international tourism as a contribution towards much needed economic growth. At the end of the first decade of independence in 1990, foreign exchange receipts from tourism had become the fourth largest earner of currency and investment in accommodation and transport within Zimbabwe for tourists had greatly increased. It is estimated that tourism now contributes approximately 5% of GDP in Zimbabwe. Prior to independence, in 1980, tourism marketing was the responsibility of the state Department of Tourism and the Zimbabwe Tourist Board, and these two bodies continued operations until 1984, when the government established the Zimbabwe Tourist Development Corporation (ZTDC) to promote tourism development and to co-ordinate all aspects of the industry between the private and state sectors. The successful achievement of these two objectives was, however, hampered by two factors. The first was the chronic shortage of foreign currency within Zimbabwe, which severely restricted the extent to which tourism could be promoted effectively in the European and North American markets. Secondly, harmonious co-operation between the state-controlled Air Zimbabwe and the ZTDC on the one hand and the privately-owned hotels and tour operators within the country on the other was often difficult to achieve (Mutambirwa 2000).

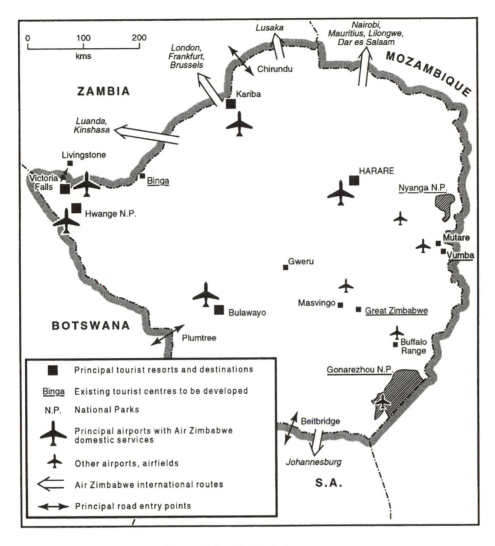

Figure 5.1: Air Zimbabwe map.

As a state-controlled corporation, Air Zimbabwe, assumed responsibility for marketing tourism through its own offices in Europe (Frankfurt and London) and North America (New York). Promotion was, however, inevitably constrained by the Air Zimbabwe Act, which stipulated that all investment decisions, which included marketing as well as aircraft purchase and fares policy, were subject to government approval through the Ministry of Transport. In the fiercely competitive world of tourism marketing the financial resources available to Air Zimbabwe and the associated tour operators for maintaining a presence in overseas markets were woefully inadequate as a result of state expenditure constraints. Initially tourism promotion was centred upon the Air Zimbabwe "Flame Lily" tours,

Table 5.1: Tourist arrivals in Zimbabwe 1995–2000.

Region	1995	1996	1997	1998	1999	2000
United Kingdom and Ireland	66,346	84,001	108,100	128,816	189,436	135,643
Other European states	85,383	145,987	119,506	173,068	187,941	133,337
USA and Canada	36,081	38,227	56,001	95,795	100,291	78,592
Other American states	4,228	10,223	6,223	23,726	14,574	37,536
Australia and New Zealand	22,609	35,564	42,481	42,743	64,984	56,053
Asia	11,693	21,176	13,805	36,552	34,968	23,477
South Africa and Botswana	475,653	567,135	394,188	686,876	550,318	812,370
Zambia	518,795	443,909	348,600	511,909	598,759	365,695
Mozambique	98,331	157,139	128,954	211,011	206,572	111,970
East Africa	10,198	13,212	12,006	24,460	40,523	30,440
Other African states	34,095	60,432	51,341	51,518	112,154	83,299

Source: Zimbabwe Tourism Authority Report (2002).

packages involving domestic air services and hotel owners, which had been introduced prior to independence by the Central African Airways group. Resorts such as Victoria Falls and the Hwange National Game Park were linked by air to Harare, the international gateway airport, and the venture was initially a success. However, Air Zimbabwe's domestic fares were not covering operational costs; furthermore, fare increases were not initially sanctioned by the Ministry of Transport. Consequently, the tours became uneconomic to operate.

Strict state control over air fare structures also inhibited Air Zimbabwe's operations and competitive position on its long haul flights between the United Kingdom, Germany and Zimbabwe. Whereas other airlines, such as British Airways, Air France, Lufthansa and KLM, were able to increase long haul fares gradually, Air Zimbabwe often had to endure a delay of up to three years before submissions for increases were sanctioned by the Ministry. During this waiting period heavy losses were sustained and when rises did take place the overall cost of a Zimbabwe holiday package increased substantially as tour operators were obliged to pass on these infrequent but substantial air fare increases to their customers. The disadvantages of this tight state control over fares became especially apparent in late 1992 when air fares between Harare, Kariba, Victoria Falls and Hwange rose by 35%. Air Zimbabwe justified this substantial increase as being necessary to cover soaring operational losses on its domestic routes. At the same time, the major tour operators recognised the potential dangers of these vastly increased air travel costs, claiming that they would discourage international tourists from coming to Zimbabwe and that Air Zimbabwe's already declining share of the long haul market would thus fall even further. Although other factors have also contributed to Zimbabwe's declining share of the southern African tourist market the misgivings of the private sector in 1992 have been proved to be correct.

In the early 1990s an attempt was made to strengthen Zimbabwe's tourism marketing strategy with the formation of the Zimbabwe Council for Tourism. Thus, in 1994, Air Zimbabwe co-operated with hotel companies and tour operators in a new programme to publicise Zimbabwe as a destination throughout Europe, North America and Australia. Government control over tourism policy was relaxed in 1996 when the Zimbabwe Tourist Development Corporation was replaced by the Zimbabwe Tourism Authority (ZTA) which had the responsibility for marketing Zimbabwe as a destination across the world. ZTA had responsibility for a number of other tourism functions such as inspecting hotel and other accommodation in the main resorts.

Air Zimbabwe

Although the late twentieth century saw the relaxation of many of the state-imposed restrictions upon its operations, Air Zimbabwe was, for most of the first two decades of independence, one of a group of parastatals which were firmly controlled by government bodies. When the airline was formed in 1980 it inherited the aircraft and supporting facilities of the previous organisation, Air Rhodesia, whose antecedents in turn can be traced back to 1933 in the Rhodesia and Nyasaland Airways company. The joint daily service between London and Harare provided by British Airways and Air Zimbabwe dates from the declaration of independence in April 1980 but direct flights were later also introduced by Lufthansa, Air France, Swissair and the Portuguese airline TAP. The joint Qantas-Air Zimbabwe route between Harare and Perth is the only regular link with a non-European destination. The strict constraints upon Air Zimbabwe's air fares policy have already been noted and similar restrictions were imposed upon the purchase of replacement aircraft for the obsolete planes inherited from Air Rhodesia.

Although the urgent needs for fleet modernisation, the opening of new routes and airport modernisation were identified in the First National Development Plan little was achieved in the first few years of independence. The airline lacked planes suited to the varying requirements of its long haul, regional (within Africa) and domestic services and for many years the principal airports at Harare and Victoria Falls were unable to accept the larger long haul Boeing aircraft of the 1980s. On the principal London–Harare route, British Airways was able to operate its large capacity Boeing aircraft but its partner Air Zimbabwe could only offer the smaller Boeing 707s which had been acquired from Lufthansa.

Within Zimbabwe, and on routes to other African states, the airline was obliged to make use of old aircraft that were inefficient in their fuel consumption, a serious factor as 40% of Air Zimbabwe's expenditure of its foreign currency allocation was on aviation spirit. Requests were made in 1983 to the Ministry of Transport by the airline for the purchase of a fleet of Boeing 747s for long haul routes and 737s for shorter routes but agreement was delayed until 1985. Various options for the acquisition of different types of aircraft were pursued. The inability of many of the smaller domestic airports to accept the proposed planes further delayed the purchase of a fleet of aircraft capable of allowing Air Zimbabwe to meet tourist passenger demands in an acceptable manner.

The airline has rarely made a profit as a result of these inefficient operations and losses of up to 25% of total annual receipts were common in the 1990s before privatisation. Air Zimbabwe had always therefore been reliant upon the government for annual subsidies to meet these deficits (Hofton 1989). Passenger flows on the long haul routes between Harare, London, Frankfurt and Athens normally account for about 10% of all traffic and in the pre-privatisation period these services remained profitable and made some contribution towards meeting losses on the domestic flights. Although load factors on the Air Zimbabwe regional African services were usually lower than on the European flights all routes covered their direct costs and profitability increased in the late 1980s and 1990s. Despite the process of privatisation, Air Zimbabwe still relies on the government for support and thus suffers from interference, for example, in relation to buying aircraft or engaging in maintenance deals with other companies.

The inadequacies of international tourist travel facilities in Zimbabwe are best illustrated by the continuing delays in plans to improve the major airport at Harare. The airport is the focus for all Air Zimbabwe domestic, regional and international routes and the terminal for many of the other airlines serving the country. Until the early twenty-first century it continued to rely upon the passenger handling facilities provided in the colonial era, with the use of a former freight warehouse as the domestic terminal. Although the runway may now be used by all modern high-capacity aircraft, passenger processing has until very recently involved long delays for incoming flights. As tourist travel increased in the early 1980s with the devaluation of the Zimbabwean dollar, six long haul airlines with large capacity aircraft were using Harare by 1983 and congestion increased at the terminal. Despite the outdated passenger handling facilities aircraft landing and parking fees were raised by almost 1,000% between 1994 and 1995 and many airlines saw this as the time to reappraise the viability of their African routes which made use of Harare airport. A new terminal is now available but the number of overseas airlines making use of Harare as a major terminal has sharply declined.

The continuing viability of the established Harare-Kariba-Victoria Falls-Hwange-Harare tourist circuit has also been threatened by the inability of Kariba airport to accept aircraft such as the Boeing 737. If the Lake Kariba tourist traffic is to be maintained as part of the popular Victoria Falls circuit there must be either be investment in runway improvements or an increase in the number of smaller planes to cope with the passenger traffic from Harare.

Air Transport and Tourism in the 21st Century

Between 1995 and 2000 tourists entering Zimbabwe from all overseas sources increased in number by 37% with a doubling in the totals from destinations outside Africa. Visitors from Europe, and especially the United Kingdom, peaked in 1999. There has been a downward trend since then, according to provisional data for 2000 and 2001 partly as internal strife over land reforms continues to be a major de-stabilising issue. A similar trend is being witnessed in relation to North American, Asian and Australian arrivals and by visitors from some

African countries. Receipts from tourism in the period 1990–2000 peaked at US$231.8 million in 1996 but by 2000 this had fallen to US$124.7 million, although this was more than double the total income in 1990.

Traffic between South Africa, Botswana, Zambia and Zimbabwe continues to rise but, as previously stated, most of this involves localised short stay visitors rather than commercial tourism. This latter traffic is largely responsible for the fact that over 75% of all recorded tourists enter and leave Zimbabwe by road, with the remainder using principally Harare airport and Victoria Falls and Bulawayo airports.

The contribution made by Air Zimbabwe towards the international tourist industry has changed substantially in the last decade as a result of three significant changes. Firstly, there has been a liberalisation of air transport within Zimbabwe and the emergence of some limited competition with the national carrier. Secondly, the establishment of an African government in South Africa has encouraged the development of international tourism and the consolidation of Johannesburg as the major airline terminal in southern Africa. The third factor is the continued current unsettled political situation within Zimbabwe resulting from the government's controversial land settlement policy. In addition, the challenge of a vigorous opposition party and intense media scrutiny regarding human rights issues means that Zimbabwe has lost considerable goodwill in the international community. This has compounded the declining economic position with rapid inflation, widespread unemployment and the loss of foreign currency earnings formerly gained from commercial agricultural exports of maize and tobacco. There may well be short-term tourism gains from a de-stabilised Middle East but the future is not promising.

Air transport deregulation and privatisation had a substantial impact upon the large undertakings of Europe and the United States in the late twentieth century. They have been analysed in some detail, and the changes that have taken place have also had an impact upon the fortunes of much smaller companies such as Air Zimbabwe. In the 1990s Zimbabwe, in common with other developing states, embarked upon a programme of economic structural adjustment. Many of the state undertakings, such as Air Zimbabwe, were subjected to a reappraisal by independent advisers and the report by a European consultancy recommended a policy of liberalisation for the airline and the loosening of constraints upon competition for traffic from other airlines. Within this competitive framework, long haul flights into Harare were introduced by Air France, KLM and Sabena and the national airline was ill-equipped to counter this with its limited financial resources and lack of aircraft suited to its various routes. However, the restructuring of Air Zimbabwe, with a loosening of state control, was viewed by the government as an opportunity for the airline to improve its performance on all routes and to compete more effectively in the tourism market.

Competition was also introduced on internal routes and in 1995 the independent Zimbabwe Express airline began flights between Harare and Victoria Falls, using a B.Ae 146 aircraft that had previously been leased to the national airline. This was followed by flights between the capital, Harare and Bulawayo and by the late 1990s Zimbabwe Express was providing 52 flights each week between the major internal airports, with more services on the Bulawayo route than those operated by Air Zimbabwe. In such a competitive environment it is not possible to obtain reliable passenger carrying data from the airlines but on the basis of total flights operated the new independent airline now provides over 30% of all flights on the Harare-Victoria Falls and Harare-Bulawayo routes. Zimbabwe Express also began operations on the Harare-Johannesburg and Victoria Falls-Johannesburg routes and, as within Zimbabwe, soon secured a substantial share of the available traffic.

Attempts are being made to widen the appeal of Zimbabwe's natural tourist attractions in order to reduce the heavy dependence upon Victoria Falls and the nearby Hwange game reserves for tourist revenue. The Zimbabwe Council for Tourism and the Zimbabwe Tourism Authority have embarked upon an ambitious programme to further promote the World Heritage Site incorporating the ancient ruins at Great Zimbabwe and to develop as international centres the popular domestic resorts in the eastern highlands bordering Mozambique. The latter include the Nyanga National Park, the border town of Mutare and the Vumba mountain region with its botanical gardens and golf facilities. However, access by air to this region from Harare is restricted and up to the present the majority of tourists received have been from within Zimbabwe or from South Africa. The military airport near Mutare and the group of smaller airfields in the region can only accept small capacity aircraft and it is very doubtful if finance could be made available for upgrading these to allow Air Zimbabwe planes to use them. Accommodation is limited to a few large hotels in Nyanga, Mutare and the Vumba, supplemented by groups of informal forest and lakeside lodges and chalets, and further growth will probably involve the expansion of this informal accommodation sector. The distance between this region and Harare involves road journeys of at least 175 km and although an air connection would clearly provide a shorter transit time for any international tourists the potential for development is currently limited given the size of available airfields.

Air Transport and Tourism Within the Southern African Region

As the process of liberalisation of air transport within Zimbabwe progressed in the late twentieth century the national airline also had to prepare to counter competition for tourist traffic in the wider southern African region (Debbage 1994; Ellison 1990).

The sub-standard quality passenger facilities at Harare airport already discussed discouraged several of the European-based airlines which had started flying into Zimbabwe in the 1990s. In effect, Harare was replaced by Johannesburg as a terminal for southern African flights. A large proportion of tourists from Europe and North America destined for southern Africa still see the Victoria Falls as a prime attraction but Harare is no longer the major gateway airport for these visitors. In the mid-1990s Air Zimbabwe provided three flights daily from Harare to Victoria Falls between 8.15 a.m. and 2.00 p.m. but these services could not always cope with the volume of international visitors brought in by Air Zimbabwe and other long haul flights from Europe; tourists booked for the two or three-day package stays in Victoria Falls and Hwange often had to stay over in the capital until the next day. This delay was seen, by private sector tour operators, as an unacceptable and frustrating hindrance to the further growth of tourism within Zimbabwe.

Direct flights to the Falls from Johannesburg and other South African airports have led to a reduction in the relative importance of Harare as a gateway, and the Air Zimbabwe flights operated from there to Victoria Falls. One United Kingdom tour operator has also offered visits to the Falls based upon flights to Livingstone, in Zambia, and a short road journey across the Zambesi river into Zimbabwe. In an effort to regain some of the Europe-Victoria

Falls traffic, Air Zimbabwe introduced a direct flight once a week between London and the Falls airport in 2001 but this was withdrawn later.

The consolidation of Johannesburg as the principal gateway airport for southern Africa reflects the accessibility that the airport provides to the principal tourist attractions of the region, including not only Victoria Falls and the Hwange National Park within Zimbabwe but also sites within South Africa. European-based tourists now have the opportunity to fly on package holidays into Johannesburg and visit a group of resorts in both South Africa and Zimbabwe, whereas Air Zimbabwe and its associated tour operators were only able to offer attractions within Zimbabwe. The latter airline is now the minority carrier for traffic into and out of Victoria Falls, which currently receives a substantial amount of charter flights. International scheduled passenger traffic at the Falls airport increased by over 600% in the 1990–1996 period compared with a rise of only 30% at Harare. Reliable data for chartered traffic at Victoria Falls airport is not available for the period after 1994 but between 1987 and 1994 flows increased by almost 1,500% (Mutambirwa & Turton 2000).

Although the overall amount of traffic handled at Harare airport continues to increase the national airline has been unable to maintain its level of tourist traffic transferring to Victoria Falls because of competition from the direct flights to the latter from South African centres. Whereas other airlines in the region have developed a thriving charter traffic the income derived from this source by Air Zimbabwe is usually less than 5% of its total revenue.

Conclusions

Both the Zimbabwe tourism industry and Air Zimbabwe have had to make very substantial changes in their management and marketing structure in order to adapt to the demands made by international tourists for air transport. In common with many other small developing nations the Zimbabwe government has been obliged to support its national airline with regular subsidies to enable it to compete with much larger undertakings based in Europe and with routes to southern African destinations. The liberalisation of Air Zimbabwe in the mid-1990s exposed the weaknesses of an undertaking which had previously been shielded from competition by state protection and financial support. At the December 1997 conference of the International Air Transport Association held at Victoria Falls, the implications of competition were discussed in relation to African states, such as Zimbabwe. Countries operating their own small airlines were advised to pool their resources to combat the continuing threats to their traffic from large European companies and from South African Airways. The latter, for example, has a fleet of over 50 aircraft, including several Boeing 747s, whereas Air Zimbabwe has only 9 planes, the largest being the Boeing 767 with a total capacity of less than 300 passengers.

South African Airways has continued to increase its share of international traffic which is routed through Johannesburg to and from Victoria Falls, and several European airlines which previously operated direct routes to Harare now fly direct to Johannesburg for a transfer to the Victoria Falls service. Air Zimbabwe continues to operate flights to other east and southern African countries, although direct links with Windhoek, Gaberone, Capetown and Maputo were severed in the late twentieth century and these towns are now only accessible from Harare via Johannesburg. If competition from larger airlines continues to increase, then Air Zimbabwe, if it is to remain commercially viable, may have to confine its activities to domestic services together with selected routes, shared with neighbouring airlines, to a few centres in other states in southern and east Africa.

National airlines, however uneconomic, have always been regarded as an essential and prestigious component of an independent state's structure. If current trends persist then the only solution may be for Air Zimbabwe to lose its separate identity and to form a new regional southern African undertaking with neighbouring small airlines which face similar problems.

Tourism development in a country such as Zimbabwe, in the short term at least, is heavily dependent on a long haul international market. The discussion presented in this chapter offers a preliminary analysis of the relationship and discontinuities present between government, tourism policy formulation and airlines as a tool of development. Despite continued efforts to develop a vision for tourism in Zimbabwe the limitations afforded by a disjointed airline strategy will continue to hamper opportunities to encourage the tourism sector to compete effectively against neighbouring destinations. The future does not look promising.

References

Britton, S. G. (1992). The political economy of tourism in the Third World. *Annals of Tourism Research*, *9*, 331–356.

Cooper, C., & Wanhill, S. (1997). *Tourism development: Environment and community issues*. New York: Wiley.

Debbage, K. G. (1994). The international airline industry: Globalisation, regulation and strategic alliances. *Journal of Transport Geography*, *2*(3), 190–203.

De Kadt, E. (1979). *Tourism; passport to development?* Oxford: Oxford University Press.

Ellison, A. P. (1990). Southern Africa — rehabilitation and regulation. *Journal of Transport Economics and Policy*, *24*(2), 215–218.

Graham, B. J. (1995). *Geography and air transport*. Chichester: Wiley.

Hilling, D. (1996). *Transport and developing countries*. London: Routledge.

Hofton, A. (1989). Developing world airlines — how they can survive and prosper. In: M. J. Heraty (Ed.), *Developing World Transport* (pp. 309–312). London: Grosvenor.

Mutambirwa, C., & Turton, B. J. (2000). Air transport operations and policy in Zimbabwe 1980–1998. *Journal of Transport Geography*, *8*, 67–76.

Page, S. (1994). *Transport for tourism*. London: Routledge.

Pearce, D. (1987). *Tourism today: A geographical analysis*. Harlow: Longman.

Simon, D. (1996). *Transport and development in the third World*. London: Routledge.

Turton, B. J., & Mutambirwa, C. (1996). Air transport services and the expansion of international tourism in Zimbabwe. *Tourism Management*, *17*(6), 453–462.

Zimbabwe Tourism Authority (2002).

Zinyama, L. (1989). Some recent trends in tourist arrivals in Zimbabwe. *Geography*, *74*(1), 62–65.

Chapter 6

Transport and Destination Development

Bruce Prideaux

Introduction

Destinations are a key feature of the tourism industry and their evolution, structure, operation, image, economy and marketing have featured widely in the research literature. Destinations are also one of the key building blocks for developing both domestic and international tourism through their function of providing a focus for visitors and investment in tourism-related activities. Over time, and as growth occurs, some destinations will also become generators of visitors. This chapter examines a range of transport issues involved in destination development and demonstrates how the transport system can stimulate tourism by analysing the emergence of Cairns (Queensland, Australia) as an international destination. The chapter draws together previous research in this area to build a theoretical basis of future study of the role of transport in destination development. Given the significant impact that new transport technologies have had on the shape, structure and economics of travel and tourism since Thomas Cook's addition of rail as the third passenger mode (road and sea being the first and second respectively), and the significance of that journey as the start of the contemporary tourism era[1] (Prideaux 2002a), an understanding of the central position that transport occupies in the tourism industry is important if the future evolution of destinations is to be comprehensively understood.

This chapter looks at the impact of transport on destination development but the term *destination* is not clearly defined in the literature either in a spatial sense, functional sense, political sense, or economic sense. Often, the literature uses the terms destination and resorts interchangeably. Thus, a seaside tourist city such as Brighton in the U.K. is referred to as a resort in the literature emanating from the U.K. but a similar size seaside tourist city in Australia and parts of Asia is often referred to as a destination. Given this lack of definitional clarity this chapter combines two views of destinations. The broad view refers to any definable spatial area where tourism is an established industry and draws visitors from regions or countries outside that destination. A destination in this sense can be as small as a seaside village or mountain vacation town or, as large as a region, state or nation. The second view of destinations is much narrower and combines the European concept of *resort* used to describe a specific urban area specialising in tourism, with the term

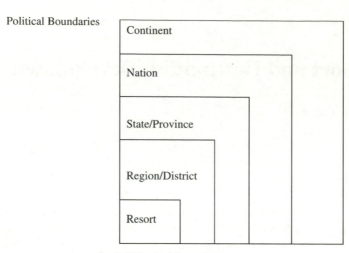

Figure 6.1: The destination classification matrix.

destination when used to describe a similar area, to create the term *resort destination*. Used in this sense, the term resort destination describes a specific urban locality that specialises in tourism and is defined by the functions that are provided including: a designated area set aside for human leisure consumption; provision of leisure services for short term visitors; contain a range of touristic attractions; and provide commercial accommodation. Irrespective of size, the destination's visitors must travel from their home, in an origin or generating region, to the destination via some form of transport.

To add clarity to the concept of destination and the variety of senses in which the term is applied in the literature and in practice, Figure 6.1, The Destination Classification Matrix, was developed. The Matrix illustrates destinations on a spatial scale commencing with a resort and growing in scale to encompass a continent. On the vertical axis destinations are identified according to their political boundaries. In many areas of the world political boundaries transect spatial areas that exhibit the features of a tourism destination (Timothy 1995, 2001). Thus, Niagara Falls is divided between the USA and Canada in the same manner that Victoria Falls sits astride the Zambian-Zimbabwe border.

In the destination matrix the following classes of destinations are identified by political and spatial boundaries. The designation of destination status to a specific tourism orientated locality is often a function of the perspective of the visitor or tour operator. Thus, in Japan, France may be marketed as a single destination. The French, however, would see France as a series of discrete destinations.

Resort Destinations

These are the smallest destinations and include towns and cities that focus on beach, spa, lake, mountain, marine, heritage, city life (Hong Kong and Singapore) and ski tourism.

Region/District Regions and districts are areas bound together by at least one physical or cultural characteristic that differentiates them from surrounding areas. For example, the Lake District of the U.K. is a region where the physical landscape (i.e. a series of lakes) is the focus of tourist activity. In the USA, Washington, DC is a city which comprises the District of Columbia and is a separate political region/entity from the states that surround it.

State/Province This term refers to a nation, or country, and in some cases to political units within a nation. Thus, while the USA is a state, it is also comprised of 50 states. In Australia, also a state, there are sub-national entities known as states while in Canada sub-national units of this structure are known as provinces.

Nation From the perspective of a foreigner visitor a nation may be seen as a single destination. While small nations may have only one major focus of tourism activity, Monaco for example, larger nations may be generally regarded as having many destinations.

Continent The Antarctic is a continent and usually regarded as a destination. Australia falls in to a similar category for many non-Australian visitors.

The Role of Transport

In the twenty-first century travel has become safe, comfortable, fast and relatively inexpensive. The journey from a point of origin to a destination has become routine and if complaints are made it is often about the comfort of seats or the service quality offered by transport operators. But travel was not always safe, fast, comfortable or inexpensive and history has left us many accounts of the adventures and hardships that early travellers had to endure as they explored the world in the pre-contemporary era (Prideaux 2002a). Historical records give us some understanding of the role played by transport in the past. Herodotus, history's first recorded travel writer, has left us with many fascinating insights into life and travel in the Mediterranean and Middle East in the fifth century BC (Casson 1974). In the third century BC, a list of the Seven Wonders of the World (Casson 1974) was compiled by an unknown scholar for the travellers of that era. Most of these sites were old even in the third century BC and constituted the icons of the contemporary traveller of that era. In the Christian Bible a harrowing account of sea travel in the Mediterranean was recorded by the Apostle Paul (1984 edn) (Acts of the Apostles, Chapter 27). Prideaux (2000a) provides a detailed account of the development of transport and its impact on the development of tourism from Herodotus to the present and emphasises the significance of the transport system and its technology as a facilitator of travel in the past, in the present and also into the future.

A number of researchers have recognised that efficient transport networks are a necessary precondition for the development of the tourism industry (Abeyratne 1993; Chew 1987; Page 1999; Prideaux 2000b) and play a critical role in the development of domestic and international tourism (Teye 1992). However, the relationship between tourism and transport, and more specifically the relationship between transport and destination growth, has been largely ignored. This is surprising, however, as Prideaux (2000b) observed that the operation of the transport system is often taken as a given and the impact that transport can exert over the shape and welfare of the tourism industry is often ignored. History illustrates the role of transport in destination development. The massive expansion of seaside resorts in nineteenth century Britain was made possible by the building of rail networks that offered fast and comfortable travel arrangements (Gilbert 1939: Kaiser & Helber 1978). In a similar manner, the enhanced mobility offered by the automobile and aeroplane underpinned the development of both domestic and international tourism in the twentieth century. Chew (1987) described the impact of railway, cars and planes as the three transport revolutions that shaped tourism.

The role of transport in destination growth can be measured from a number of perspectives that involve consideration of the location of origin and destination regions, the transport infrastructure that is required to connect them and contemporary economic production systems. From an origin perspective, distance and the type of transport services that connect the origin to the destination are important factors and can be described by application of the concept of peripherality. From a destination perspective, the distance that separates it from the various origin markets that it draws visitors from will have a significant impact on the structure of the destination's infrastructure and the classification of visitor segments that it services. From another perspective the mass tourism phenomenon of the twentieth century, and the sand and sun destinations that characterise mass tourism, was underpinned by a juxtaposition of new transport technology and Fordist patterns of production and consumption. In the future emerging forms of tourism (Torres 2002) such as neo-Fordist tourism described as niche market mass tourism and post-Fordist tourism described as specialised/individualised niche mass tourism will become more popular and require new responses by the transport sector.

The Origin Perspective

The structure, operation and role of peripheries have attracted some attention in the tourism literature and is a suitable concept around which to commence a discussion of the place of transport in destination development. Essentially, a periphery is a spatial concept that measures the location of a point of interest in a remote location by the distance, or perception of distance, that separates it from the core. In tourism, the core is taken to be a tourism generating region and the further the periphery is from the core the more difficult it is to encourage flows of visitors from the core to the periphery. Periphery can be determined by a number of factors including accessibility, distance, visitor perceptions and scale. Researchers, including Oppermann (1993), Pearce (1995) and Weaver (1998), have developed a range of interpretations of the concept including an international core-periphery dynamic, an internal core-internal periphery dynamic (Weaver 1998), "plantation tourism model" (Weaver 1988) and the distinction between formal and informal tourism space (Oppermann 1993).

As transport technology has reduced travel times and costs, the concept of periphery has changed and areas that were once regarded as inaccessible have become accessible. Frontier regions such as the Antarctic, once the preserve of explorers and well-funded expeditions, now attract a limited number of travellers although travel remains expensive

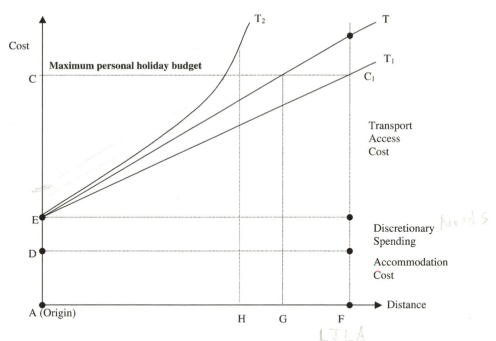

Figure 6.2: Impact of travel cost on demand for attractions in peripheral areas. *Source: Adapted and modified from Prideaux (2000c).*

and difficult and for travellers without either the time or funds required to travel to this region, it remains a periphery. Before the introduction of commercial jet passenger services, countries in Asia and the Caribbean lay in Europe's periphery. This is no longer the case for many Asian and Caribbean destinations where suitable transport infrastructure has been established to minimise the time and cost of travel from the origin region to the destination region. Where adequate transport infrastructure has not been established the constraints of periphery remain. Thus, while Beijing is directly accessible from many European capital cities, Tibet, over which many China-Europe flights pass, remains a difficult and expensive locality to travel to. Factors that determine the scale or degree of the periphery from the core include actual distance, perceived distance and the cost of travel.

Figure 6.2 illustrates the impact of transport as a factor that influences travel decisions by reducing the degree of peripherality of a destination through enhanced transport infrastructure.

In Figure 6.2, the horizontal axis represents the distance of travel while the vertical axis represents the cost of travel. The visitor origin point is represented by Point A and points H, G and F represent destinations that receive visitors from A. Discretionary expenditure is represented by DE while accommodation cost is represented by AD. Tourist may substitute between these expenditure categories. For example, a tourist may trade expenditure on discretionary goods and services (such as shopping, tours and entertainment) for superior accommodation. EC represents transport access costs which can be grouped into three categories:

- The actual fare cost;
- Time taken to travel from the origin to the destination (where the individual places a cost on the time taken to travel between the origin and destination); and
- The cost of comfort (an example in rail travel is first class air vs. economy seats).

Because transport costs increase with distance from an origin point they are treated as a variable cost. In Figure 6.2, CC_1 represents a maximum personal holiday budget. For the purpose of this chapter, CC_1 is assumed to represent the travel budget of all travellers from origin A but in reality each individual will have their own unique budget which will determine their individual travel decisions. In this example, travellers to destinations G and F have two travel options with ET_1 being the least expensive while ET is the most expensive. Travellers to H have no options of this nature and because of the structure of the transport system servicing the destination, incur the higher transport cost T_2 which is greater than the maximum holiday budget CC_1. Although G and F are physically more distant they are cheaper to travel to. Tourists travelling to destination G have the option of selecting the least expensive transport option and reallocating the savings to other classes of expenditure. Travel to destination F is affordable if mode T_1 is used but not if mode T is used. Because of the high cost of travel, destination H is unlikely to attract visitors unless they can increase their maximum travel budget. This example illustrates the significance of transport in travel decision making. Thus, while H is physically closer to the origin point, it occupies a peripheral position because of the high access cost compared to more distant, but cheaper to access, destinations G and F.

This paradox is explained by viewing peripheries as more than distance-based and as suggested by Prideaux (2002b: 381), the concept of periphery should include a range of factors including "distance, accessibility, visitor perceptions, and scale which can be measured from slightly peripheral to very peripheral, or exhibit location characteristics which describe the periphery as near or far." In addition to these factors, the concept of origin push and destination pull should also be considered. Thus, while a destination may be physically closer to the origin, a destination may be perceptually more peripheral because of the cost or difficulty of access. The location of a destination in either a near or far periphery will effect investment decisions, marketing strategies, public subsidies and management strategies. There is also a relationship between the major attractions of a destination and the degree of its remoteness. As the degree of remoteness increases the scale and uniqueness of its attractions must be enhanced if the destination is to attract visitors who might otherwise confine their travel to less remote sites.

A further explanation for the paradox of H's peripheral status relative to the location of origins and other destinations can be found in the concept of push and pull (Dann 1977; Laws 1995). Push factors refer to the combination of factors that encourage travel beyond the locality where potential tourists live and work. As personal income increases, and this can be measured on a national scale by GDP, there is an increased propensity to travel although other factors including personal and national security, length of annual holidays, and attitudes to travel may be constraints. In destinations, a range of pull factors encourage visitors to select one specific destination over its competitors. Pull factors include the uniqueness of a destination's attractions, its cost structure, security, image and ease of access. In the case of destination H, if its attractions were considered to be unique or even iconic in nature, tourists may be encouraged to increase the size of their travel budgets beyond CC_1 to fund travel. This could be achieved in a number of ways including sacrificing other non travel expenditure, or by changing their holiday cycle from one trip per year to a trip cycle of one trip every two years. Either of these strategies enables H to become affordable and the magnitude of its pull factors become sufficiently large, at least for some tourists, to outweigh the negative impact of its peripheral status.

The Destination Perspective

The distance of origin markets from a destination also has a significant impact on destination development regardless of the destination's spatial or physical size. The Resort Development Spectrum (RDS) developed by Prideaux (2000d) is a multi dimensional model that takes into account the impact of location of the resort destination relative to its major origin markets by measuring the relationship between the expansion of destination infrastructure, the local economy and the emergence of market segments. The RDS identifies the role of economic forces, origin markets and infrastructure on growth and agues that the resort destination's micro-economy influences the investment decisions made by suppliers, and through these decisions, the path and format that growth will take over time. Commencing with visitors from nearby areas, the RDS traces the impact of expansion into new market sectors (see Figure 6.3) on the resort destination's infrastructure including transport, hotels and commercial facilities (see Figure 6.4). The markets that a resort destination may target include regional, national and international. Prideaux (2000d) observed that the capacity of resorts is essentially a locality specific factor and is determined by the juxtaposition of a number of elements including the availability of land, specific environment factors, the aspirations of the host community, perceptual (psychological) components, sustainability, public sector responses, infrastructure, provision of support services and transport access'.

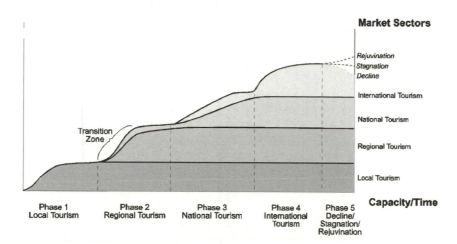

Figure 6.3: The resort development spectrum. *Source:* Prideaux (2000a).

Major Characteristics	Phase 1 Local Tourism	Phase 2 Regional Tourism	Phase 3 National Tourism	Phase 4 International Tourism
Tourist Types	* Locals * People from nearby towns	As per phase 1 plus; * Tourists travelling from areas within the state or region * Possibly limited interstate tourist traffic passing through the area on route to a larger resort	As per phase 2 plus; * Tourist who travel long distances from all parts of the nation * State capital cities become primary markets	As per phase 3 plus; * Emphasis on international tourism
Accommodation	* Beach houses * Caravan parks * Licensed hotels (not resorts) * Inexpensive motels * Backpackers Hostels	* Unit and apartment development occurs * 2–3 star resort motels appear * Caravan parks still important * Outside investment commences in hotels	* 3–4 star hotels * Integrated resorts * Internationally known hotel chains commence hotel development i.e. Hilton, Ramada	* International hotel chains establish resort hotels * Numerous 5 star hotels which may incorporate golf courses, casinos and stage shows
Marketing	* Undertaken by local progress and/or Tourist associations * Limited funds * Limited professionalism * Emphasis on selling not marketing	* State wide * May attract government funds * Businesses operating in the resort advertise on an individual basis * Increasing professionalism of advertising campaigns	* Establish professionally staffed promotion body * Joint campaigns with state & local government and local businesses * Hotels and major attractions fund significant campaigns in national media	* Very professional approach * May attract significant government funds * Corporate advertising very significant * Well developed marketing strategy
Attractions (Major attractions are either natural or built)	Limited to beach and nearby areas of scenic beauty such as National Parks	)First man-made attractions built, generally on a small scale. * Animal parks may be constructed * At the end of the phase larger theme park type attractions will be planned	* Large theme Parks or similar attractions will be constructed. These attractions will feature active rather than passive participation	*The focus of attention will shift from the beach to non-beach activities such as theme parks and up market shopping
Transport	* Very limited in scope * Main mode is road * Possibly some traffic from rail if the resort is located close to rail services * No scheduled air services	* Road access is significantly enhanced * Other modes may be assisted by infrastructure development * Limited (if any) scheduled air services operated by local airlines	* Scheduled interstate air services commenced by national operators or affiliates * Road access continue to be improved i.e. Freeways. *Other modes may be significantly redeveloped. i.e. sea terminals & rail services	* International air services commence * Other modes continue to be developed * Depending on distance to source markets, air may become the dominant mode.
Policy	* Generally ignored by local government	* Tourism maybe incorporated in Local government policy documents	*The need for policy by local and state authorities becomes apparent	*The health of the resort becomes the concern for policy markers at all levels of government
Retailing	* Little specific tourism shopping	* Emergence of specific tourism shopping	* Shopping complexes built to service the tourism trade	* Opening of duty free shops, emphasis on international brand shopping experiences

Figure 6.4: Changes in resort infrastructure over time. *Source:* Prideaux (2000a).

The rate of growth of resort destinations varies and depends on the ability of the resort destination to satisfy twelve key criteria, including investment in new transport infrastructure, and the distance of the resort destination from its major origin regions. In effect these criteria constitute a checklist, which if satisfied will facilitate growth or if violated will hamper growth. Other factors (Prideaux 2000b: 323) that affect the rate of growth are:

- The main tourist attractions (these usually, but not always, include both natural and built attractions);
- Ability to develop an effective and representative resort marketing authority with appropriate distribution channels;
- Success in developing new tourism generating regions and new tourism sectors through marketing;
- The support given by local authorities and local residents for tourism development;
- The time that a particular resort destination take to expand its supply side capacity;
- Carrying capacity and sustainability expressed as land available for development, availability of resources such as water, environmental factors and political factors;
- Ability to attract investment and the composition of that investment;
- The level of support given by regional, state and national governments (this may include support for marketing, building infrastructure and tax concessions);
- Impact of competing resorts;
- Changes over time in the national and international economies.

Figure 6.3 illustrates the relationship between growth and expansion into new markets over time while the impact of expansion into new markets on resort destination infrastructure is shown in Figure 6.4. Thus, expansion of the resort destination from a locality that services only a local market into a locality that services more distant markets will require construction of a range of transport infrastructure that might include highways, airports, high capacity rail lines or cruise terminals. The scope of transport infrastructure required will depend on the volume of tourists, the modes used and to some extent the pooling of infrastructure that may occur where there are several resort destinations located in close proximity.

The validity of the RSD was demonstrated (Prideaux 2000b) in Cairns and the Sunshine Coast, both in Queensland. In Cairns, the opening of the Cairns international airport was the catalyst for the expansion of the resort destination into the international market while on the Sunshine Coast, the opening of a domestic airport enabled the resort destination to expand into the Australian interstate market.

The role of transport in the growth of Cairns as an international destination

The development of Cairns illustrates the role of the transport system on resort destination over time while the RDS explains how new transport infrastructure enabled Cairns to expand into more distant markets. It is apparent that the opening of the Cairns International airport reduced the image of Cairns as a peripheral Australian destination and stimulated rapid growth in international tourist arrivals.

Cairns, located in the far north of Queensland, was established as a port to service the region's mining, agricultural and pastoral industries. The scenic beauty of the town, located in the wet tropics rainforest zone, was recognised in the first part of the twentieth century but its relative isolation from the remainder of Australia and the need to travel by coastal steamer deterred many visitors. The opening of a rail link to the remainder of Australia in 1924 reduced this sense of isolation, however, Cairns still occupied a peripheral location relative to Australia's other major regional tourism regions. The completion of an all weather road to Brisbane, the state capital, did not occur until after the Second World War. However, when constructed the highway eased Cairns isolation and encouraged a boom in intrastate drive tourism. Increased car ownership levels, the long period of post-war prosperity, granting of four weeks paid annual leave and the popularity of caravanning made the five day 2,720 kilometre return trip between Cairns and Brisbane possible.

With the growth of drive tourism a number of attractions were constructed and new motels were opened. Travel times still remained a deterrent for interstate visitors and until the introduction of jet passenger aircraft following the opening of a jet standard runway in 1965, the number of visitors from the larger southern metropolitan cities of Sydney and Melbourne were limited. Introduction of jet services ended the sense of periphery that the Cairns tourism industry had previously experienced in interstate markets and by 1982/83 interstate tourist accounted for 41.8% of all visitors. Reducing the sense of periphery also paralleled the growing strength of a range of pull factors such as new tourism products, additional hotels, golf courses and shopping facilities. The significance of air travel vs. other forms of travel can be seen in the distribution of tourists by transport mode. In 1995/96, 11.8% of intrastate visitors travelled to Cairns by air compared to 73.4% who travelled by road. In the same year, 21% of interstate visitors travelled to Cairns by road compared to 61.8% who travelled by air. In some origin markets, Sydney for example, 88.3% of visitors travelled by air (Bureau of Tourism Research 1998).

Following the success of marketing campaigns to attract interstate visitors the Cairns business community became interested in expanding into off-shore markets. A report produced by PATA (Pacific Asia Travel Association) in 1981 identified the potential for international tourism, provided that an international airport was constructed. Successful lobbying of the Queensland and Federal Governments by the Cairns business community resulted in the Cairns Port Authority being authorised to rebuild the Cairns domestic airport into an international airport. Capitalising on the strong relationships previously established with the Queensland Tourist and Travel Corporation (QTTC) and the Australian Tourist Commission (ATC), familiarisation visits by key interstate and international buyers, travel writers (Commonwealth Department of Local Government and Administrative Services 1986) and journalists, and success in attracting members of the Inbound Tour Operators Association (IOTA) to visit Cairns, ensured that Cairns was featured as a destination in many overseas tour itineraries.

The opening of the Cairns International airport in 1985 allowed direct access to inter-national markets and stimulated investment in 4 and 5 star tourist hotels, golf courses and other attractions (Prideaux 2000d). By 1996/97 international visitors accounted for 43% of visitor arrivals in Cairns, up from 4.0% in 1983/84. A number of airlines, including Qantas, began hubbing some of their international services through Cairns reducing both flight times and costs for many Asian visitors. The Asian finical crisis of 1997 had a significant impact

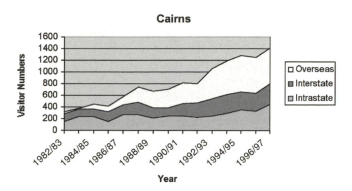

Figure 6.5: Growth of visitor types to Cairns 1982/83 to 1996/97. *Source:* Compiled from Queensland Visitors Survey 1982/83 to 1996/97 (Queensland Tourist and Travel Corporation (1998)).

on Cairns and many direct flights from Asian destinations were withdrawn or redirected through Brisbane and Sydney in the south. This action increased the time and cost of travel from Asia to Cairns thus casting it as a more peripheral destination than other competitors such as Hawaii. As a consequence, the annual growth in international passenger arrivals and departures between 1995/96 and 2000/01 averaged 0.9% compared to 2.8% average annual growth for domestic passengers over the same period (Cairns Port Authority 2002). During this period a number of international airlines including MAS, Singapore Airlines and Garuda Indonesia ceased operating services to Cairns. One consequence of the reduction in direct flights was a fall in the percentage of international visitors to 38.6% of all visitors in 2000, although in numerical terms the number had increased from 606,000 in 1996 to 777,000 in 2000, including international visitors who arrived via domestic air services.

Figure 6.5 illustrates the rapid growth in international visitors following the opening of the international airport. Investment in facilities such as retail shopping malls, golf courses, new visitor attractions, additional land and marine tours, holiday apartments and holiday hotels to support the international market also appears to have had a spill-over effect into the domestic intrastate and interstate markets attracting additional visitors because of the expanded volume and quality of tourism products.

The loss of a number of direct international air services after the Asian financial crisis had a dampening effect on the confidence of the Cairns tourism industry, however, an announcement by Qantas that it was to base a new low cost leisure airline in the city to service the international market brought renewed confidence to the Cairns tourism industry. The airline, Australian Airlines, commenced flying economy class Boeing 767 flights from October 2002 operating under a cost structure approximately 20% less than its parent airline's full service leisure/business configured aircraft (Ferguson 2002). Using four aircraft the new airline will increase the number of potential seats available to Cairns by approximately 170,000 per annum although some of this traffic would have previously travelled to the city via either Brisbane or Sydney.

It is apparent that the opening of the international airport encouraged investors to construct a range of new facilities that appealed to the international as well as the domestic market, thus laying the foundation for the growth of both domestic and international tourism after 1985. Reduction of flights after the Asian financial crisis and the commencement of flights by Australian Airlines in 2002 illustrates the considerable impact that changes to the structure of a destination's transport system can exert over tourist volumes.

Conclusion

Although often overlooked, it is apparent that the transport system can exert a major influence over the shape and direction that tourist development takes in a destination. As the distance between destinations and origins increase, the significance of transport, including both its cost and availability, becomes increasingly important. This chapter has combined a number of theories and models to explain this relationship. While there are numerous factors that influence travel decisions and destination choice, the options for travel that are provided by the transport system will either facilitate or impede any travel decision. As transport technology has improved, travel has become safer, faster, more comfortable and cheaper than at any time in the past. New transport technologies can be expected to continue this trend in future but for a destination to take advantage of existing and proposed technologies, it must have available to it an appropriate transport infrastructure.

The chapter has demonstrated the role of transport technology and enhanced transport infrastructure in overcoming the barriers imposed by periphery. Of course the availability of transport is not a panacea for tourism development as a destination must also have other tourist related infrastructure as well as a range of attractions that will generate interest by potential travellers. Transport's role is therefore one that lies in the background, noticed only when it is inadequate to the task or falls short of the expectations of the traveller and the destination.

For planners, knowledge of the limitations imposed by inadequate transport is essential as is knowledge of the relationship between transport and its supporting infrastructure, distance, access cost, and destination attractiveness. Just as there are examples of transport and its supporting infrastructure stimulating tourism development there are other examples of where the provision of these facilities has not provided the desired stimulus. For example, Biak, located in the Pacific Ocean north of Irian Jaira was identified as a site for the development of a major integrated tourism development along the lines of the Nusa Dua model (Prideaux 2000e) and a major hotel and international standard airport were constructed. The failure of Indonesia's Garuda Airline to operate direct international flights to Biak because of the inability of the project to attract customers resulted in low occupancy rates and the failure of the area to gain other tourism investment (BTE 1999).

In the opening paragraph to this chapter it was stated that an understanding of the central position of transport in destination development is essential if the destination growth process is to be comprehensively understood. In the following discussion many of the key relationships between transport and destination development were discussed. In the future there is an urgent need to pursue further research into the relationship between transport and destination development. This research might include: ongoing analysis into the impact of new technologies; developing more efficient transport networks to service destinations; negative impacts such as pollution, civil and military conflict and the ease with which efficient transport systems can spread disease as recently demonstrated by the SARS (Severe Acute Respiratory Syndrome) epidemic that traveled from China via Hong Kong to many countries via air travelers (Lemonick 2003); and from a more philosophical perspective the role of transport in emerging Post-Fordist, Neo-Fordist and Post Modernist patterns of tourism demand.

Note

1. Prideaux (2002b) proposed a new tourism metaphor, the Tourism Evolution Model, to describe the development of tourism from the past, to the present and into the future. The Tourism Evolution Model identifies three eras: Contemporary to describe the present era and commencing with the first organised rail tour in 1841, Pre-contemporary to describe the past and Post-contemporary to describe the future where current production systems will be replaced by new and as yet unknown production systems. Existing production systems described by the Modernist and Fordist models and their derivatives are encompassed within the Contemporary era.

References

Abeyratne, R. I. R. (1993). Air transport tax and its consequences on tourism. *Annals of Tourism Research, 20*, 450–460.

Bureau of Tourism Research (1998). *Domestic tourism monitor 1996/97*. Canberra: Bureau of Tourism Research.

Bureau of Transport Economics (1999). *Adequacy of tourism transport infrastructure in Eastern Indonesia Report 99*. Canberra: Bureau of Transport Economics.

Cairns Port Authority (2002). *Annual Report 2001*. Cairns: Cairns Port Authority.

Casson, L. (1974). *Travel in the ancient world*. London: John Hopkins.

Chew, J. (1987). Transport and tourism in the year 2000. *Tourism Management, 18*(2), 83–85.

Commonwealth Department of Local Government and Administrative Services (1986). *Cairns region joint tourism research study*. Canberra: Commonwealth Department of Local Government and Administrative Services.

Dann, G. (1977). Anomie, ego-enhancement and tourism. *Annals of Tourism Research, 6*(4), 184–194.

Ferguson, A. (2002). In a time of aviation upheaval, Qantas has big plans to grow and prosper. *Business review Weekly*, August 29 to September 4, *24* (34), 50–53.

Gilbert, E. W. (1939). The growth of inland and seaside health resorts in England. *The Scottish Geographical Magazine, 55*(1), 16–35.

Kaiser, C., & Helber, L. E. (1978). *Tourism planning and development* (p. 144). Boston: CBI Publishing.

Laws, E. (1995). *Tourist destination management: Issues, analysis and policies*. London: Routledge.

Lemonick, M. D. (2003). Will SARS strike here? *Time*, April 14, 72–73.

Oppermann, M. (1993). Tourism space in developing countries. *Annals of Tourism Research, 20*, 535–556.

Pacific Asia Tourism Association (1981). *Cairns — A preview of increased tourism potential*. Bangkok: PATA.

Page, S. J. (1999). *Transport and tourism: "themes in tourism" series*. London: Addison Wesley Longman.

Paul (Apostle) (1984). Acts Chapter 27. In: *The Holy Bible*. New International Version. Grand Rapids: Zondervan Publishing.

Pearce, D. (1995). *Tourism today a geographical analysis* (2nd ed.). Harlow: Longman Scientific.

Prideaux, B. (2000a). Transport and tourism, past present and future. In: E. Laws, B. Faulkner, & G. Moscardo (Eds), *Tourism in the Twenty-First Century: Lessons from Experience* (pp. 91–109). London: Continuum.

Prideaux, B. (2000b). The role of transport in destination development. *Tourism Management, 21*(1), 53–64.

Prideaux, B. (2000c). *The role of the transport system in the growth of coastal resorts — An examination of resort development in South East Queensland* (pp. 1–309). Unpublished Ph.D. thesis, The Department of Tourism and Leisure Management, The University of Queensland.

Prideaux, B. (2000d). The resort development spectrum. *Tourism Management, 21*(3), 225–241.

Prideaux, B. (2000e). Transport aspects of ecotourism development in Eastern Indonesia. In: Gnawn, M. P. (Ed.), *Parahiatal Indonesia Menghadapi Adad XXI* (Vol. 3, pp. 30–40). Bandung: Bandung Institute of Technology.

Prideaux, B. (2002a). The cybertourist. In: Dann, G. (Ed.), *The Tourist as a Metaphor of the Social World* (pp. 317–339). Wallingford (Oxon): CAB International.

Prideaux, B. (2002b). Building visitor attractions in peripheral areas. *International Journal of Tourism Research, 4*, 379–391.

Queensland Tourist and Travel Corporation (1998). *Executive summaries results of the Queensland visitors survey 1982/83 to 1996/97*. Brisbane: QTTC.

Teye, V. B. (1992). Land transportation and tourism in Bermuda. *Tourism Management*, December, 395–405.

Timothy, D. J. (1995). Political boundaries and tourism: Borders as tourist attractions. *Tourism Management, 16*, 525–532.

Timothy, D. J. (2001). *Tourism and political boundaries*. London: Routledge.

Torres, R. (2002). Cancun's tourism development from a Fordist spectrum of analysis. *Tourist Studies, 2*(1), 87–116.

Weaver, D. (1988). The evolution of a plantation: Tourism landscape on the Caribbean Island of Antigua. *Tijdschrift voorEconomische en Sociale Geografie, 79*, 319–331.

Weaver, D. (1998). Peripheries of the periphery tourism in Tobago and Barbuda. *Annals of Tourism Research, 25*(2), 292–313.

Chapter 7

Transport and Visitors in Historic Cities

Aylin Orbaşlı and Steve Shaw

Introduction

The critical qualities that make historic cities attractive places to visit are links to the past, diversity of architectural periods and styles, a sense of place and a pedestrian scale which combine to offer a distinctive character. Tourism is playing a greater part in the economic life of cities than ever before, and a developing visitor economy is increasingly valued as a catalyst for urban regeneration. In a competitive, global market for destinations, historic cities in the U.K. and mainland Europe, like their counterparts in other continents, are being marketed and promoted by urban authorities, as well as by national and regional tourism organisations (Ashworth 1994; Orbaşlı 2000). With very few exceptions, however, the traffic generated by tourism is problematic in sensitive and sometimes fragile historic settings.

Historic cities offer visitors a mixture of cultural heritage attractions and leisure activities in a unique setting, particularly evident in the visual character of the public realm. Although the needs and wants of the different tourism sectors will vary, all visitors are, in some sense, buying into a heritage "experience" or "product" that they "consume." They will come with certain expectations, from accommodation standards to the service level and facilities provided at cultural attractions and shopping opportunities. All this must take place in a high quality and unique environment. Context in historic cities is as important as the individual attractions themselves, and an important contributing factor will be the infrastructure, provision and network of transport. The *spaces in-between* and the *links* between key attractions or activity nodes are the unifying elements of urban tourism.

The sustainable circulation of people and goods is a key factor in maintaining this integrity, and ensuring long-term success as an attractive place for the local population, as well as for visitors. Appropriate planning and management of transport — including walking — is required to ensure that a historic city continues to function and prosper as a living place. Without such intervention, there is a very real danger that the ebb and flow of visitors will conflict with the day-to-day activities and movement of local people. In time, this will alienate, if not displace those who wish to live, work and enjoy their own leisure time in the locality, leaving the historic core as a museum-like environment, disconnected and isolated from the "real life" of the city.

This chapter will examine these problems and issues, and assess the extent to which they can be resolved. Specific problems that build up over time and demand action include traffic congestion and parking, visual intrusion, danger, vibration and atmospheric pollution that causes damage to historic buildings, as well as to the health and safety of those on foot or using non-motorised transport. In some cases, the sheer volume of sightseers in confined public spaces may be problematic, compromising the spontaneous enjoyment of the historic city that most visitors seek. In this chapter, the emphasis will be on what can be learned from historic cities dealing with such problems, and how this can inform proactive and sustainable transport strategies for historic urban areas in the earlier stages of tourism development.

Traffic and Transportation in Historic Cities: Change and Conflict

While some historic cities have become well-established and popular destinations, others have emerging and fast-developing visitor economies. Urban cultural heritage is now widely appreciated as an economic and social asset. Urban authorities are thus deliberately nurturing high yield cultural tourism based on heritage and the arts, especially where older industries have declined or relocated (Evans 2001). Some may be promoted as "cultural quarters" with venues for live performances, museums and art galleries, and may include "must see" or "flagship" attractions. Typically, there will also be a range of small and medium-sized businesses, some of which are oriented towards local needs, as well as smaller attractions and facilities concerned with place-history and contemporary arts that attract local and specialist audiences.

In many cases, considerable commitment and resources will be required to create the basic tourist infrastructure and facilities that are required, but this is seen as an investment that will help regenerate the local economy. Public funding may be invested to make the area accessible, safe and visually appealing to visitors, including international tourists. Residents may benefit if this results in improvements to local transport, community facilities and the public realm that they use on a day-to-day basis, as well as from the expenditure of visitors if this increases local income and creates attractive, well-paid jobs that residents are able to take up. Within an appropriate planning framework, inward investment may help fund conservation of the built heritage and public spaces, enhancing the environment for urban communities. Less tangibly, the interest of outsiders may also foster a sense of confidence and civic pride: a significant benefit in poorer areas where low self-esteem has been reinforced by the negative perceptions of outsiders (Shaw 2003).

The arrival of visitors by car or tour bus, may nevertheless have an impact that is far from positive in historic quarters whose built form was developed in pre-industrial times for more traditional forms of transport. In many Islamic towns of Spain, North Africa and the Middle East, for example, the only means of carrying people and goods was on the backs of animals, especially camels and donkeys (Bairoch 1988). The narrow streets of these great cities designed for pedestrian movement are unsuitable for most wheeled vehicles. Narrow streets, tight corners and steep hills that make up historic cities are a challenge to motorised traffic and the presence of vehicles can restrict safe pedestrian movement. Large service vehicles trying to negotiate narrow junctions frequently damage the historic fabric.

Nevertheless, the majority of visitors who want to experience the atmosphere of historic cities arrive by private car, and in developed countries such as the U.K. this rises to over 70% in small to medium-sized historic cities such as Durham, Cambridge and Canterbury (English Historic Towns Forum 1994). The provision of sufficient, appropriate and accessible car parking space, especially off-street, thus remains a major priority for cities that want to develop as a tourism destination. The highest visitor spend in historic cities is from visitors staying overnight, and when they stay in the centre of cities they are more likely to patronise local establishments and spend longer wondering around shops. However, public provision for a highly seasonal influx of car-borne visitors close to the historic core is an important issue for land use allocation, and a delicate balance has to be struck with local demand. Parking restrictions in central areas thus make larger and often chain hotels on the periphery with car parks more attractive to visitors arriving by car.

Indeed, car parking has become a significant problem and issue for urban authorities in historic cities throughout the world. Not only is there limited available space in which to park cars, once parked they are often an unwelcome visual intrusion to the unique qualities that make historic cities so appealing to visitors. While underground car parks are visually less intrusive, they may well destroy archaeological remains below the ground, and multi-storey car parks rarely sit comfortably in a low rise and small-scale urban environment. Limited parking, compounded by blanket pedestrian schemes, also becomes a deterrent for residents living in historic centres. Madrid is just one example where residents are moving out of the historic centre as parking problems are escalating. Yet, it is the life in cities that is one of the attractions for visitors and also what stops them from being "dead" tourist places.

Second only to cars are visitors arriving by coach, and coaches parking up against a major monument or in the context of an historic city can be unsightly. Coaches provide a more efficient means of transporting large numbers of visitors than cars, but with no place to park, their drivers may have no option but to start circling while their group visits the attraction. This not only adds to traffic congestion, but also increases pollution levels. In London, coaches circling while groups visit St Paul's cathedral have, for several decades, had a major impact on traffic levels as well as on air quality in the City. In the early 1990s, Salzburg was inundated with up to 600 coaches a day, including many from Eastern Europe, whose passengers seldom spent more than two hours in the city. The coaches were generally old, noisy and emitted excessive fumes. In response to public pressure, the city council prohibited coaches from entering the centre without proof of overnight accommodation or restaurant booking, but these restrictions proved unpopular as local businesses suffered from a greater than anticipated fall in coach numbers (English Historic Towns Forum 1999).

Urban authorities throughout Europe are experiencing the problems of historic cultural quarters that have become "victims of their own success," including the problems of excess demand over capacity. Large visitor flows put pressure on infrastructure, and can be detrimental to environment and amenity, especially if they arrive by private car or tour-coach. Even predominantly pedestrian cities like Venice become congested at peak periods. The presence of tourists may cause local people to avoid some areas altogether or reschedule their daily activities (Shaw & MacLeod 2000). In such circumstances, local people may feel alienated, as tourism-related development and commercial activities constrain them from enjoying the public realm of their own city (Goodey 1994), at times isolating historic centres into tourist enclaves (Bianchini & Schwengel 1991).

In time, tourists and the industry that caters for their requirements, may overwhelm and dominate the historic urban landscape to such an extent that it destroys the very qualities that the visitors found appealing in the first place. Rising land values may displace established local residents and small businesses that contribute to the neighbourhood's distinctive qualities. The success of tourism in historic cities and urban areas is dependent on planning strategy approaches and the sensitive management of visitors in complex urban situations, both physical and social. Transport issues are closely linked to both planning and management, from how visitors arrive at a destination to their movement within them.

Planning for Tourism and Transport in Historic Cities

The development of tourism in historic cities is, to some extent, supply-driven with the availability of transport routes and services exerting a strong influence on the volume and type of tourism demand in particular places at particular times. From the visitor's point of view, transport is part of the experience from choice of transport to travel to a historic city destination, to the point of arrival and movement within the historic area. Transport and land use planning by urban authorities, and the commercial policies and practices of transport operators, both play an important role in determining the quality of the "experience" for visitors. Ideally, provision for tourism should be complementary, but in many cases, conflicts occur between provision for the movement of visitors and local demand.

Getting There

The significance of supply-driven tourism in historic cities has been powerfully demonstrated by full-scale deregulation of European scheduled air services in 1997, and the rapid growth of low-cost operators such as Ryanair and easyJet that promote short breaks to independent travellers. This has opened up heritage tourism to lesser-known and hitherto "unspoilt" destinations, such as Perpignan and Palma de Mallorca; it has contributed to the dynamism of cities such as Barcelona and Dublin; but it has also added to the pressures on popular destinations such as Venice and Prague that already faced capacity problems.

The capacity and quality of trunk roads and the orientation of routes can also play a significant part in determining the pattern of tourism where fast roads connect historic cities directly with major population centres or with airports and holiday resorts. However, easy access also signals quick departure. Good road connections have made the city of Granada, and particularly the Alhambra Palace, a popular day trip destination for coaches from the coastal resorts of Southern Spain, causing significant congestion and strain on local infrastructure with little contribution to the local economy (Orbaşlı 2000).

How visitors reach a destination is an important consideration in both the marketing of places and also in the facilities that have to be provided and where links and interpretation has to be developed. Given the high dependence on cars and coaches, urban authorities must address the need for effective strategies for parking and onward movement of large flows of visitors that are appropriate both to the pattern of demand and the nature of local conditions, especially the capacity of the road and public transport system, the mix of land uses, and the availability as well as the suitability of sites for parking. Despite the predominance of the private car and tour bus, however, other more sustainable forms of transport should be promoted in the interest of both the city as destination and the region as a whole.

High speed and other inter-city rail services also continue to influence arrivals, and fast, reliable services may be promoted as a more sustainable means of transporting visitors than road vehicles. For example, in the U.K., fast and frequent services from London carry large numbers of international as well as domestic tourists to York, and this was given a further boost by "First Stop York by Rail": a campaign initiated by the train operating companies. Discounts at over 50 attractions, accommodation and restaurants were used to encourage off-season short breaks (English Historic Towns Forum 1999). Some historic cities are, however, less well served. For example, another cathedral town, Lincoln, is less visited for not being located on major rail or road networks. Furthermore, the constraints of railway timetables, awkward connections and difficulties transferring luggage, may present a less attractive option than the door-to-door convenience and instant availability of cars and coaches.

Arrival

When the railways came in the nineteenth century, most stations were located on the outskirts of what were then the existing urban centres. Airports, introduced in the twentieth century were located even further away. Consequently, the arrival points for many domestic and international visitors to historic cities may be at a considerable distance from the heritage attractions or tourist accommodation. The railway operators of the late nineteenth and early twentieth century left a legacy of grand and imposing termini, which in cities such as Copenhagen, Helsinki and Antwerp provide arrival points that are heritage attractions in their own right.

There are also some fine examples of well-designed modern "gateways," where tourism has justified new facilities that also benefit local residents and businesses, such as the new airports and rail links built for the Barcelona (1992) and Athens (2004) Olympics. Some new high-speed rail terminals also provide impressive gateways, including the TGV station at Lyon Satolas and Eurostar's London Waterloo International. Unfortunately, however, there are many other transport interchanges — airports, ferry ports, railway and coach stations — that are less well designed, maintained and managed, which provide a cold welcome and inconvenience visitors with poor onward connections.

To encourage people, especially first-time visitors unfamiliar with the city to use local public transport systems and/or walk to reach historic city destinations, it is important to provide good links between the point of arrival and the destination area. This will not only be in frequent and reliable transport, and adequate sign posting in pictograms or in a number of languages, but also in determining desirable and attractive routes. For example, visitors arriving with certain expectations of "historic" will not want to walk from a railway or coach station through a run down or industrial and unwelcoming part of town to reach their destination. In Bristol the "Millennium Walk," a scheme of maps, signposting and dedicated routes connects Temple Meads railway station with the old docks area, which is being developed as a leisure and activity hub.

The provision of a coach park needs to be combined with a drop off and pick up point close to a major attraction or central area in a historic quarter. This is particularly important as coach visitors are likely to be older people or school groups, and in some cases parents with young children. There will be a need for integrated planning for tourism development and promotion as to how much coach tourism is to be encouraged and how it will be managed. Where land is available and compatible with neighbouring uses, coach parks and rest facilities for drivers may be sited in peripheral locations where they will not · obstruct local traffic and have good access to trunk roads. For example, the coach park in Windsor has been specially designed to meet the needs of coach operators, drivers and visitors, and the charging system encourages longer stays. It has a reception centre with cafés, shops, toilets, information and a bureau de change. With the castle in view, visitors follow multi-lingual signs to a pedestrian link through the new Windsor Royal Station shopping area.

For most visitors the car park is the point of arrival, a first impression and a point of orientation. Facilities such as toilets, information points, orientation in car parks are important components of welcoming visitors to a location. Park + Ride schemes can be developed, inviting visitors to use car parks on the outskirts of a city and catch a regular shuttle bus into the centre. But, even when car parks are located on the periphery, provision needs to be made for disabled parking in a central location. In historic city centres a delicate balance has to be achieved between providing sufficient parking space without detracting from the unique character of the place. Furthermore, visitor parking must not impact on residents' parking.

Travelling Around

Most cities have a wide range of activities to offer, some of which might be spread over a large area not always navigable on foot. Alongside a historic core there might be an attractive riverside or another leisure activity; or the historic core might be located on a steep hill. Despite the desirability of encouraging alternative means of transport, private cars and tour buses, with their door-to-door convenience, remain highly attractive and convenient modes of transport for visitors, especially if their time to explore is limited. In contrast, local public transport is often perceived as a poor and inconvenient alternative for travel within historic areas.

One solution is to develop scheduled services dedicated to visitor travel, if such special-purpose transport is commercially viable. Examples include hop-on hop-off buses in cities such as London, Barcelona and Dublin. These can also offer visitor information, guided commentaries and even discounts to attractions. They provide useful orientation for first-time visitors, and those with open top decks offer particular opportunities to view famous landmarks and take photographs. Compared with tour-buses, they offer greater flexibility to their passengers as well as a practical way of moving large numbers of visitors between sites without the associated parking and circling problems. Nevertheless, they may sometimes be seen as visually intrusive, especially in smaller historic cities. Residents in Bath, U.K. have campaigned vigorously against the sightseeing buses, including drenching passengers on open-top buses with their garden hoses. On the grounds that they were both visually disruptive and impacting on the historic road surface, buses are no longer permitted on the famous Royal Crescent.

Underground and metropolitan railways (metros) penetrate to the heart of major cities, providing access for large numbers of visitors as well as local people without congesting the streets on the surface. In contrast to small and medium-sized historic cities, where arrivals by car and coach predominate, metro stations can provide the main means of visitor access to historic quarters such as the Le Marais in Paris, Gamla Stan in Stockholm, the Barri Gotic in Barcelona, as well as Bankside in London described below. Nevertheless, the fragile fabric of historic cities and underlying archaeological remains may restrict the possibilities of building underground systems, whether it is metro lines or lowered roads. The building of the Athens and more recently Istanbul metro was met with much obstruction from the discovery of significant archaeological remains.

In cities with a population of 0.5 to 3 million and suburbs of larger metropolitan centres, tramway or light rail systems may provide fast electrically-powered, non-polluting mass transit, especially if their track can be segregated from other traffic. Relative to suburban railways and other heavy rail system, they can climb steep gradients and their track is flexible so they can negotiate tight curves and weave through historic streets in cities such as Lisbon, where the vintage trams have become a heritage tourist attraction in their own right. Their routes may also have underground sections, for example, the Lewisham extension of London's Docklands Light railway, which opened in 1999, tunnels under the River Thames to a subsurface station that provides an important gateway to Maritime Greenwich: a World Heritage site that receives over two million visitors per annum (Evans 1994; Evans & Shaw 2001).

From a visitor's point of view, urban public transport should offer a well-integrated city-wide system, i.e. a co-ordinated network of connecting modes (e.g. local rail, bus, tram) and services (routes). Key features would include the following (Shaw 1993):

- Interchanges designed to provide access for people with special needs and minimise walking distance, suitable waiting facilities, sense of personal security, signage and passenger information that is intelligible in different languages, staff available to provide information with language skills;
- Schedules that are reliable and which minimise waiting time for passengers changing mode/service;
- Through ticketing that is easy to purchase and use on different services and modes of public transport;
- Service information available off-system, including Websites that offer prospective visitors passenger information to plan their journey and perhaps to book in advance on-line from home.

Unfortunately, however, many public transport systems fall short of this ideal. Incremental and piecemeal development, interchanges inherited from earlier phases of development and the physical configuration of sites may make it difficult or impossible to upgrade. Services are likely to be less frequent between peeks and at weekends when visitors are most likely to use them. Some historic cities have, nevertheless, developed well-integrated and tourist-friendly public transport, notable examples being Amsterdam's metro, tram, bus and ferry services and Munich with its local rail (S-bahn), metro (U-bahn), trams and buses (Cervero 1998). Some historic cities of Central and Eastern Europe such as Prague, Czech Republic and Cracow, Poland have relatively good public transport systems with modern vehicles and well-maintained infrastructure. These have considerable potential to carry international tourists sustainably and bring additional revenue to their municipal operators, but service information and ticket-outlets make little concession to those who speak other languages.

Innovative Solutions

The use of other forms of transportation could become an added attraction. In some places there is the opportunity to make better use of waterways for example. This form of transport might have novelty value but can also be very effective as a means of transport and in reducing pressures. While the waterways are the main form of transport in Venice, in Bruges canal transport is predominantly a tourist attraction. London's branded Riverside One (RV1) bus service, introduced in 2002, is integrated with the city-wide system of public transport and links more than thirty cultural and heritage attractions north and south of the Thames. The drivers carry free guidebooks and an information system shows passengers where they are on the route and images of the attractions at the nearest stop. To serve the needs of residents and employees as well as visitors to the capital, the vehicles are designed to be accessible for people with physical disabilities, those with small children or encumbered with heavy luggage or shopping.

Although a relatively small percentage of visitors arrive by this mode, cycling holidays are increasingly popular throughout Europe, and some urban authorities in the U.K. are improving facilities. For example, in Taunton a franchise-operated bike park, five minutes walk from the city centre, provides secure lockers for cycles and clothes, showers and bicycle repairs. Opportunities for rental and easy to follow maps will promote cycling and reduce pressures on other forms of transport, as demonstrated in Copenhagen and other historic cities in Scandinavia where urban routes for cyclists are well segregated from motorised traffic. Cycle routes in historic centres must, however, respect designated pedestrian environments. Other alternative and novel forms of transport include low impact road "trains," people movers, pedal-rickshaws. Horse carriages are popularly used in cities such as York as an added visitor attraction and alternative tour of the city in summer months.

Pedestrian Zones

Pedestrian areas are a solution to providing safe pedestrian access in historic cities as well as reducing the visual and physical impact of cars. The "spaces in-between" are as much a part of the tourism product as are the heritage attractions, retail outlets and hospitality businesses. This network of public spaces provides a web of connections that offers people a range of choices when deciding to make local journeys in the course of their daily lives. Safe, well maintained, attractive and uncluttered open spaces play a crucial role in strengthening communities.

In tourism management there is a very important link between good urban design and transport planning which is often overlooked. The nature, materials and design of pedestrian areas not only help define what is known as the public realm and but can also enhance the character of an historic area. In the broad context of an urban renaissance founded on design excellence, social well-being and environmental responsibility, the Urban Task Force (1999) report highlights some examples of imaginative strategic planning where high quality urban design has enabled historic areas to be well connected with modern development. Cities such as Amsterdam, Barcelona or Copenhagen are cited as cities where comprehensive developments to improve pedestrian and cycle movement have been undertaken.

Nevertheless, by creating pedestrian-only areas, traffic problems can be moved to neighbouring areas or a distinct border zone created where shops and businesses immediately outside such a zone lose out on key business. The interface between pedestrian and traffic zones need not be "rigid," so long as differences are clearly indicated for safety purposes, speed limitations set and surfaces differentiated. Schemes that integrate pedestrian and traffic in a clear scheme that provides sufficient access throughout the day and one that doesn't create a large boundary area can also be successful. Other initiatives such as widening pavements or narrowing roads to make easier crossing points can be just as effective in combining desirable and active pedestrian areas with traffic management.

Links between the various activity areas in a city need to be made attractive, safe and accessible for the benefit of all. Overall, interventions need to remain in keeping with the character and local distinctiveness of the historic area. This does not mean the use of standard street furniture and fittings in "heritage" styles.

Throughout Europe the population is an ageing one and considerations for their safety and easy accessibility in the urban environment is becoming a priority which is also reflected in recent legislation. This group represents a substantial tourism market segment for historic cities, and their needs cannot be overlooked when developing transport solutions and designing open spaces in cities. Some considerations include:

- Surfaces suitable for wheelchairs and others with mobility difficulties;
- Level paving but clear (visual and physical) differentiation between traffic and pedestrian areas;
- Provision for alternative means of transport in pedestrian areas.

The servicing needs of shops and businesses that serve the needs of local people and tourists must also be planned and managed sensitively, especially with regard to the routing and timing of deliveries to replenish retail stock and to service restaurants, bars, hotels and so on. The collection of refuse and other waste as well as street cleansing is also an important consideration as the vehicles are likely to impact both physically and visually on the historic environment, as well as on the daily lives of residents and other local users. Physical solutions include providing guidance on the paving to ensure that damage to the historic fabric is avoided and the use of quieter and short wheel-base vehicles with low emission levels.

Signage is an important visitor management tool, but too many and visually conflicting signs regularly detract from the sought after qualities of a historic environment. Good traffic planning, the design of surfaces and choice of paving can significantly reduce the number of signs that are required. Bollards for example indicate that vehicular access is not permitted, and can reduce the need for a large "no access" sign.

Transport as a Means of Improving Tourism Potential

Solutions are necessary not only for historic cities which are already popular as tourist destinations, and which experience pressures due to large seasonal flows of visitors, but also for the less well known neighbourhoods that have the *potential* to attract more visitors and may help relieve visitor pressure elsewhere. In such cases, there is scope to adopt a more pro-active approach where visitors are encouraged to travel by public transport and make use of walking and cycling routes.

The concept of the public realm, provides a useful starting point, especially to understand the quality and interconnection between urban public spaces, and the vision needed to make improvements. Nevertheless, it should be regarded as a key element within a more holistic framework of action to develop sustainable access. In sensitive areas, the need to minimise the intrusive effects of tourism on the daily lives of residents, as well as the historic built environment, may require the control of entry/parking for visitors' cars and tour-coaches. Instead, convenient access by rail/metro/rapid transit, bus and water transport — as well as for exploring safely on foot and by cycle — may be developed. Thus, visitors will be encouraged to share facilities used by local communities. The expenditure of tourists may help provide the rationale to upgrade and improve dilapidated infrastructure such as metro or bus stations, street lighting and paving of public spaces, and contribute to the upkeep of services which are also used by local people, especially public transport.

Where major new infrastructure is planned, there may be opportunities to influence the pattern of visitor flow and, in the longer term, change the tourism geography of a city by linking in the lesser-known, less-visited historic quarters that can accommodate and benefit from the development of a local visitor economy. Examples include the extension of the Lisbon metro for the World Expo (1998); Manchester Metrolink (light rail) extension to the industrial/maritime heritage quarter at Salford Quays (2000); and the extension of the Athens Metro in anticipation of the Olympic Games in 2004.

In 1993, the U.K. government confirmed the funding and detailed route of the £3.5 billion Jubilee Line Extension (JLE) that, for the first time, directly connected central London/West End with Docklands/Southwark and East London by the Underground. Although the primary rationale for the orientation of London's new tube route was to provide a fast, high-capacity link between the city centre and the new "office-city" at Canary Wharf on the Isle of Dogs, it was recognised that it could also provide a "tourist route," connecting the existing clusters of major "honeypot" attractions at Westminster and Waterloo with emerging cultural quarters and attractions further east. The JLE route also provided interchanges with international gateways that included London City Airport (via a shuttle bus) and the Eurostar terminal, Waterloo International.

In a study commissioned by Transport for London, the emerging visitor economy is being monitored along the JLE "corridor," within 1,000 metres of each of the new stations before and after opening of the new tube line in 2000 (Evans & Shaw 2001). Although it is hard to prove that the tourism-led regeneration is entirely due to the "JLE effect," it is apparent that new flagship attractions decided to locate in the "poorer" Borough of Southwark because the JLE would offer a high quality public transport link in an area where little parking for cars or coaches would be provided, and where local roads were often congested. The most notable being the conversion of Bankside power station to the Tate Modern art gallery (2000), attracting 3.53 million visitors in the first year of opening. The major attractions have, in turn, stimulated the development of secondary ones, as well as bars and restaurants along the riverside walk through the historic area of Bankside in Southwark: an area with a weaker local economy that had seldom appeared on the tourist map of London a decade earlier. The riverside walk has been further improved and new pedestrian bridges crossing the Thames link the City with the South Bank and Bankside.

Conclusion

Cities are complex living places with conflicting demands on urban land use and enjoyment of the public realm. No two historic cities are the same, and transport solutions must respond to each individual place. Nevertheless, in planning and managing the transport needs of visitors in historic towns the following key areas need to be addressed:

- Make certain that transport strategies are integrated and the various transport systems are compatible and coordinated;
- Ensure that information on transport is clearly relayed to visitors;
- Promote alternative means of transport to reduce pressures and develop links between conventional and non conventional means of transport;
- Recognise that open spaces, car parks, pedestrian zones, the areas "in-between" are all part of the historic city and any intervention in the urban realm must enhance rather than detract from the character of the historic environment;
- Address local needs first: transport solutions that serve local needs will provide an infrastructure from which successful tourist services can be developed.

An integrated approach is essential and an historic quarter cannot be isolated from city-wide transport policies, or indeed regional transport planning. The ultimate aim of pedestrian and vehicular planning must be to create safe and accessible environments for residents, local workers and visitors alike.

References

Ashworth, G. (1994). From history to heritage; from heritage to identity: In search of concepts and models. In: G. Ashworth, & P. Larkham (Eds), *Building a New Heritage: Tourism, Culture and Identity in the New Europe*. London and New York: Routledge.

Bairoch, P. (1988). *Cities and economic development: From the dawn of history to the present*. London: Mansell.

Bianchini, F., & Schwengel, H. (1991). Reimagining the city. In: J. Corner, & S. Harvey (Eds), *Enterprise and Heritage: Crosscurrents of National Culture*. London and New York: Routledge.

Cervero, R. (1998). *The transit metropolis: A global inquiry*. Washington: Island Press.

English Historic Towns Forum (1994). *Getting it right: A guide to visitor management in historic towns*. Bath: EHTF.

English Historic Towns Forum, English Tourism Council and English Heritage (1999). *Making the connections: A practical guide to tourism management in historic towns*. Bath: EHTF.

Evans, G. (1994). *Cutty Sark 2000 — Visitor validation and forecast for Greenwich Town 1995–2010*. London: Greenwich Waterfront Development Partnership.

Evans, G. (2001). *Cultural planning: An urban renaissance?* London and New York: Routledge.

Evans, G., & Shaw, S. (2001). Urban leisure and transport: Regeneration effects. *Journal of Leisure Property, 1*(4), 350–372.

Goodey, B. (1994). Spreading the benefits of heritage visitor quarters. *International Journal of Heritage Studies, 1*, 18–29.

Orbaşlı, A. (2000). *Tourists in historic towns: Urban conservation and heritage management*. London and New York: Spon Press.

Shaw, S. (1993). *Transport: Strategy and policy*. Oxford: Blackwell.

Shaw, S. (2003). Multicultural heritage and urban regeneration in London's city fringe. In: *Conference Proceedings: Cultural Heritage Research: A Pan-European Challenge*. Cracow: European Commission and Polish Academy of Sciences.

Shaw, S., & MacLeod, N. (2000). Creativity and conflict: Cultural tourism in London's city fringe. *Tourism, Culture and Communication, 2*(3), 165–175.

Urban Task Force (1999). *Towards an urban renaissance: Final report of the urban task force, chaired by Lord Rogers of Riverside*. London: Department of the Environment, Transport and the Regions.

Chapter 8

The Changing Airport Environment: Past, Present and Future Imperfect?

Paul Freathy

Introduction

In recent years airports have undergone significant change as political, economic and social factors have reconfigured their structure and operations. Yet many airports continue to remain a primary link in the development of their country's business and tourism economy. For example, in 2000, 180 million passengers passed through U.K. airports and by 2030 this is forecast to increase to between 400 million and 600 million. Both inbound and outbound passengers represent important consumer markets. For example, in 2001 almost 50% of the U.K. population made at least one journey by air. Furthermore, the U.K. attracts a large and growing number of tourists from overseas, many of them travelling by air. The Department for Transport (2002) estimate that inward tourism is worth about £13 billion each year (approximately 1.5% of Gross Domestic Product).

The aim of this chapter will be to detail the nature of the changes that airports have experienced over the last two decades, identify the primary drivers behind these developments and consider the future challenges that the airport sector face.

Past

Perhaps surprisingly, the role and purpose of an airport would seem to be far from defined. There are those who remain close to the traditional view of an airport, i.e. that it exists to ensure the efficient movement of passengers between one destination and another. An alternative and perhaps more eclectic approach, views airports within a broader framework of economic change and commercial opportunity. Airports may be seen not only as modal interfaces but as leisure attractions and primary destinations in their own right. This change of emphasis represents one of the most significant developments in the last two decades. Travelling passengers have been viewed as potentially lucrative revenue streams and have been targeted with co-ordinated commercial offers.[1]

Tourism and Transport: Issues and Agenda for the New Millennium
Copyright © 2004 by Elsevier Ltd.
All rights of reproduction in any form reserved.
ISBN: 0-08-044172-6

This is not to argue that all airports have followed a similar strategic trajectory. The priority assigned to the generation of commercial revenues will depend upon a number of factors, not least the extent of state support for such a strategy, the nature of the competitive environment and the strength of senior commercial representation within an airport's management structure.

A number of airports continue to follow what Doganis (1992) described as a traditional model. This views commercial activities as supplemental to the airport's main activities of ensuring consistent passenger flow, the servicing of aeroplanes and the maintenance of the airport. However, a series of factors have compelled many airports to re-appraise this approach and adopt a more commercial ethos. These include.

Competition Between Airlines

Airports have seen the income they derive from aeronautical activities decline as a result of intense competition within the airline industry. The charges levied on airlines by airports, for using their facilities have remained relatively static since the late nineteen eighties. This has partly been in response to government policies aimed at encouraging in-bound tourism and travel and partly due to the airline authorities operating on limited margins and keeping fares low. For example, between 1997 and 2002 Heathrow and Gatwick airports set the annual increase in airport charges below the rate of inflation.

Deregulation and Liberalisation

The early 1980s witnessed the deregulation of air travel in the United States and represented a catalyst for major structural change within the industry. The development of "wheel and spoke" and "hubbing"[2] in the U.S., established major transfer points through which the majority of flights were routed. The airports involved expanded significantly while others on the periphery saw traffic diminish. A similar situation was experienced in Europe when a number of airports began to emerge as hubs, drawing an increasing number of the newly created airlines to them they intensified the pressure upon established airlines to embark upon a price competitive strategy. (Doganis 1992, 1995). As many of Europe's established airlines were state owned, they had cost structures related to a regime of regulated air fares and route monopolies.

The structure of the air transport industry within Europe would have been considered mature with established carriers, airport operators and an existing infrastructure. However, the liberalisation of air travel within the European Union and the movement towards an "open skies" policy within the United States has led to a number of new airline operators entering the market. New point-to-point routes have opened using secondary airports such as Beauvais, Charleroi, Luton and Prestwick and offering the consumer lower fare alternatives (Symons Travers Morgan 1997). While barriers to entry still exist and new entrants continue to find it difficult to gain slots and gate space at primary airports, market liberalisation has led to an intensification of competition within the air industry (Freathy & O'Connell 1998).

Decline in State Control

Traditionally airports have been administered and controlled directly by the state or by a body appointed on its behalf. A number of reasons have been put forward to account for the state's involvement in managing airports. Smith (1994), for example, maintains that because many cities have only a single airport, their role becomes central to a region's economic development. Control over the country's airports is therefore central in ensuring not only general economic growth but also as a way of assisting in tourism, rural re-development and regional policy.

While it remains accurate to suggest that the majority of airports throughout the world still have some form of public sector ownership, the level of operational control exercised by central government may be balanced against a greater participation from private sector interests. A reduction in state control and regulation of the air transport industry in favour of greater commercial sector involvement can be identified.

Deregulation has been prompted primarily by the state's desire to avoid the financial burdens associated with subsidising airport capital investment. Airports have traditionally had to compete with other areas of public expenditure such as education, health and defence. The increasing cost associated with operating an airport has prompted the view that airports are in an intensely competitive market and need to be run on commercial rather than state principles (Freathy & O'Connell 1998).

Allowing private sector organisations a financial interest in airport operations is arguably an efficient and cost effective way for the state to maximise revenue while at the same time improving customer service and quality standards. The level of return is increased while the degree of risk is minimised as the state draws upon a specialised set of management skills (Doganis 1995; Sewell-Rutter 1995).

Abolition of Duty Free on Intra EU Travel

Arguably the biggest influence upon the structure of operations in European airports were the legislative provisions relating to fiscal harmonisation across EU member states. In particular, the removal of a passenger's right to purchase duty and tax free products when travelling within the EU. Intra-EU sales of tax and duty free were of fundamental importance to many airports as the revenues it generated could be used for infrastructure projects such as terminal redevelopment.

The rationale for the abolition is that since the movement of goods between member states will no longer be treated as "exports" or "imports" for tax purposes, it would be inappropriate to waive the tax and duty on purchases which are currently exempt (Netherlands Economic Institute 1989). The legal basis for duty and tax free allowances is the 1969 Directive 69/169/EEC which stated that passengers can import limited quantities of products without paying VAT and Excise duties when travelling.

Airports such as Cork in Ireland, derived over 90% of its income from commercial activities and it was estimated up to US$1.8 billion (52% of total sales) would be lost if duty free was abolished (ETRF 1996; O'Connell 1993). The original intention was to create a single market amongst member states by December 1991, however, two EU Directives

(91/680 and 92/12) delayed the implementation of the provision by a further a seven and a half years.

Despite an intensive lobbying campaign from the air transport industry, that highlighted job losses, fare increases and service decline, a further extension was not forthcoming. The entitlement of passengers to purchase tax and duty free goods on intra EU travel ended on the June 30th, 1999. This effectively removed a primary source of income for many airport authorities and created a further impetus to proactively seek and develop other commercial opportunities.

Present

Airport authorities recognised that the external factors identified above had the potential to reconfigure the air industry. Such imperatives have prompted a series of strategic measures designed to ensure the future viability of many European airports.

Segmentation of Customer Base

One approach has been to develop a more sophisticated approach to marketing and create a commercial strategy that further segments the airport's customer base. In addition to improved customer service and better communications, this strategy provides a more tightly focused merchandise range, eliminates inappropriate product groups and allows the better utilisation of in-store space.

Airport segmentation strategies have therefore gone beyond the simple delineation of traveller/non-traveller. The process of segmentation within airports may be conceptualised as comprising a hierarchy. Passengers are initially segmented on their purpose of travel, while non-passengers are segmented on their purpose of visit. The increase in persons visiting an airport has led to a further segmentation of these two categories. Moreover, the customs and security requirement to record passenger details has also assisted this process and allowed airports to compile a detailed customer database. The outcome has been a series of broad, identifiable sub-segments that include:

- Domestic vs. International v Transit;
- Short Haul vs. Long Haul; Scheduled vs. Non-Scheduled;
- Business vs. Pleasure;
- Intra EU vs. Non-Intra EU;
- Airport Staff, Taxi Drivers and Airline Crews;
- Meeters and greeters/Weepers and wavers;
- Local residents.

Commercial Expansion

The detailed segmentation of consumers has been accompanied by a marked increase in the amount of space now dedicated to specialist shopping facilities. In many of the larger airports there has been a marked increase in the number and mix of retail operators. For example, in the U.K., BAA increased its retail floor space (including catering) from 400,000 square feet in 1991 to 928,000 square feet in 1998 and by August 2002 had 40 different retailers at Heathrow Terminal 4 including Harrods, Hamleys, Dunhill and Escada. Similarly, Milan airport devotes 15% of its total terminal space to retailing while Schiphol airport offers a range of over 120,000 different products. It was hoped that the existence of a diverse range of shopping facilities could represent a credible commercial proposition that provided airport authorities with an income stream that compensated for the loss of intra-EU duty free sales.

In an attempt to further reinforce the commercial viability of European airports, a number of authorities have embarked upon a number of other strategic undertakings. These have included 24-hour trading, direct mail, catalogue shopping and the development of consumer loyalty schemes. More fundamentally, authorities such as Schiphol International have taken the process of commercialisation further by developing a landside shopping centre aimed at the local population.

Strategic Alliances

In an attempt to expand operations into developing markets, a number of airport authorities have embarked upon a strategy of acquisition and joint venture activity with overseas partners. While neither of these approaches are particularly new, both strategies have become increasingly widespread within the air industry. The benefits derived from joint ventures includes access to local knowledge and expertise, the use of an existing infrastructure and distribution network and the opportunity to develop management skills through overseas experience (Freathy & O'Connell 1998; Keogh 1994). Aer Rianta, for example, operate the three main airports in Ireland and have commercial interests in airports in Europe, North America, Middle East and the CIS.

Diversification

A number of airport authorities have also sought to develop activities unrelated to airport management. While arguably a diversification strategy carries with it a higher degree of risk, such an approach has been actively pursued by a number of European airport authorities. For example, Aer Rianta own and operate a group of hotels in Ireland, similarly after privatisation the BAA, also began developing hotels on its own property as well as opening a separate hotel in Belgium. In addition, it has jointly constructed a £450 million rail link between London Paddington and Heathrow airport. The company has also invested in property, manages shopping facilities within a hospital and has bought a freight forwarding company.

Significantly, BAA also entered into an agreement with the U.S. property developer McArthur/Glenn to establish a series of designer outlet centres. The first in the U.K. was a 200,000 sq. ft, 60-unit operation in Cheshire, followed by a 155,000 sq. ft, 40-outlet centre in Troyes, France. By 2002 the BAA/McArthurGlen joint venture had developed seven centres in the United Kingdom and five across Europe in France, Austria, Italy and the Netherlands.

Export of Intellectual Capital

Sanderson (1998) maintained that intellectual capital will be one of the major determinants of differential advantage and that strategic policy will be increasingly influenced by an organisation's ability to manage its knowledge base. The expertise that operators have developed in managing their airports has a commercial value and a number of authorities have established subsidiary international companies. Skills transfer has therefore been at the centre of a number of airport operators future growth strategies. For example, in Cyprus, the French operator ADP assisted in the redesign and refurbishment of Larnaca airport, while the Frankfurt authority helped develop a marketing strategy for the new airport at Spata in Greece.

Airport authorities have been required to offer a wide portfolio of operational and commercial services that cover every aspect of an airport's activity. This includes master-planning, traffic forecasting and market research, through to retail space planning, leasing and marketing.

Future

As the above discussion illustrates, the airport industry has reacted in a proactive way to the challenges it has faced over the past decade. Despite being in a mature market, the sector remains dynamic and constant change continues to affect its structure and operation. In this section, we highlight the major challenges that airports can expect to face over the next decade.

Changing Patterns of Consumer Behaviour

The arrival of the low cost operators such as EasyJet and Ryanair have been well documented. In addition to encouraging some individuals to switch from the traditional state run and state controlled airlines, these carriers have encouraged new groups of persons to use air transport. For example, the introduction of a Ryanair service from London to France's Strasbourg airport tripled passenger numbers and boosted local spending. DFNI (2003) report that a survey conducted in November 2002 showed that the low-cost airline had attracted a wide passenger profile including managing directors, students and retired persons. Similarly, the reasons for travelling varied, from business trips to holidays and family visits.

One consequence of these changes will be new patterns of consumer behaviour at the airport. Passenger purchasing behaviour has already begun to alter and evidence suggests that this trend is likely to continue. Airports will be required to monitor how changes in the passenger profile influence shopping behaviour and adjust both the product mix and tenant mix accordingly.

While it is likely that new consumer groups will continue to utilise air travel, there will still be the requirement for many airports to provide for the business passenger. Amongst both developed and developing nations, air travel has become an increasingly important method of travel for the business community. Schilling & Hill (1998) note how trade agreements have reduced trade barriers between the world's economic zones and increased both the propensity and incentive for international business travel. Increasingly businesses are looking to expand on an international scale rather than being confined to national boundaries.

Business travellers have higher levels of disposable income and have identifiable spending patterns. Furthermore business passengers are considered to have only a limited time to shop in the country in which they are visiting. Airports may therefore represent one of the primary opportunities for them to purchase products. However, as a segment, business travellers represent a challenge for the commercial operator. They are less likely to browse, may regard shopping as unnecessary and often spend less on any single journey due to their high frequency of travel.

Increased Airport Congestion

One consequence of the growth in passenger numbers has been considerable terminal and airfield capacity problems. Some view congestion as one of the biggest challenges facing the air transport industry (Airports Council International (ACI) 2003). Airports such as Heathrow maintain that terminal capacity is close to saturation. Research has estimated that without a fifth terminal, foreign tourists would make fewer leisure trips to the U.K. than would otherwise be the case. By 2010, this could result in lost potential income of £1 billion a year and lost job opportunities in the tourism industry (Coopers & Lybrand 1995).

Many airports therefore face the prospect of having to extend their existing terminal buildings (Dublin), attempt to construct a completely new terminal (Heathrow) or develop an entirely new airport (Athens Spata). To accommodate the growth in passenger numbers, increasing levels of investment in the airport infrastructure will be required. O'Toole (1997) estimated that in order to maintain their current level of construction and redevelopment, Europe's airports require in the region of $4bn per annum.

Doganis (1995) highlighted the problem of runway shortage maintaining that the rapid growth in air travel has been outstripping available capacity. Duty Free News International (DFNI 2001) noted that 24% of European flight departures were delayed by more than 15 minutes. A number of airports have therefore embarked upon major capital investment programmes not only to accommodate increased passenger traffic but also to cater for a new generation of aircraft. If the creation of the 800–1,000 seat supercarriers becomes a reality, check-in times may be increased up to three hours and dwell times will be longer in order to facilitate the increased number of passengers embarking and disembarking. Airports will be required to enlarge current terminal capacities, as well as provide specific taxiing, parking and take-off facilities.

Increasing Environmental Concerns

Airports and the airlines that use them have an adverse effect upon the environment. This influence needs to be balanced against the economic and social benefits an airport can provide to both the local community and country as a whole. Graham (2001) notes that there are five primary areas of environmental concern for airports. These are:

- Noise;
- Emissions;
- Water pollution and use;
- Waste and energy management;
- Wildlife, heritage and landscape.

Many airport operators are acutely aware of the need to manage these areas and have sought to limit their impact by incorporating them into their overall business strategy. While significant improvements have been made in areas such as noise pollution, emissions and fuel efficiency (IATA 2003), concerns over the environmental damage that an airport can have, has continued to grow. Some within the EU have called for additional taxes to be levied upon airlines as a way of encouraging travelling passengers to seek alternative transport methods (FoE 1999). Other groups have been more cautious. Some such as the TUC (2002) have highlighted the need for a sustained programme of expansion in the field of aviation, noting its importance to a country's economic sustainability. It appears therefore that environmental issues will continue to play a central role in influencing the future strategy of airport development.

Political/Terrorist Threat

External events such as September 11th and the bombing of a nightclub in Bali has had a major impact upon the numbers of persons travelling by air in the short/medium term. Although a recovery appears to be underway it is still not possible to be entirely clear what the longer term effects will be (Department for Transport 2002). The market is characterised by a high degree of uncertainty and, with the conflict in the Middle East, there is no guarantee that any recovery will be enduring.

The economic implications of political unrest and terrorist activity has been well documented. For example, in the aftermath of September 11th, transatlantic travel declined by 30% while European traffic fell by 15%. In addition to the decline in aeronautical revenues, Generation AB (2002) estimated that sales of duty free goods worldwide fell by over a billion dollars (or 5% of the total market) in the following twelve months. In addition, Goodrich (2002) estimated that there have been in excess of 100,000 persons made redundant in the airline industry.

The Growth of Alternative Tourist Locations

There is evidence to suggest that some groups of tourists are switching to alternative locations (Hooper 2002). For example, the combination of terrorist threats, a poor yen to dollar exchange rate and continued economic recession has led many Japanese travellers to consider alternative vacation options. In particular, Korea and China have been viewed as relatively "safe" tourist destinations (Raven Fox Research 2002). Such a change has serious implications for a number of airport authorities and duty free retailers who rely upon the revenues that Japanese tourists provide. In 2000, Japanese travellers accounted for between 50% and 55% of the U.S. retailer DFS' US$1.5 billion sales. Such a high level of dependency upon a particular consumer group obviously creates a degree of vulnerability for the company.

Within the Asia/Oceania market some airports and indeed some countries remain more attractive than others. The entry of China into the World Trade Organisation (WTO) is likely to boost tourism and, as the Chinese government increases the number of approved overseas destinations, inbound and outbound travel will increase. While in 2000, China had 83.4 million visitors, this is set to reach 135 million by 2020, making it the world's most popular destination. Given the potential level of discretionary spending this can generate, China will remain a primary market against which other countries (and airports) will be required to compete.

Increased Market Concentration

Reflecting a trend that is characteristic of economic internationalisation, the travel sector will continue to undergo a period of market concentration. A number of authorities have already grown significantly by competing for airport contracts overseas and this trend is likely to continue. For example, in addition to owning seven airports in the U.K., BAA have contracts in the USA, Italy, Oman and Australia. Similarly, the Schiphol Group who operate airports in the Netherlands also manage JFK Terminal 4 in New York and Brisbane airport in Australia.

Market concentration is particularly evident in the travel retail sector. Of the estimated 2,500 retailers that operate in the sector, the top three account for nearly 16% of the total duty free market, while the top 20 retailers account for over 50% of global duty free sales (Generation AB 2002). Suppliers to the retail industry also mirror this trend, for example, in 2002 Imperial Tobacco acquired the world's fourth largest cigarette supplier Reemtsma (owners of the West and Davidoff brands) for $5.2 billion. This has allowed the company to penetrate markets where previously it was largely under-represented. For example, in the Czech republic Reemtsma had an 18% market share while in Germany it has an 11%. Equally important, the acquisition provided Imperial Tobacco with an entry to the Taiwanese market as previously the company held a 13% market share.

WHO Framework Convention on Tobacco Control

While the tobacco industry is no stranger to controversy, the proposal by the WHO to ban duty free tobacco sales by 2003 is viewed as one of the most serious threats yet. While the demand for tobacco products in airports has been dropping in recent years it still represents a US$2.19 billion market and accounts for 11.6% of all duty free sales (Generation AB 2002). It therefore represents a significant source of revenue for both the retailer and the airport authority. For example, in Japan's Kansai airport, it is estimated that 30% of all retail revenues are derived from tobacco sales (DFNI 2002). Moreover it is seen as a product that draws customers into stores and encourages additional purchases.

Two reasons have been put forward for a ban. First, tax-free sales make cigarettes available cheaply, thereby increasing consumption. To end all duty-free tobacco would be consistent with WHO health policy targets of reducing tobacco use. Second, an end to all duty-free tobacco would facilitate the fight against smuggling.

Some airlines and ferries rely heavily on tobacco sales as a way of generating income and subsidising less profitable routes. It is feared that its removal could lead to consolidation within the industry and a removal of some of the less financially viable routes (DFNI 2002). Perhaps unsurprisingly therefore, the proposal has been strongly resisted by many retailers, suppliers and airport authorities who have campaigned vociferously against its implementation.

Conclusions

In conclusion, the configuration of the airport industry needs to be understood in the context of social reform, economic expediency and political upheaval. The factors that have driven change have remained largely outside the control of the sector itself. As a consequence, the competitive environment within which airports operate have become increasingly intense. Moreover, there is little to suggest this situation has abated, the sector continues to remain dynamic and constantly changing. The challenge for the airport authorities will be to develop coherent yet flexible strategies that provide the direction and growth required in order to remain competitive, while at the same time being responsive to changing market circumstances.

Notes

1. Duty free and tax-free retailing represents a complex industry where the boundaries between retailer, wholesaler, airport operator and manufacturer have become increasingly blurred. Companies such as Heinemann are retailers, distributors and agents; BAA and Aer Rianta are both retailers and airport managers; LVMH are retailers, manufacturers as well as suppliers to the competition. In this chapter, the term airport retailer may refer to an airport authority who undertakes its own retail activities or an independent retail group operating within an airport environment.
2. Recognised methods of organising the routing and scheduling of aircraft.

References

ACI (2003). Key challenges facing the worlds airports. http://www.airports.org/about/challenges.asp

Coopers & Lybrand (1995). *Heathrow Airport Terminal 5 — Assessment of wider economic benefits*. London: Coopers & Lybrand.

Department for Transport (2002). *The future development of air transport in the United Kingdom: Midlands a national consultation*. http://www.aviation.dft.gov.uk/consult/airconsult/midlands/mainconsult/01.htm

DFNI (2001). *New-generation airports: Are we ready or already too late?* http://www.dfni. travelretailworld.com/Features.asp?ID=137&Action=View&Search=True

DFNI (2002). *Review says Kansai faces tough time.* http://www.dfni.travelretailworld.com/ RetailNews.asp?Action=View&ID=792

DFNI (2003). Strasbourg survey reveals power of low-cost business. *Duty Free News International Confidential*, 15 January 2003. http://www.dfni.travelretailworld.com/RetailNews. asp?ID=898&Action=View

Doganis, R. (1992). *The airport business.* London: Routledge.

Doganis, R. (1995). Airport economics — Some fundamental principles. Paper presented at Economics and Finance Symposium, University of Westminster and Cranfield University.

ETRF (1996). *Facts about the duty and tax free industry in the EU: 1995 Statistics.* Surrey: European Travel Research Foundation.

FoE (1999). Dutch transport minister calls on key nations to lead by example with an aviation emission charge, Friends of the Earth Press Release, Brussels, June 17. http://www.foeeurope.org/press/ luxembourg_action.htm

Freathy, P., & O'Connell, F. (1998). *European airport retailing.* Macmillan: Basingstoke.

Generation AB (2002). Best 'n Most 2002: Introduction and general statistics. *Generation AB* (Vol. 1) Sweden.

Goodrich, J. (2002). September 11, 2001 attack on America: A record of the immediate impacts and reaction in the USA travel and tourism industry. *Tourism Management*, *23*, 573–580.

Graham, A. (2001). *Managing airports: An international perspective.* London: Butterworth-Heinemann.

Hooper, P. (2002). Privatisation of airports in Asia. *Journal of Air Transport Management*, *8*, 289–300.

IATA (2003). *Environment overview.* International Air Transport Association, http://www.iata.org/ priorities/environment/index

Keogh, D. (1994). An airport authority with a difference — the Irish experience. *Commercial Airport 1994/95.* London: Stirling Publications.

Netherlands Economic Institute (1989). *The impact of abolishing duty and tax free allowances in the European community.* Rotterdam: Department for Society and Policy.

O'Connell, F. (1993). An Aer Rianta response to aspects of change in the Micro, Task and Organisation Environments. Unpublished mimeo Aer Rianta, Dublin.

O'Toole, K. (1997). European lead: Europe's hubs begin to face to face up to the new commercialism. *Flight International*, *151*(4572), 34.

Raven Fox Research (2002). *Duty free database and directory.* London: Raven Fox Publications.

Sanderson, S. (1998). New approaches to strategy: New ways of thinking for the millennium. *Management Decision*, *36*(1), 9–13.

Schilling, M., & Hill, C. (1998). Managing the new product development process: Strategic imperatives. *The Academy of Management Executive*, *12*(3), 67–81.

Sewell-Rutter, C. (1995). Experiences of Privatisation. Paper presented at the Airport Economics and Finance Symposium, University of Westminster/Cranfield University.

Smith, C. (1994). Airport industry structure: The trend towards commercialization. Report prepared by Coopers and Lybrand, London.

Symons, Travers, Morgan (1997). Assessment of the impact of the Abolition of Intra-EU Duty and Tax Free Allowances on Low cost Airlines. Report commissioned by the European Travel Research Foundation, London.

TUC (2002). The future development of air transport in the U.K. The TUC response, Trades Union Congress. http://www.tuc.org.uk/economy/tuc-5886-f0.cfm#tuc-5886–1

Chapter 9

Tourism Development and Airlines in the New Millennium: An Operations Management Perspective

David Briggs

Introduction

The advent of the jet age, and the process of deregulation have been the principal factors to shape the airline industry in the twentieth century. The current literature has focused on the strategic development of companies and role of alliances within the industry as an indicator of future trends (Evans 2001; Hannegan & Mulvey 1995). Whilst accepting the importance of strategic alliances and other dimensions such as regulation, geographical constraints, manufacturing and market dynamics this chapter suggests that there are other important factors such as technological acquisition and operational interfaces which also help to determine the future of airline development (Weber & Williams 2001). Taking what Fitzsimmons & Fitzsimmons (1994) describe as an "open systems" perspective, three core areas are discussed: capacity planning issues, capacity management and service quality strategies. The aim of the chapter is to provide a synthesis of several operations management perspectives which warrant further research.

Background

Managing operations in any field of business calls for an understanding of "technical issues" surrounding operating equipment and related technologies. This is the hard interface where airlines facilitate the business of tourism and other activities such as business travel. Whilst the spotlight has focused on supersonic travel such as *Concorde*, it is the workhorse products of the 1960s such as the Boeing 747 that continue to lift millions of passengers to global destinations at affordable prices. As Copeland (1992) indicates, 747s flying from main tourism generating countries have contributed to the growth of long haul mass tourism. On shorter distance routes, 737s and comparable craft make significant contributions in the rapidly expanding "no frills" sector. The changing patterns of demand, environmental pressures and the web of regulatory frameworks now concentrate the minds of the airline industry when drafting specifications for next generation of aircraft. For example, achieving higher throughput of passengers from increasingly congested "hub" airports has caused airlines to seek "technical" solutions in the form of "super jumbo" aircraft such as the 550 seat capacity Airbus A380. Should this type of equipment offer reductions in operating costs and some scope for fare reductions, new opportunities would also arise to grow the price sensitive end of the long haul market in a way not seen since the advent of the jet age. More radical solutions and consequences might follow from the development of a "sonic cruiser" type airplane offering improvements in speed, but without excessive increases in costs per passenger kilometre. As in the past, "hard" technological advances may provide some of the drivers which fuel the process of creating new airline and tourism products.

⌈Elsewhere, whilst recent expansion in the "low-cost" sector owes much to the liberalisation of North American and European markets, it is new information technologies that are making significant contributions as enablers for different types of service delivery. Low-cost carriers utilise what Levitt (1972: 22) described (in another context) as "the carefully planned use and positioning of technology." However, expansion of low-cost airlines, serving standardised products does not mean we are witnessing a "McDonaldisation" (as discussed by Ritzer (1993) in the context of the hospitality sector) of the skies. Instead, the twenty-first century is likely to see greater diversity as more appropriate operating strategies and structures emerge. Kangis & O'Reilly (2003) point towards two "archetypal" strategies: one where focus is on "core" activities, the other being "value-added" driven. The latter path is one where, for example, new information technologies may take those operators labelled "traditional carriers."⌋

Incremental movement towards this position can be traced using a business model developed by Olassen & Revang (1991). Here, differentiation is expressed in terms of service systems which are labelled; "standard," "complex" and "sensitive." In the context of Scandinavian Air Services a shift in mission is a classic example of this. The transition through these forms can be seen: from a system where aircraft-oriented technologies is a main component, to one based upon advanced information systems. In a "sensitive" service system, "travel engineering" through information technology may share common ground with the techniques known as value analysis and value engineering, which are normally encountered in a manufacturing setting. However, a significant difference is that "rational" service customer *and* service provider become engaged in the task of data gathering and analysis to secure maximum utility from the relationship.

It is clear that the advances in technology, namely tools such as the Internet, are increasingly instrumental in blurring the scope and boundaries of the airline industry. Overall the customer interface is changing, there is greater empowerment through timely information and improved buyer search skills which affords the customer in a growing bargaining position with tourism suppliers (Zakreski 1998). Rising expectations and more sophisticated consumers will challenge how low-cost and traditional carriers conduct their business (McIvor *et al.* 2003). With distribution costs making up 17% of airlines' total operating costs, relationships between airlines and other stakeholders in the market, seems likely to change (Alamdari 2002). The pace at which internal drivers deliver promise from twenty-first century globalisation may well be governed by the desire to shed twentieth-century regulatory frameworks. As Evans (2001) indicates, strategic alliances in the airline industry are an inevitable outcome of a regulatory framework that produces patterns of ownership falling short of what might be expected in other industrial sectors. Chan (2000a), for example, refers to stifled development given such an international regulatory framework. Several authors suggest that moves towards an open skies policy will be thwarted by incremental and defensive strategies of countries and clusters of companies (Elek 1999; Lyle 1995).

Capacity Configuration and Market Requirements

Given that there are a number of driving factors that have shaped the sector, which ones will become increasingly important? Firstly, capacity configuration, in line with market requirements, has been a challenge for airlines during the past decade of intensifying privatisation. How will this be extended?

Next Generation Aircraft

Hanlon (1999) describes a trend whereby aircraft size increased considerably from 1960 to 1980, then underwent downsizing in the 1980s and remained fairly constant in the 1990s but with an increased schedule frequency. During the 1990s industry growth also failed to generate high levels of profitability: a return on capital of 6% falling below the 8–10% norm associated with this sector (Button 2003). Not surprisingly, Lockwood (1995) concluded that losses of the 1990s, well in excess of earnings made during the industry's entire history, left airlines unable to purchase new aircraft. Additionally, the high costs of aircraft replacement speeded up the privatisation process for some airlines, which in turn, forced significant restructuring of operating capacity. With continued growth likely to come through already congested hubs, "technical" solutions have been the most important of the limited options available to airlines and other industry planners. Gate capacity and competition for scarce air slots have cemented the case for airlines to use significantly larger aircraft, such as Airbus A380s. Manufacturers' publicity thus places particular emphasis upon airport compatibility and hails the aircraft's environmental credentials: "the largest most advanced and efficient commercial airliner ever conceived" (Airbus 2001). With limited modifications to existing infrastructure, some scale economies may be achieved and pressure for new airport developments reduced. However, increased feeder traffic (air and land based) together with potential changes to land use patterns have long been regarded as negative forces on the environment (Wheatcroft 1991).

An alternative path may be taken by airlines choosing to exploit "point-to-point" operations from regional centres where spare capacity is likely to be available. Boeing's "sonic cruiser" concept offered promise to achieve this. In March 2001, Boeing unveiled plans for a "sonic cruiser" capable of delivering shorter journey times through speeds up to Mach 0.98. However, by December 2002 Boeing had replaced its efforts to produce a plane that would "change the way the world flies" with a development offering a more conventional "super efficient airplane" (Boeing 2001).

Route Configurations

Current trends suggest North America and Europe will see more prominent changes in regional markets. Changing structures will continue to emerge as low cost carriers alter constituents in business travel and leisure sectors (Archambault & Roy 2002). In Asia, developments through super hubs may continue to exert the strongest influence. As Chan (2000b) indicates, Asia is potentially the richest travel market and, centres such as Hong Kong have half of the world's population within a four-hour flight.

However, network changes through new operating capabilities may transcend developments, for example, in relation to spatial factors such as economic geography. The current economic and world political climate is holding back confidence in aircraft such a Boeing's "sonic cruiser" which if adopted could, eventually, transform route networks on a scale not witnessed since the advent of the 1950s. Delivering faster flight, meeting aggressive environmental constraints and having fuel consumption per passenger equivalent to today's aircraft (Boeing 2001), puts this type of equipment high up on airline procurement list. "Sonic cruiser" and "super jumbo" classes of aircraft would offer airlines complementary operating capabilities relevant to twenty-first century needs.

Current long range aircraft have capabilities varying between 6,600 to 8,500 nautical miles (12,223–15,742 kilometres). Speeds at Mach 0.95 from a sonic cruiser represent a 15–20% reduction in journey times. However, Boeing have indicated that a range would become a critical factor in the deployment of faster aircraft (Figure 9.1).

Should advances in operating equipment enhance airline product portfolios, a new equilibrium may be formed as a result of changes to both push and pull influences on business and tourism related travel.

Delivery Systems

Efficiency gains and increased consumer benefits have, and may continue, to come from less high technology sources; namely changes to delivery systems. Although low cost airlines make extensive use of information technologies, it is the nature of their delivery systems that enable them to outperform operators in other sectors of the airline industry. Reflecting on the current state of the Canadian market, Archambault & Roy (2002) consider whether economic climate or a process of transformation account for success in the low cost sector. Overall growth, and increased share of traffic from leisure passengers, is a major factor; but in terms of cause and effect, the now widespread phenomenon of lean production systems is a significant factor (Holloway 2002).

A much vaunted benchmark for this sector, SouthWest Airlines is far removed from a basic "production-line approach." Instead, its operational strategy reflects what Bowen & Youngdahl (1998) describe as a "common industrial paradigm" arising from convergence of service and manufacturing production orientation.

Levitt (1972) used the example of fast food operations to demonstrate the case for a technocratic (manufacturing) approach to service operations. Early developments with call centres and central reservation systems, in many parts of the service sector, reflect this move towards the production and delivery of standardized products in high volume. Manufacturers

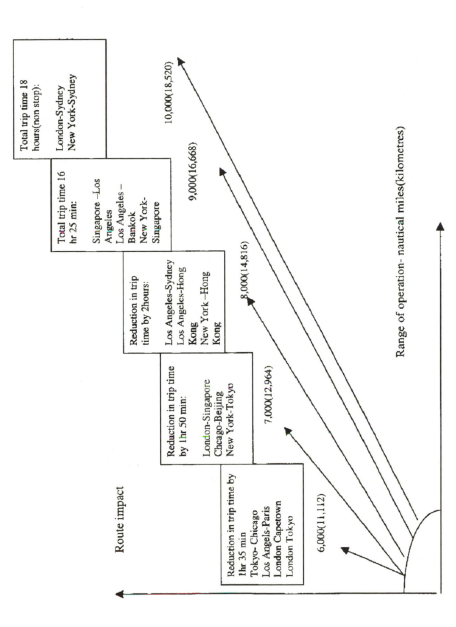

Figure 9.1: Potential trade-offs for route impact and range capabilities for Boeing sonic cruiser. *Source:* Boeing news release: New Boeing airplane to include range of possibilities, April 2001.

long capable of mass production in the factory learned how to deliver the "extra" components making up the (albeit standardized) total product package purchased by consumers. Later, at a time when many successful tour operators saw the dominance of standardized package holidays (inclusive tours) change, manufacturers were increasingly expected to cater for distinctiveness through what became regarded as "designer label" phenomenon.

For both manufacturing and services, common ground has emerged with a need to deliver products containing some element of distinctiveness from an operating facility geared up to high volume outputs. Thus "lean" production systems have emerged in both sectors to meet the challenge of "mass customization." In the airline industry, low cost entrants derive operational efficiencies through concentrating upon a lean core to deliver principal elements required by the consumer. The remainder of the product package is then fashioned to the required specification by consumers themselves. Low cost provision in the airline industry is nothing new; achieving this through an operational structure divested of what were traditionally regarded as essential supporting components is a significant development.

Cost-driven charter airlines have long had much in common with their low cost counterparts. For example, as Lobbenberg (1995) indicates, fast/low cost turnaround at airports is critical to charter operations. However, some not so lean differences exist in the means used to secure operational efficiency:

- charter airlines typically provide "standardised" products — no frills airlines allow consumers to customise product;
- charter airlines sometimes derive economies through vertical integration;
- no frills airlines often use streamlined capacity outsourcing.

Managing Capacity

A second dimension relates to the potential to extend the use of information technology as a demand management tool and as a competitive weapon.

Yield management   An open-systems view of services emphasises the overlap in production and marketing functions (Fitzsimmons & Fitzsimmons 1994). In capacity constrained services, this linking and certain industry characteristics make a compelling case for a yield based approach (Kimes 1994). Airlines fit the conditions normally associated with a case favouring the application of yield management:

- high fixed costs;
- low variable costs;
- ability to segment customers;
- ability to forecast demand;
- time perishable capacity.

When American Airlines Decision Technology (AADT) team pioneered yield management systems, the strategies and tactics used to maximise revenue were already familiar to other operators:

- capacity management — overbooking to compensate for "no shows";
- discriminatory pricing — to minimise unrealised revenue potential associated with single pricing;
- length of haul controls — to minimise revenue displacement on multiple leg (long haul) flights where demand is uneven between sectors;
- group booking controls — to minimise displacement caused by sales negotiated with groups.

AADT's success has come through harnessing precision in application from GDS/CRS interfaces capable of feeding into the central task of demand forecasting. Load factor, a key measure of operational performance to airlines, is also influenced by the way strategic alliances play out through computer reservation systems, code sharing being the most dominant feature (Chen & Chen 2003). Capacity utilisation through yield management, which utilises a culture of practices to which consumers have now become accustomed, is not without its critics. Lee & Ng (2001) suggest that there are improved results when advance sales are not undertaken, provided excess capacity can be tolerated. Advance sales and other yield management practices (such as overbooking) are now well established in the minds of consumers. What is less certain is the consumer's attitude towards what Kimes (1994) terms "perceived fairness." Presumably, an argument could be constructed along the lines that, in coping with variable demand from a very fixed supply position, airlines through yield management secure better capacity utilisation, lower operating costs which in turn, may benefit consumers. With overbooking, acceptance by consumers (especially those who get "bumped") is a state not helped by publicised information adding up to little more than small print on an IATA flight coupon.

Discriminatory pricing probably fares no better in the minds of many consumers. For many years consumers have been accustomed to yield management "fences" that produce variations in price according to booking condition such as:

- advance payment;
- advance reservation;
- refundable/non-refundable;
- changes/no changes permitted to date of travel;
- specified length of stay.

Fencing off capacity to stop lucrative business travellers trading down to lower fares pitched predominantly at leisure travellers has been the forte of traditional carriers. Again, uneven demand and the pursuit of better capacity utilisation would be factors used in an airline's justification of these tactics. With consumers, being accustomed to rather than accepting without question these conditions (such as an APEX fare requiring a Saturday night stay), may be nearer the truth. Consumers in business and leisure travel markets are showing signs that fare structures with traditional carriers do not meet with approval (Archambault & Roy 2002).

On fares, traditional carriers are under attack from low cost competitors with pressures arising from the aftermath of "9/11," forcing some carriers to ease restrictions on some tickets (e.g. length of stay). However, the problem is more deep-rooted because of the differences in the product each type of operator supplies.

No-frills cost/benefit challenge   Yield management systems pioneered by American Airlines and sold on to other capacity constrained operators (e.g. hotels, rail operators, car rental) offer customers benefits in the form of discounted fares for sacrifices; such as the opportunity to book late. Low cost operators that emerged in North America used relatively unsophisticated yield management systems and offered customers low fares with minimum restrictions (Pender & Baum 2000). In Europe, consumers now enjoy a substantial package of benefits at what might be judged a tolerable level of sacrifice. Traditional carriers are locked into booking restrictions probably because "constrained" capacity is considerable, in that it extends well beyond core capacity (seats on aircraft). Indeed one of the hall-marks of a "world class" carrier such as Singapore Airlines (SIA) is the high level of investment at "home base," Changi Airport. For SIA, this covers dedicated cargo terminals, maintenance facilities, in-flight services and so on. Similarly, Cathay Pacific has undertaken substantial investment following opportunities opened up through Hong Kong's new airport, Chek Lap Kok. However, more recently, other global players such as British Airways have faced pressures to reduce home base operating capacities through use of out-sourcing.

Pender & Baum (2000) outline the cost advantages and consumer benefits exploited by low cost carriers. In many instances, operating efficiencies also enhance monetary and non-monetary consumer benefits, (Gilbert *et al.* 2001). Table 9.1 summarises themes discussed in recent literature.

The principal reason here for linking operating features and consumer impacts is, that it may be important to separate those items which might be described as "service innovations" from those merely representing cost advantages. This is particularly important when considering the airline/airport relationship since low cost carriers as new entrants may be pushing against open doors at regional airports keen to promote traffic growth. By way of contrast, traditional carriers are often products of (political) history and/or have complex operating structures.

Seristo & Vepsalainen (1996: 12) present an appropriate model covering cost drivers and revenue factors in airline operations. It offers a good basis for comparisons between traditional carriers as well as traditional and low cost carriers. However, by extending scope and time frame a wider picture showing operations equilibrium and cost/revenue influences can be shown. As indicated in sections above, additional cost drivers such as level of service, age of aircraft, level of automation, outsourcing and traffic charges may be significant. With respect to revenues, cargo yield (lack of) and traffic composition are also critical differences (Figure 9.2).

If some erosion of current cost advantage occurs for European-based low-cost carriers, growth opportunity may rest on differentiation through elements in the product package that are non-price related. Piga & Filppi (2002) conclude that ticket price is only one element in consumers' cost calculations. "Transfer distance," the journey between airport and place of residence, is introduced; this together with other determinants could be used to develop a more comprehensive consumer utility function based upon "total travel experience." "Transfer distance" enters consumer cost calculations (Piga & Filppi 2002) but other variables, such as alternative forms of transport, may play a part in consumer decisions. Low cost airlines owe much of their strong presence in Britain to a relatively flexible labour market, but another influence may be location and performance of other

Table 9.1: Operations and consumer benefits.

Operations feature	Impact on consumer
Simplified pricing — through single/flexible return fares	Fewer restrictions, greater flexibility in travel. "Bumping" through overbooking less likely because of non refundable fares
In-flight services — simplified "leaner" service enables faster turnaround and higher aircraft utilisation	Increased choice: purchase of services consumed determined by consumer
Aircraft fleet — standardised on one/few aircraft types • Cabins configured for one class • Maintenance regimes simplified through standardisation of parts and servicing	Confidence — safety standards maintained through use of aircraft fleet with low average age
Airport related facilities • Homogeneity/streamlining eliminates differentiation and duplication in areas such as check-in and waiting lounges • Lower costs and complexity from baggage handling transfer activities	Customer processing • Standardised with waiting line fairness achieved through first come first served basis instead of price paid BUT • Lack of transfer facility may mean increased complexity and time for multiple flight journies
Departure points • Developing regional airports tend to offer lower access costs	Convenience • From lower "transfer distances" and total journey times • Flight schedules independent of hub activity
Customer interfaces • "lean" and simplified with low operating costs from application of latest technology, elimination of airline to airline interfaces from through ticketing, elimination of tickets and intermediaries needed to issue them and collect payment	Simplified access • With 24/7 availability time BUT • Consumers required to be active participants and • Conform to more tightly structured process of interaction

modes of transport. In mainland Europe, cities are often served by rail services working to an internationally co-ordinated timetable. In this context, integrated or "seamless" transport may be more of a reality than in Britain where fragmentation and congestion are order of the day. Thus, "transfer distance" may be relevant to passengers engaging low-cost operators because:

• excessive concentration of airline operations through hubs such as Heathrow may exclude large percentages of the population on grounds of cost and total journey time;

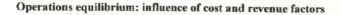

Operations equilibrium: influence of cost and revenue factors

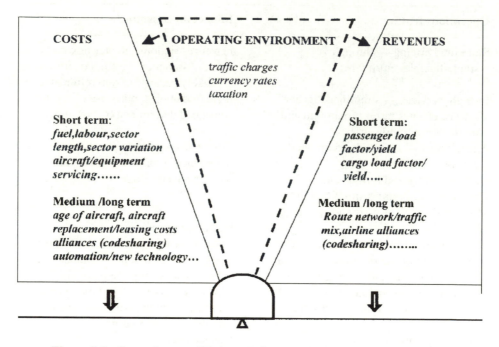

COSTS

OPERATING ENVIRONMENT

REVENUES

traffic charges
currency rates
taxation

Short term:
fuel,labour,sector
length,sector variation
aircraft/equipment
servicing......

Medium /long term
age of aircraft, aircraft
replacement/leasing costs
alliances (codesharing)
automation/new technology...

Short term:
passenger load
factor/yield
cargo load factor/
yield.....

Medium /long term
Route network/traffic
mix,airline alliances
(codesharing)........

Figure 9.2: Operations equilibrium: Influence of cost and revenue factors.

- low-cost carriers competing on routes serving same final destination tend to use different departure points (Piga & Filppi 2002).

Also, as providers of inclusive and other tours know, transfer distance at final destination is a factor in consumer choice of product package.

Taking the "total travel experience" low cost carriers and regional airports may be extending to the traveller improved access to air travel on the basis of cost and total journey time. In the nineteenth century, rail transport had similar liberating effects upon large sections of the population. Thus, for some consumers, low cost carriers may turn air travel into a commodity of "routine" consumption whereas others may be drawn in on the basis of "novelty" appeal. From banking to fast food, operating systems geared up to deliver mass service enable latent rather than entirely new demands to be tapped.

Service Quality Strategies: New Directions Through Information Technologies

Information technologies and company interfaces will continue to change the role and position of airlines, traditional electronic tourism intermediaries and new e-Mediaries (Morgan *et al.* 2001). From a range of e-platforms; the Internet, IDTV (interactive digital television) and mobile devices, principals will form new business models (Barnett &

Standing 2001). Recent false starts may have dampened some supplier expectations, but several studies identify consumers to be major beneficiaries (Buhalis & Licata 2002; McIvor *et al.* 2003). "Virtual travellers," enabled through the internet to become more proactive and sophisticated in their dealings with airlines, reflect the position of consumers in the "sensitive service system" defined by Olassen & Revang (1991).

At a basic level, information technology in a "standard" service system acts as an assistant, is an integral part of the service process and, presents the consumer with a "hard" interface. Examples here include the virtual automation of routine transactions such that even provision of a human interface through a call center may be considered inappropriate. "Complex" service systems have information technology positioned to play the role of advisor. To the consumer, technology becomes an instrument for interaction with a softer interface. Greater consumer participation rather than a more open two-way process of communication between service provider and consumer is the underlying rationale.

New intermediaries and new approaches from existing operators utilize the communicator role of "sensitive" service systems to deliver a service process where both interaction with and isolation from the technical core are features. Here emphasis moves away from just delivering solid operational efficiency towards competitive advantage gained from more effective customization of products.

"Sensitive" service systems must deliver a high level of tolerance for individual needs and utility. Information technologies offering airlines the possibility of designing an individual service package may be the long term future for traditional carriers:

> Obtaining a patent on your systems or services you offer to the market is impossible, but the company that executes excellent service is hard to copy
> (Olassen & Revang 2002: 44):

Short term expedients used to meet the challenge of low-cost penetration and the aftermath of 9/11 suggest this point is not lost on some of those operators with vastly under-utilised networks of facilities.

Role and position of traditional carriers   Low cost carriers may be viewed as "standard service systems" using information systems to "assist" the engineering of cost reductions. Although traditional carriers seem likely candidates for using information technology to engineer service quality improvements, some studies suggest grounds for caution when considering service attributes having greatest impact up consumer perceptions of quality. For example, assessment of service quality is not always reflected in market share (Tsaur *et al.* 2002). Similarly Lafferty & van Fossen (2001) point to safe efficient travel as a priority for many travellers. This study is interesting in that it takes as a focus integration in the tourism industry; component sectors being transport, accommodation, entertainment, food and beverages. Consumption patterns of travellers and the capabilities on offer from new information technologies may point to available opportunities. However, airlines with professional and technical competence as a priority, are viewed as having different operating cultures from hotels and restaurants. Although information technologies offer enabling devices, enthusiasm for vertical integration, if on the scale of previous attempts, would not see fundamental changes in the airline customer relationship.

Conclusions

A synopsis taken during the first decade of the present century must paint a picture of mixed fortunes for the airline industry. For traditional carriers, the aftermath of "9/11" has proved a difficult storm to ride out (Golaszewski 2003). However, these adverse conditions exacerbate a paralysis of longer standing. Competition laws and the slow transition from "flag carriers" to truly trans-national airlines may account for limited prospects of "technical" solutions being applied to change the way the world flies in the twenty-first century.

Slow adaptation in some sectors may have provided a window of opportunity for operators capable of developing strategies more in tune with market requirements. Vast operations concentrated on hub and spoke networks do offer enormous operating and marketing advantages but in adverse conditions, airlines with large operating infrastructures become vulnerable. Leaner and more flexible operations, as found in the low cost sector, do not carry such millstones and prove responsive to developing trends identified in the 1990s (Figure 9.3).

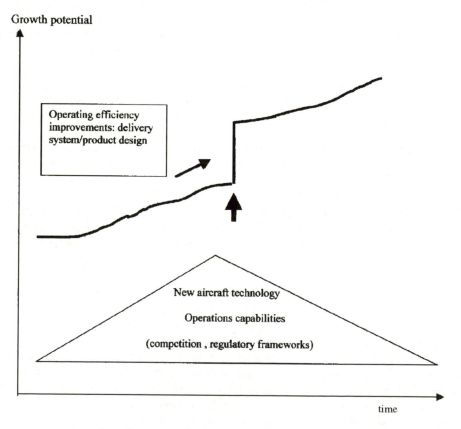

Figure 9.3: Operations improvement: Step-wise development.

Low-cost airlines represent one stage in the evolution of operating systems needed to meet the diverse requirements of the market for air travel. Parallels can be seen in other service sectors such as fast food and budget hotel operations; with boundaries being pushed out to embrace provision for mass consumption.

In three core areas, capacity configuration, capacity management and service quality, low-cost airlines deliver customer satisfaction and resource productivity through operating structures tuned more closely to market requirements. Research to test this balance in meeting operation objectives might come from studying the significance of "transfer distance" in the make up of airline/tourism product packages. Other linkages worth pursuing include the role of low-cost airlines and new information technologies in the development of short haul independent travel.

For traditional carriers the vexed question some face is whether to limit operations to niche markets or attempt to span all; especially mass provision. Whichever course is followed these operators seem likely to re-engineer their products and operating structures with the kind of rigour associated with methods such as value analysis and engineering. The potential impact of new information technologies may suggest evolution towards "sensitive" service systems; but more fundamental may be recognition that, where competition prevails, any operating system lacking a customer focus is out of alignment with its market. Thus, states of competition may reflect the varying degrees of "sensitivity" operators in the airline industry appear to have towards provision of delivery systems capable of meeting customers expectations. The direction of the research agenda should therefore be expanded to embrace further analysis of these underpinning strategic operational factors.

References

Airbus Industrie (2001). Airbus-Aircraft Families — Introduction A380 Family. (http://www.airbus. com/product/a380_backgrounder.asp) Accessed 2/3/03.

Alamdari, F. (2002). Regional developments in airlines and travel agents relationship. *Journal of Air Transport Management*, 8(5), 339–348.

Archambault, M., & Roy, J. (2002). The Canadian air transport industry: In crisis or in transition? *Journal of Vacation Marketing*, 9(1), 4–16.

Barnett, M., & Standing, C. (2001). Repositioning travel agencies on the Internet. *Journal of Vacation Marketing*, 7(2), 143–152.

Boeing (2001). New Boeing airplane to include range of possibilities. (http://www.boeing.com/news/ releases/2001/q2news_release_010426a.html) Accessed 2/5/03.

Bowen, D., & Youngdahl, W. (1998). "Lean" service: In defense of a production-line approach. *International Journal of Service Industry Management*, 9(3), 207–225.

Buhalis, D., & Licata, M. (2002). The future eTourism intermediaries. *Tourism Management*, 23(3), 207–220.

Button, K. (2003). Does the theory of the 'Core' explain why airlines fail to cover their long run costs of capital? *Journal of Air Transport Management*, 9(1), 5–14.

Chan, D. (2000a). The development of the airline industry from 1978–1998: A strategic global overview. *Journal of Management Development*, 19(16), 489–514.

Chan, D. (2000b). Air wars in Asia: Competitive and collaborative strategies and tactics in action. *Journal of Management Development*, 19(6), 473–488.

Chen, F., & Chen, C. (2003). The effects of strategic alliances and risk pooling on the load factors of international airline operations. *Transportation Research, 39*(E), 19–34.

Copeland, E. (1992). The role of airlines in the tourism and environment debate. *Tourism Management, 13*(1), 112–114.

Elek, A. (1999). Open skies or open clubs? New issues for Asia Pacific economic cooperation. *Journal of Air Transport Management, 5*(3), 143–151.

Evans, N. (2001). Collaborative strategy: An analysis of the changing world of international alliances. *Tourism Management, 22*(3), 229–243.

Fitzsimmons, M., & Fitzsimmons, J. (1994). *Service management for competitive advantage.* Singapore: McGraw-Hill.

Gilbert, D., Child, D., & Bennett, M. (2001). A qualitative study of the current practices of 'on-frills' airlines operating in the U.K. *Journal of Vacation Marketing, 7*(4), 302–315.

Golaszewski, R. (2003). Network industries in collision: Aviation infrastructure capacity financing and the exposure to traffic declines. *Journal of Air Transport Management, 9*(1), 57–65.

Hanlon, P. (1999). *Global Airlines* (2nd ed.). Oxford: Butterworth Heineman.

Hannegan, T. F., & Mulvey, F. P. (1995). International airline alliances: An analysis of code sharing's impact on airlines and consumers. *Journal of Air Transport Management, 2*(2), 131–137.

Holloway, S. (2002). *Airlines: Managing to make money.* Aldershot: Ashgate.

Kangis, P., & O'Reilly, M. (2003). Strategies in a dynamic marketplace. A case study in the airline industry. *Journal of Business Research, 56*(2), 105–111.

Kimes, S. (1994). Perceived fairness of yield management. *The Cornell Hotel and Restaurant Administration Quarterly, 35*(1), 22–29.

Lafferty, G., & Van Fossen, A. (2001). Integrating the tourism industry: Problems and strategies. *Tourism Management, 22*(1), 11–19.

Lee, K., & Ng, I. (2001). Advance sale of service capacities: A theoretical analysis of the impact of price sensitivity on pricing and capacity allocations. *Journal of Business Research, 54*(3), 219–225.

Levitt, T. (1972). Production-line approach to service. *Harvard Business Review, 50*(5), 20–31.

Lobbenberg, A. (1995). The impact of turnaround costs on inclusive tour prices. *Tourism Management, 16*(7), 501–505.

Lockwood, R. (1995). Goal-directed development of new products. *World Class Design to Manufacture, 2*(1), 34–37.

Lyle, C. (1995). The future of international airline transport regulation. *Journal of Air Transport Management, 2*(1), 3–10.

McIvor, R., O'Reilly, D., & Ponsonby, S. (2003). The impact of Internet technologies on the airline industry: Current strategies and future developments. *Strategic Change, 12*(1), 31–47.

Morgan, N., Pritchard, A., & Abbott, S. (2001). Consumers, travel technology: A bright future for the Web or television shopping. *Journal of Vacation Marketing, 7*(2), 110–124.

Olassen, J., & Revang, I. (1991). The significance of information technology for service quality: From market segmentation to individual service. *International Journal of Service Industry Management, 2*(3), 26–46.

Pender, L., & Baum, T. (2000). Have the frills really left the European airline industry? *International Journal of Tourism Research, 2*(6), 423–436.

Piga, C., & Filppi, N. (2002). Booking and flying with low-cost airlines. *International Journal of Tourism Research, 4*(3), 237–249.

Ritzer, G. (1993). *The Mcdonaldisation of society: An investigation into the changing character of contemporary social life.* Newbury Park: Pine Forge Press.

Seristo, H., & Vepsalainen, A. (1996). Airline cost drivers: Implications of fleet, routes, and personnel policies. *Journal of Air Transport Management, 3*(1), 11–22.

Tsaur, S.-H., Chang, T.-Y., & Yen, C.-H. (2002). The evaluation of airline service quality by Fuzzy MCDM. *Tourism Management, 23*(2), 107–115.

Weber, M., & Williams, G. (2001). Drivers of long-haul air transport route development. *Journal of Transport Geography, 9,* 243–254.

Wheatcroft, S. (1991). Airlines, tourism and the environment. *Tourism Management, 12*(2), 119–124.

Zakreski, E. (1998). Beyond frequent fliers: Knowing customers as a foundation for airline growth. In: G. F. Butler, & M. R. Keller (Eds), *Handbook of Airline Marketing.* New York: Aviation Week Group.

Chapter 10

Cruise Ships: Deterritorialized Destinations

Robert E. Wood

Introduction

The growth of cruising in recent decades has been roughly double the overall rate of growth of tourism. From its predominantly Caribbean base, cruise tourism has spread across the world, increasing ports of call in all regions. As well as this, river and canal cruising has grown rapidly, particularly in Europe and China. In order both to meet and create this demand, cruise ships have increased in size; there appears to be no limit in sight. The clientele has expanded far beyond its traditional older and affluent market base. With only about 13% of Americans, and even smaller proportions elsewhere, having cruised, the cruise industry is confident about its future.

In 2002, the global cruise fleet consisted of 223 ships with an annual passenger capacity 11,358,203, and with sales revenues of over $15 billion. The North American market dominates and the growth rate there has been spectacular, rising from a mere 330,000 passengers in 1965 to 7.6 million in 2002. It is estimated that between 10–12 million people took cruises worldwide in 2002. By 2006, it is predicted that a fleet of 251 ships will deliver sales revenues of over $19 billion (Cruise Industry News Annual 2002: 14).

Foster (1986) noted, with astonishment, how cruise ships and their culture had escaped social scientific attention, and he noted: "Clearly, cruising the cruise industry is a major frontier for tourism research" (Foster 1986: 216–217). Almost twenty years later, despite periodic reviews of the industry (Dowling & Vasudavan 2000; Hall & Braithwaite 1990; Hobson 1993; Mancini 2000; Peisley 1996; Ritter & Schafer 1998), and analyses of consumer choice, patterns of passenger expenditure, and impact on ports and the broader economy (De La Vina & Ford 2001; Dwyer & Forsyth 1998; Henthorne 2000; Marti 1992; Mescon & Vozikis 1985; Moscardo *et al.* 1996; Teye & Leclerc 1998), it remains broadly the case that there continues to be "a paucity of studies and little academic literature on cruise ship tourism" (Robertson 2002: 1). Apart from a special issue of the Australian-based *Journal of Tourism Studies* in December 1996, cruise tourism has received very little organized or sustained attention within the academic literature. Several authors have also focused on its negative environmental impacts and on its limited economic contribution to the poor regions it visits (Klein 2002; Pattullo 1996; Uebersax 1996). However, in terms of the cruise experience there has been little written.

The relative neglect of the cruise industry in tourism studies is unfortunate not only because it involves an increasingly important sector, but also because it has several unique features which have implications for other forms of tourism. Two will be emphasized in this chapter. The first involves the uniquely-global nature of cruise tourism sector. A variety of factors, notably its sea-based mobility and the weakness of international regulatory regimes, has enabled cruise ships to function in a uniquely deterritorialized environment. This is related to the second unique feature, that to a very significant extent, the cruise ship is not only a form of transport but the destination itself. This phenomenon is not entirely new, nor is it universal; there definitely remains "destinational cruising" where the itinerary is more important than the ship. Destinational cruising, however, is generally seen as a "niche" market within the industry.

This makes cruise ships a unique form of tourism transport. People go on a "cruise" more than they go to a place. And yet their major competition is not other forms of transport but real places. As Morrison *et al.* (1996: 15) put it:

> Instead of competing with the airlines, the cruise lines have become their partners and now compete with destinations, resorts, and other vacation alternatives. The cruise ship itself has become a floating resort providing the maximum possible leisure and entertainment facilities.

Cruise ships have become more like mobile versions of their land-based competitors.

Pursuing these themes, this chapter proceeds as follows. The first section provides an overview of the history and structure of the cruise industry. The second section explores how a key aspect of globalization, the process of deterritorialization, is at the heart of the cruise industry's success and yet poses some of its greatest challenges. The third section examines the cruise ship as a deterritorialized destination, exploring the ongoing evolution of the cruise experience and addressing the issue of the relationship of cruise tourism to stay over land-based tourism. A final section summarizes key issues that are likely to shape the future of cruising.

History and Structure

In marketing and sometimes ship décor, the contemporary cruise industry pays homage to the Golden Age of the great trans-Atlantic liners, which sailed from the 1860s to the 1960s (Fox 1999; Maxtone-Graham 2000). Passenger levels in the post-second world war period peaked in 1957, then declined rapidly with the advent of non-stop jet flights in the late 1950s. Many liner companies went out of business; few remain today. The current leading cruise companies, Carnival and Royal Caribbean, came into existence after the collapse of the trans-Atlantic liner industry.

The first vessel designed entirely for the North American cruise market, *Oceanic*, was built in 1965 for the company Home Lines, and some have chronicled this as the beginning of modern cruising. Others cite December 19 1966, when the fledgling Norwegian Caribbean

Line became the first company to offer a year-round schedule of cruises on the *Sunward* aimed at a mass market. There have been several fundamental developments. Firstly, there was no need to design for high speed or for cargo storage and handling. Secondly the use of hulls with stabilizers fostered the shift away from the "wedding-cake" design of the traditional liners to the box designs of most contemporary cruise ships which maximize revenue-generating space (Cudahy 2001; Dawson 2000). The aesthetic appeal of the earlier generation of ships explains the nostalgia associated with cruise tourism, especially in relation to the classic liners.

The central achievement of the post-1960s cruise industry has been the repositioning of cruising as a mass market product. The social life of cruising portrayed on the *Love Boat* TV series of the 1970s remained intimidatingly up market, and in this context Carnival Cruise Line's "fun ship" marketing is often credited with making the decisive break with this perspective (e.g. Dickinson & Vladimir 1997). The cruise industry has moved toward offering a diverse and stratified set of cruising options with a view to expanding market reach.

The mass market sector is generally divided into three categories. The "budget" segment is the domain of relatively small companies with older ships, some of them converted liners or cargo vessels from an earlier era. Various charter operations, sometimes linked to travel agencies, as well as some purely-local, small-scale companies, populate this sector as well. Most focus on the European market, for example, Airtours Cruises. While their cruise prices are lower than the higher sectors, the difference between "budget" pricing and those in the next tier are relatively minor. For consumers who prefer older ships and the style of shipboard life they sustain, a budget cruise is one of the few available options.

The second segment is what is generally referred to as the "contemporary" sector. The term is not very revealing, apart perhaps from the hedonistic orientation of the aging baby boomers, who constitute the largest demographic passenger group in this sector. The major lines and the majority of ships serve this market segment: Carnival, Royal Caribbean, Princess, Norwegian Cruise Line (NCL), Costa, Disney, Festival/First European, and Malaysian-based Star Cruises, although Star's smaller ships also accommodate the luxury sector. The bottom end of the contemporary segment overlaps with the budget sector. It has been seriously depleted in recent years with the collapse of such cruise companies as Commodore, Premier, Dolphin, Royal, Majesty, Renaissance and Regal. The large profits to be made in this sector, due to economies of scale with the new generation of mega-ships (Vogel 2001) have enabled its dominant players to consolidate in this and other sectors.

The top echelon of the mass market sector is generally referred to as the "premium" segment. Price and ship design are not very different from the contemporary sector, but the premium markets are decidedly an older and upscale population segment. Major lines in this category are Holland America, Celebrity, and Orient — all owned by dominant companies in the contemporary sector. In varying degrees, their cruises tend to be somewhat more destination-oriented than those in the budget and contemporary sector.

Above the mass market sector may be placed the "niche" sector. By its nature, this involves a highly-diverse group of cruise options: sailing ships and high-end yachts; small cruise vessels with unusual itineraries; river cruises; various kinds of exploration, adventure, and special-interest cruises; etc. Although the degree of luxury varies considerably in this category, prices tend to be consistently higher. There are no opportunities for economies of scale and they often do not fly flags of convenience (which will be discussed in more detail below). There are a large number of companies in the niche sector, but most are small. The larger companies in this sector tend to be the river and coastal cruise companies, e.g. Viking River Cruises, CroisiEurope, Peter Deilmann, Victoria Cruises, and Norwegian Costal Voyage.

At the top end of the entire market is the luxury sector, with the major companies being Cunard, Seabourn, Windstar (all owned by Carnival), Crystal, Radisson Seven Seas, and Silversea cruise lines. There is considerable diversity in what is on offer in these different cruises, but the average price tends to be well above the premium and much of the niche market, although it overlaps to some extent with the latter. For example, ResidenSea introduced a new type of cruising vessel, the 43,000-ton *The World*, in 2002. This was in essence a floating resort apartment complex, which includes 110 privately-owned two to six bedroom condominium apartments (at $2 million to $6.8 million each) and 88 guest suites that can be rented by the night for $1800 to $5640 (Hamilton 2002). Constantly navigating the world with a new itinerary each year, the ship's club carries reciprocal privileges with the most exclusive clubs in its ports of call. For an elite, cruising has become a permanent lifestyle.

It needs to be emphasized that the schema above necessarily simplifies a very complex picture. Some companies offer cruises in several categories. On a single ship there are often very considerable differences in cabin accommodation, and some have observed that the ostensibly-discarded class system on ships is gradually returning (Klein 2002). In the substantial European market, which to date is less oligopolistic than the North American market, there is diversity in regional ownership and operational styles that is not fully captured here. On the other hand, the global reach of the largest cruise companies, along with their enormous financial resources, suggests a long-term trend towards this kind of stratified homogenization.

Globalization and the Cruise Industry

The cruise industry is uniquely global. There is virtually no region of the world that does not experience cruise tourism. The Caribbean, although it remains by far the most significant cruise market, is in a process of long-term decline in its market share, as other regions become more developed. For example, the Alaskan cruise market has seen significant growth in recent years, as has the European market. Despite turbulence associated with the Asian financial crisis and SARS, the most rapidly-growing market over the past decade has been in Southeast Asia, where the extraordinary growth of Star Cruises fueled an annual growth of 60% between 1994 and 1998 (Singh 1999). With over a million cruise arrivals a year, Singapore has emerged as the most important international cruise destination and hub in the Asian Pacific region; the gap between Asian and South Pacific and European cruising is narrowing (Wood 2002).

The growth of Star Cruises reflects the fact that cruise tourism has become a global form of middle class leisure. Star has introduced cruising to the middle classes of Southeast Asia, and it sees its future in fostering similar growth in China. Furthermore, the less formal "free style" cruising pioneered by Star has been exported through its subsidiary, NCL, into the Caribbean and European markets. Thus, innovations and trends in the industry increasingly tend to be global rather than purely at a regional level.

Globalization is often accompanied by economic concentration, and this has been particularly true in the cruise industry. A large number of smaller and medium-sized companies collapsed in the 1980s and 1990s. This process has intensified as mainstream companies consolidate their position. For example, Malaysian-based Star Cruises, launched a surprise takeover of NCL in early 2000. With Carnival's takeover in 2003 of the former number three company, Princess, the top three parent companies, Carnival, Royal Caribbean, and Star Cruises, now account for 79.7% of the global and 91.5% of the North American cruise market share, thus making the cruise industry one of the most concentrated in the world (Cruise Industry News Annual 2002).

The globalization of the cruise industry involves more than geographical spread and economic concentration. Unlike its land-based competitors, the cruise ship and the experience it offers can be repositioned in a short period of time virtually anywhere in the world. Furthermore, since its ships operate most of the time in international waters, they are largely free from national regulation and only loosely-governed by international regulations. If deterritorialization is viewed as the central defining feature of globalization (e.g. Bauman 1998; Scholte 2000; Tomlinson 1999), then the cruise industry can be seen as global in a particularly pure sense of the term. It operates in a unique environment, one that approaches the neo-liberal ideal of a minimally-regulated global market.

The two major lines and most of their subsidiaries have their home offices in, and mainly sail out of, the United States. Carnival and Royal Caribbean are, however, incorporated in Panama and Liberia respectively. Provisions in the U.S. tax code exempt income from ships and airplanes belonging to foreign corporations as long as their home country provides reciprocal privileges. While most airlines are incorporated in home countries that tax their income (e.g. British Airways, Lufthansa, etc.), both cruise and cargo ship companies routinely avoid such taxation by incorporating themselves in offshore financial centers that attract capital by taxing it minimally or not at all. This represents a very substantial tax saving that is not available to the land-based competition. It has been supplemented by numerous special tax breaks that the powerful cruise companies have successfully lobbied for (Frantz 1999; Klein 2001), as well as government subsidies for the ships they order from European shipyards.

However, it is the open-registry (flag-of-convenience) regime that most underpins the entire industry. Almost all of the larger cruise ships are registered either in 'flag of convenience' state or else in "second registries" of other states that serve roughly the same function.[1] This allows all the major companies to recruit their crews on a global basis, and frees them from having to abide by most national labor, minimum wage, health, safety and environmental laws. This is a major saving, one which enables cruise ships to offer accommodation, meals, and free entertainment for substantially less than such a package would cost in most of the ports they visit. The flag of convenience regime is at the heart of the cruise industry's economic competitiveness.[2]

In contrast, the cruise industry asserts that theirs in fact is one of the most regulated industries in the world. These assertions cannot be substantiated. While cruise ships may theoretically come under the jurisdiction of many sovereignties, the effect of this has been largely vitiated by the fact that enforcement has generally been to the flag states, which attract companies by making it known that they will not be unduly taxed or regulated. Nonetheless, the past decade has seen a gradual although uneven assertion of greater control over certain cruise ship activities, particularly in the United States. While this falls far short of what the industry's critics believe is necessary, it seems likely that the industry's regulatory environment will be strengthened over time, rather than weakened. However, this appears to apply only to some areas, most notably pollution and passenger rights. The industry's largely-unregulated prerogatives in the areas of employment and tax-avoidance have so far remained largely unscathed, despite the flag of convenience and anti-"sweatship" campaigns of the International Transport Workers Federation (ITF) and other similar organisations.

Take, for example, the current situation regarding pollution at sea. A single large cruise ship generates in a week's voyage 210,000 gallons of sewage. It will also produce one million gallons of gray water (wastewater from sinks, showers, galleys and laundry), at least 130 gallons of hazardous wastes, eight tons of solid waste, and 25,000 gallons of oily bilge water (Schmidt 2000). Cruise ships emit large quantities of air pollutants as well (Bluewater Network 2000). Existing international law bans the disposal of plastics at sea, but allows just about everything else to be dumped, subject to certain conditions. Untreated sewage may legally be dumped twelve miles from shore. Despite the limited nature of the pollution regulatory regime, cruise ship violations of both national and international laws have been commonplace. A U.S. Government Accounting Office (GAO) study reported 104 known illegal discharge cases involving cruise ships between 1993 and 1998. Of 111 cases of marine pollution referred to foreign flag states in a slightly earlier period, no penalties were imposed in any of them except for two minor fines (GAO 2000). Because of the failure of flag registry states to live up to the responsibilities given them by the International Maritime Organization (IMO), governments have had to look for other mechanisms.

U.S. prosecutors pioneered an innovative strategy against Royal Caribbean in the mid-1990s when they realized that the company was engaging in a fleetwide criminal conspiracy to dump oily waste by rigging pipes to bypass the onboard anti-pollution equipment. Instead of seeking to pursue Royal Caribbean for violating international pollution laws, whose enforcement is officially delegated to the registry states, the company was prosecuted only for presenting falsified logs to U.S. Coast Guard officials in a U.S. port, a violation of U.S. law. After failing to convince U.S. courts that they lacked jurisdiction, Royal Caribbean pleaded guilty and was fined $27 million in 1999. The same U.S. strategy resulted in guilty pleas and substantial penalties for similar offenses by NCL in 2002 and by Carnival in December 2001. During this period, fines for violating air pollution laws in Alaskan ports were imposed on Holland America, Carnival, NCL, Celebrity, Princess, Crystal and World Explorer Cruises as part of the state's Alaska Cruise Initiative, which also resulted in new legislation setting higher standards for the discharge of gray water and air pollutants.

The lack of volition to pursue international anti-pollution laws reflects the continuing weakness of enforcement in open registry maritime regime. However, there are mounting concerns which cannot be ignored., For example, the U.S. Environmental Protection Agency accepted in 2000 a petition from fifty-three environmental organizations to investigate cruise ship pollution and to establish new rules and mechanisms of enforcement (USEPA 2000). The industry is beginning to show signs of addressing a workplace culture (both on the ships and in the home office) that has not taken environmental laws seriously and of being ready to make investments in a new generation of substantially less-polluting ships. The International Council of Cruise Lines (ICCL) and the Florida-Caribbean Cruise Association (FCCA) have scrambled to introduce voluntary industry standards and to reach voluntary agreements with Florida and Hawaii, but as an Ocean Conservancy (2002: 25) study states: "Experience has shown that when it comes to the protection of the marine environment, enforceable standards are preferable to voluntary standards, no matter how well intentioned." European countries reached an agreement in 2001 (the Paris Memorandum of Understanding on Port State Control) to target cruise ships for regular inspections that started in 2003 (Klein 2002).

Passenger safety is the other area of increased regulation. In a technical sense, most cruise ships on the high seas are sailing under the jurisdiction of Liberia, Panama or the Bahamas, and passengers with complaints must seek recourse in the courts of those countries. In response to negative publicity resulting from Carnival's admission that 108 sexual assaults had taken place on its ships in the previous five years, however, the ICCL announced a council-wide policy of henceforth reporting such cases to the proper port authorities. Subsequently, the Florida Supreme Court ruled that the state can prosecute crimes committed on the high seas if the ship sails in and out of Florida ports. The Court noted:

> "Florida's tourism industry could be significantly affected if crimes that occur on board cruise ships where a majority of the fare-paying passengers embark and disembark in Florida were to go unprosecuted"
>
> (Corzo 2000: 1E).

Similarly a U.S. federal appeals court ruled in 2000 that foreign-flagged ships were not exempt from U.S. anti-discrimination laws, and that cruise ships must comply with the American Disabilities Act.[3]

These developments suggest a new dimension of globalization: a movement towards the enforcement of global standards in the area of ocean pollution by local authorities and towards more homeport regulation in the area of passenger rights and safety (Goldberg 2000). Further steps in this direction seem likely, but the cruise industry remains uniquely free from enforced regulation in other areas.

The Cruise Ship As Destination

The cruise ship is often considered to be the destination in itself. Carnival President Dickinson (1993: 115) observes: "The limited number of countries and ports offered is not a deterrent to Carnival customers; after all, the ship is the attraction, not the port of call."[4]

While the degree to which this form of transport is the destination varies according to the clientele and the type of cruise, cruise passengers generally spend far more of their vacation on the cruise ship than on land. Furthermore, the focus of guidebooks for would-be cruisers emphasize differences between companies and ships rather than choice of destination. The passenger onboard is vital to cruise ship economics and hence the design of cruise ships and package itineraries maximize opportunities to spend on board. Ritzer (1999: 9) characterizes modern cruise ships as "cathedrals of consumption."

Apart from unpublished market research, much of what is written on the cruise experience involves personal reminiscences within the modes of journalism and travel literature (for an interesting example, see Wallace 1996). The democratization of publishing brought about by the internet has supplemented this with literally thousands of online postings of cruise reviews by cruise passengers. While these reviews tend to focus more on the physical architecture of the ship, the quality of the food and service, and on what the writer did at the various ports of call, they are nonetheless a useful source for gleaning elements of the cruise experience from the passenger point of view.

Wood (2000) has identified several aspects of the mass market cruise experience that seem broadly verifiable. The first starts from the observation that the onboard cruise experience is a fundamentally deterritorialized one. The mass-market cruise ship experience is deliberately manufactured to be detached from the region in which it cruises. To some degree this reflects the fact that cruise ships often cruise in diverse regions of the world in different times of the year. The issue here, however, is not simply one of the material environment of the ship. Very few other concessions are made to feature the surrounding region or ports of call either. Port information sessions are almost always exclusively about what things to buy and which shops to spend your money in. Entertainment is "Las Vegas" style. Food and drink on board do not reflect the cruise region.[5] By and large, generally with only minor exceptions, the regional culture where cruising takes place is almost invisible in terms of what is experienced onboard the mass market ships.

A second theme involves the experience and representation of crew ethnic diversity and stratification. Parallel to the reemerging class stratification of passengers is a hierarchy of officers, staff and crew often closely linked to nationality, race, and ethnicity. Captains from traditionally sea-faring European nations are extolled in cruise industry marketing, while below the almost exclusively white officer class is an increasingly global crew. Crew recruitment policies vary with different lines. For example, Holland America relies heavily on Filipino and Indonesian workers, so much so that on one Caribbean sailing in 2001, there was exactly one person of African descent (an American citizen originally from Haiti) among the entire crew of 650 (author's inquiry aboard the *Zaandam*). In a virtually universal ritual on mass market Caribbean cruises, the predominantly Third World crew sings "God Bless America" to the foot-stomping and cheering U.S. passengers.

A third theme involves the centrality of simulation in the cruise environment. With their pastiche of often garish decors, cruise ships offer a broad range of simulated environments and have often been characterized as floating theme parks — "Disney World for adults," as Carnival's founder put it (Showker & Sehlinger 1998: 223). As with Disney World, this simulated world is deliberately juxtaposed to the less-perfect shoreside "real" world. In a striking extension of this principle, six cruise companies include their own private islands in their Caribbean itineraries, even marketing these entirely-simulated environments as providing an "authentic" Caribbean experience no longer possible in the real place (Showalter 1994; Wood 2000: 361–362).

In the Caribbean, the issues of the deterritorialized, stratified, and simulated cruise experience are major concerns. Cruise tourism has grown far more rapidly than land-based stayover tourism, and in fact on some islands stayovers have declined in absolute terms as cruise visits have increased dramatically. According to the Caribbean Tourism Organization (CTO), there were 19.5 million stayover tourist arrivals in Caribbean countries in 2001 and 15.2 million cruise passenger arrivals. Cruise arrivals as a percentage of total tourist arrivals ranged from 5.8% (Dominican Republic) to 77.5% (Dominica). In 13 out of 23 Caribbean island countries, cruise arrivals were greater than stayover arrivals (CTO 2002). A study commissioned by the FCCA estimated cruise passenger expenditure in ports of call to average $103.83 in 2000, with a range extending from $56.22 to $173.24 (PWC/BREA 2001: vi) The bulk of Caribbean cruise passenger expenditure is for jewelry, watches, and clothing, all of which are imported from outside the region.

The situation has preoccupied the Caribbean Tourism Organization for years, and its member states committed themselves for the first time in 2002 to develop a united approach in dealing with the cruise industry. The Caribbean Hotel Association has long complained about the lack of a level playing field in a situation where their cruise competitors are exempt from most of the tax, labor, environmental and other regulations and costs that its members must shoulder. Caribbean governments have been concerned about the low port charges in the region along with the limited and focused spending of cruise tourists. All would prefer to increase the proportion of stayover to cruise tourists, since the former spend much more and spend in ways that benefit the local economy more. The CTO has undertaken a "cruise conversion" campaign to increase the number of cruise passengers who return for stayover vacations.

The cruise companies claim that they generate stayover visitors by providing a sampling of Caribbean offerings that passengers may choose to return to. For example, a study commissioned by the FCCA in 2000 reports that 51.6% of the passengers surveyed expressed interest in returning to a port of all for a land-based vacation (PWC/BREA 2001).

There is little hard evidence either to support or refute the assertion that cruise tourists subsequently return as stayover tourists. The FCCA study's indication that almost half of the respondents did *not* expect to return for a land-based vacation is perhaps more striking. Wilkinson (1999) reports that an estimated 6.2% of stayover tourists to the Bahamas in 1996 had been influenced by a previous cruise visit. Since cruise tourists to the Bahamas outnumber stayover tourists, this represents a low conversion rate. Cruise companies depend heavily on repeat cruisers, typically over half on any given cruise, and they engage in a variety of strategies to keep cruisers coming back. Clubs and special onboard perks for past cruisers, lavishly-illustrated company magazines and brochures, specially-discounted fares and upgrades, and careful cultivation of travel agents are all designed to keep passengers coming back to the ship.

Some research suggests that there are significant differences overall between cruise tourists and land-based tourists that do not auger well for the major resort destinations the cruise industry competes with. One comparative study (Morrison *et al.* 1996) concludes that the ability of cruises to combine elements from several alternative vacation types with unique cruise attributes suggests that cruise passengers may be a quite specific travel segment and that cruises will remain as major competitors to land-based resorts.

There is little in the onboard cruise experience that would facilitate or encourage stayover return visits to ports of call. Cruise companies often exhort their regional counterparts to make land facilities and destinations more interesting and attractive, but bringing the region more onboard — reterritorializing the cruise ship environment — would also be a desirable goal from this point of view.

Conclusion: Cruising Into the Future

Given its unique combination of transport and destination, along with the advantages it gains from its unique deterritorialization, the cruise industry is likely to continue to grow at a rate above the growth rate of tourism overall. Cruise bookings rebounded quickly after the events of September 11, 2001, and the CLIA announced a record year for its members in 2002. The industry has reason to be confident about its future, although how this is viewed by the land-based tourism sector depends on whether the industry is seen to be primarily complementary or competitive. Even in the latter case, primarily the Caribbean, there is a weary sense that the regional tourism industry has to "come to terms" with growth in the cruise market as a fact of life.

However, the industry's continued ability to rely on its deterritorialization — most notably its freedom from regulation in a broad range of areas — for its profitability and competitive position is not entirely assured. Governance reforms are in the air, and much depends on how far they go.

Campaigns against the "flag-of-convenience" system to date have had only limited effects, although some cruise ships have signed agreements with the ITF (War on Want & ITF 2002). These fall far short of negotiated union contracts (just about the entire cruise sector remains non-unionized) but elicit some forms of voluntary compliance in terms of the treatment of labor. In the aftermath of September 11th, however, the flag-of-convenience regime has come under increased scrutiny. The Maritime Administrator of the U.S. Department of Transportation linked flag-of-convenience ships to terrorism in testimony to the U.S. House of Representatives in June 2002, criticizing the flag-of-convenience system and calling for policies to facilitate a return to the U.S. flag. Concerns about the loss of flag registry has likewise been a concern in a number of European countries. It is conceivable that the war on terrorism could threaten the existing flag-of-convenience regime.

Existing international treaties give the flag registry states with the most tonnage, notably Panama, Liberia, and the Bahamas, the power to veto regarding changes in the system, so the likelihood of fundamental change is not great. It does appear possible that flag registry states may be forced to make ownership more transparent and to take their enforcement responsibilities in areas of ship safety and pollution more seriously. For the cruise industry, this probably will have only a limited economic impact, since it is already shouldering the cost of building more-advanced waste disposal and anti-pollution systems into new ship design. If on the other hand its current labor and tax prerogatives are challenged by flag-of-convenience reforms, the industry's ability to offer all-inclusive vacations at such highly-competitive prices could be undermined.

Environmental sustainability has been embraced by the industry, but it continues to resist enforceable agreements and continues to violate environmental laws routinely. As a reaction, port states in North America and Europe have become more assertive and creative in finding ways to enforce both national and international standards. Various non-governmental organization (NGO) initiatives are also underway, such as the Cruise Ship Stewardship Initiative of the Oceans Blue Foundation (2002) and Bluewater Network's cruise ship campaign. Both initiatives emphasize the common interests of land and cruise stakeholders. As with the issue of the deterritorialization of the cruise experience, a reterritorialized approach that would involve a joint effort of the cruise and land-based tourism industries in addressing environmental issues that affect them both would be a welcome development.

How the continuing process of industry concentration plays itself out will also have consequences for the future of cruising. On the one hand, the major companies have generally chosen to maintain separate brands within an overall marketing framework, as Carnival does under its "World's Leading Cruise Lines" label. On the other hand, the dissolution of many smaller cruise companies and the desire to reach economies of scale are leading to an increasingly homogenized cruise product in many respects. Ritzer (1999) has argued that a tension exists between rationalization and reenchantment in such "cathedrals of consumption." Whether the cruise product can be successfully "re-enchanted" to keep cruisers coming back to a floating version of what they can find on land remains an open question, as is the ability of a highly oligopolistic industry to sustain or recreate the kind of diversity of options that has existed in the past. A reterritorialization of the cruise experience may be necessary both to retain its sea-based attractiveness and to sustain the health of its ports of call.

Notes

1. Second registries have been introduced by such countries as Norway and the Netherlands to retain or attract back to their registries ships that otherwise would be registered in flag of convenience states. The second registries generally exempt these ships from much of the usual regulation of a national registry.
2. According to Schulkin (2002, p. 125), the elimination of the flag of convenience system would be "financially devastating to the cruise system."
3. It is interesting to consider how revolutionary this might be if cruise ship hiring was subject to U.S. anti-discrimination laws. Much of cruise company hiring is ethnically-based. It has been estimated that only 7% of all Caribbean cruise ship employees hail from the region (Wise 1999).
4. This is reflected in cruise guidebook writer Anne Campbell's (2002) recommendation to take Caribbean cruises during hurricane season: "The worst thing that can happen is that the cruise line might substitute one port for another as the ship moves away from an area threatened by a hurricane." The implication seems to be that the ports are entirely substitutable with each other.
5. This is less true of regional cruise companies in Europe. However, growing concentration is imposing some quirky deterritorialized results there too. Viking River Cruises, which with its acquisition of KD River Cruises in 2000 is now the world's largest river cruise company, stresses Viking themes on its cruises across Europe, regardless of their lack of relevance to the immediate environment. On a Rhine cruise by the author in 2002, not only was information on the ancient Vikings more emphasized than anything else, but as the ship passed through the famous Rhine wine region, the recommended wines of the evening were from Chile and Australia!

References

Bauman, Z. (1998). *Globalization: The human consequences.* New York: Columbia University Press.
Bluewater Network (2000). *A stacked deck: Air pollution from large ships.* (http://www.earthisland. org/bw/stacked.pdf) Accessed 26 June 2001.
Campbell, A. (2002). *Hurricane season? Time to cruise.* (http://www.cruisemates.com/articles/ humop/hurricane.cfm) Accessed 3 December 2002.
Caribbean Tourism Organization (CTO) (2002). *Caribbean tourism statistical report: 2000–2001 edition.* St. Michael, Barbados.
Corzo, C. (2000). U.S. courts are getting tougher on cruise lines. *Miami Herald*, 30 July, 1E.
Cruise Industry News Annual 2002 (2002). New York: Cruise Industry News.

Cudahy, B. J. (2001). *The cruise ship phenomenon in North America.* Centerville, Maryland: Cornell Maritime Press.

Dawson, P. (2000). *Cruise ships: An evolution in design.* London: Conway Maritime Press.

De La Vina, L., & Ford, J. (2001). Logistic regression analysis of cruise vacation market potential: Demographic and trip attribute perception factors. *Journal of Travel Research, 39,* 406–410.

Dickinson, R. (1993). Cruise industry outlook in the Caribbean. In: D. J. Gayle, & J. N. Goodrich (Eds), *Tourism Marketing and Management in the Caribbean* (pp. 113–128). London: Routledge.

Dickinson, B., & Vladimir, A. (1997). *Selling the sea: An inside look at the cruise industry.* New York: Wiley.

Dowling, R. K., & Vasudavan, T. (2000). Cruising in the new millenium. *Tourism Recreation Research, 25*(3), 17–27.

Dwyer, L., & Forsyth, P. (1998). Economic significance of cruise tourism. *Annals of Tourism Research, 25,* 393–415.

Foster, G. M. (1986). South seas cruise: A case study of a short-lived society. *Annals of Tourism Research, 13,* 215–238.

Fox, R. (1999). *Liners: The golden age.* Köln: Könnemann Verlagsgesellschaft.

Frantz, D. (1999). Cruise lines profit from friends in congress. *New York Times,* 19 February, A1, A18.

General Accounting Office (GAO) (2000). *Marine pollution: Progress made to reduce marine pollution by cruise ships, but important issues remain.* Washington, DC.

Goldberg, W. A. (2000). Cruise ships, pollution, and international law: The United States takes on Royal Caribbean Cruise Lines. *Wisconsin International Law Journal, 19,* 71–93.

Hall, J. A., & Braithwaite, R. (1990). Caribbean cruise tourism: A business of transnational partnerships. *Tourism Management, 11*(4), 339–347.

Hamilton, W. L. (2002). On ship of Condos, life's an endless cruise. *New York Times,* 1 September.

Henthorne, T. L. (2000). An analysis of expenditures by cruise ship passengers in Jamaica. *Journal of Travel Research, 38*(3), 246–250.

Hobson, J. S. P. (1993). Analysis of the U.S. cruise line industry. *Tourism Management, 14*(6), 453–462.

Klein, R. A. (2001). *Death by chocolate: What you must know before taking a cruise.* St. John's, NF: Breakwater.

Klein, R. A. (2002). *Cruise ship blues: The underside of the cruise industry.* Gabriola Island, BC: New Society Publishers.

Mancini, M. (2000). *Cruising: A guide to the cruise line industry.* Albany, NY: Delmar Thomson Learning.

Marti, B. E. (1992). Passenger perceptions of cruise itineraries: A Royal Viking Line case study. *Marine Policy, 16,* 360–370.

Maxtone-Graham, J. (2000). *Liners to the Sun.* Dobbs Ferry, NY: Sheridon House.

Mescon, T. S., & Vozikis, G. S. (1985). The economic impact of tourism at the Port of Miami. *Annals of Tourism Research, 12,* 515–528.

Morrison, A., Yang, C.-H., O'Leary, J. T., & Nadkarni, N. (1996). Comparative profiles of travellers on cruises and land-based resort vacations. *Journal of Tourism Studies, 7*(2), 15–27.

Moscardo, G., Morrison, A. M., Cai, L., Nadkarni, N., & O'Leary, J. T. (1996). Tourist perspectives on cruising: Multidimensional scaling analyses of cruising and other holiday types. *Journal of Tourism Studies, 7*(2), 54–63.

Ocean Conservancy (2002). *Cruise control: A report on how cruise ships affect the marine environment.* (http://www.oceanconservancy.org/dynamic/aboutUs/publications/cruiseControl.pdf) Accessed 9 September 2002.

Oceans Blue Foundation (2002). *'Blowing the whistle' and the case for cruise certification: A matter of environmental and social justice under international law.* Vancouver, BC.

Pattullo, P. (1996). *Last resorts: The cost of tourism in the Caribbean*. London: Cassell.

Peisley, T. (1996). *The world cruise ship industry to 2000*. London: Travel and Tourism Intelligence.

PriceWaterhouseCoopers (PWC) & Business Research and Economic Advisors (BREA) (2001). *Cruise industry's economic impact on the Caribbean*. Miami: Florida-Caribbean Cruise Assocation.

Ritter, W., & Schafer, C. (1998). Cruise-tourism: A chance of sustainability. *Tourism Recreation Research*, *23*(1), 65–71.

Ritzer, G. (1999). *Enchanting a disenchanting world: Revolutionizing the means of consumption*. Thousand Oaks, CA: Pine Forge Press.

Robertson, G. (2002). *Cruise ship tourism industry*. (http://www.lighthouse-foundation.org/ lighthouse-foundation.org/eng/forum/artikel00304eng.html) Accessed 17 July 2002.

Schmidt, K. (2000). Bluewater network. *Crusing for trouble: Stemming the tide of cruise ship pollution*. San Francisco. (http://www.bluewaternetwork.org/reports/rep_ss_cruise_trouble.pdf) Accessed 30 April 2003.

Scholte, J. A. (2000). *Globalization: A critical introduction*. New York: St. Martin's Press.

Schulkin, A. (2002). Safe harbors: Crafting an international solution to cruise ship pollution. *Georgetown International Environmental Law Review*, *15*(1), 105–132.

Showalter, G. R. (1994). Cruise ships and private islands in the Caribbean. *Journal of Travel and Tourism Marketing*, *3*(4), 107–118.

Showker, K., & Sehlinger, B. (1998). *The unofficial guide to cruises*. New York: Macmillan.

Singh, A. (1999). Growth and development of the cruise line industry in Southeast Asia. *Asia Pacific Journal of Tourism Research*, *3*(2), 24–31.

Teye, V. B., & Leclerc, D. (1998). Product and service delivery satisfaction among North American cruise passengers. *Tourism Management*, *19*(2), 153–160.

Tomlinson, J. (1999). *Globalization and culture*. Chicago: University of Chicago Press.

Uebersax, M. B. (1996). *Indecent proposal: Cruise ship pollution in the Caribbean*. (http://www.planeta.com/planeta/96/0896cruise.html) Accessed 23 August 2002.

United States Environmental Protection Agency (USEPA) (2000). *Cruise ship white paper*. Washington, DC.

Vogel, H. (2001). *Travel industry economics: A guide for financial analysis*. Cambridge: Cambridge University Press.

Wallace, D. F. (1996). Shipping out: On the (nearly lethal) comforts of a luxury cruise. *Harper's Magazine*, *292*(1748), 33–56.

War on Want & International Transport Workers Federation (ITF) (2002). *Sweatships*. (http://www. waronwant.org/download.php?id=71) Accessed 30 April 2003.

Wilkinson, P. F. (1999). Caribbean cruise tourism: Delusion? Illusion? *Tourism Geographies*, *1*(3), 261–282.

Wise, J. (1999). How cruise ships shortchange the Caribbean. *Fortune*, *139*(6), 44–46.

Wood, R. E. (2000). Caribbean cruise tourism: Globalization at sea. *Annals of Tourism Research*, *27*(2), 345–370.

Wood, R. E. (2002). Caribbean of the East? Global interconnections and the Southeast Asian cruise industry. *Asian Journal of Social Science*, *30*(2), 420–440.

Chapter 11

Non-Motorised Transport and Tourism: A Case Study — Cycle Tourism

Les Lumsdon and Rodney Tolley

Introduction

The importance of non-motorised transport in tourism is often understated. Most trips, regardless of purpose, happen to be short distance journeys and walking is by far the most important mode of transport for this type of journey. In many developing countries walking is the only mode of transport for much of the population especially in the rural economy (Barwell 1996). Cycling is the second most common form of non-motorised transport across the world and is important in several countries, for example, in China where over 65% of all trips are still made using this mode say in contrast to the USA where only 3% of trips are by cycle. In Europe, cycling is a popular form of transport in Denmark, Germany and The Netherlands. The use of horses and other animals for transport purposes is very limited in developed countries and is losing ground in most developing countries even in the rural areas. Motorization is a priority for most countries as in the eyes of the transport planner it symbolises modernisation.

This chapter, however, focuses on a dilemma facing tourism planners, i.e. the need to improve access at destinations whilst simultaneously managing demand for tourism transport in a way which reduces energy consumption and detrimental environmental impacts (Becken *et al.* 2003). Apart from these aspects transport can have a role in enhancing the quality of life for residents and maintaining an appealing environment for the visitor. Non-motorized transport is important in this context (Lumsdon & Tolley 1999).

Despite the inherent advantages of non-motorised transport as a form of sustainable development, walking and cycling for utility purposes is in decline in many countries (Tolley 1997). In contrast, trips made for recreational or tourism purposes are increasing in the major generating countries. A delphi study undertaken by the authors in 2000 reported wide expert opinion across Europe indicating continued growth of these forms of transport for recreational and tourism purposes (Tolley *et al.* 2001). There is also a renaissance of interest in walking and cycling in North America, Australasia and in Eastern Europe where quality of life is moving higher up the political agenda (Feldt 1996; Forward 2000).

Tourism and Transport: Issues and Agenda for the New Millennium
Copyright © 2004 Published by Elsevier Ltd.
ISBN: 0-08-044172-6

There is little firm evidence of parallel trends in the developing world. However, there is a realisation at some destinations that unbridled provision for the car is creating massive pollution and health problems which negatively affects tourism imagery. For example, Latin American cities suffer badly from increasing traffic demand fuelled by sprawling cities, migration from rural zones in addition to ailing public transport systems. As a consequence, most suffer from severe congestion and poor air quality. This is considered to be the major drawback by many tour operators especially in relation to cities such as Mexico City (Lumsdon & Swift 2001). In contrast, a number of Latin American cities have adopted radical measures to overcome this car dependency such as creating car-free zones on Sundays. Bogotá, the capital of Colombia and Quito in Perú, for example, close several highways to enable residents and visitors to enjoy cycling and walking in safety throughout the central zones of the cities. There have been cycling infrastructure improvements in Santiago de Chile (Ortúzar *et al.* 2000), renowned for its poor air quality, and a regeneration of the waterfront at Buenas Aires, bringing a return of promenading, cycling and skate boarding to a city dominated by traffic. Such developments are small islands in relation the tide of motorization occurring throughout the developing world where many city destinations such as Bangkok, Cairo and Delhi are at gridlock.

The term "non-motorised" refers to human powered forms of transport (not powered by a combustion engine) and these include:

- Walking;
- Cycling;
- Wheeled carriages such as rickshaws and horse drawn vehicles;
- Animals such as camels and horses;
- Water based transport such as canoes, kayaks and rowing boats.

Some of these forms of transport are important at all destination as discussed by Orbaşlı & Shaw (see Chapter 7) in their discussion of the management of historic cities. However, few authors have given consideration to this topic. There are a number of reasons for the omission of non-motorised transport in the overall discussion of tourism management at destinations. It is partly because of a lack of clarity in defining what constitutes a visit and more significantly that short trips are not measured as such (Seekings 1989).

Secondly, non-motorised forms of transport are overlooked or have been paid scant attention in practitioner studies (Whitelegg 1993). Thus, the travel modes of walking and cycling tend to be marginalised in tourism development (Lumsdon 1999). The exception has been the proliferation of pedestrian zones which are favoured in enclave-leisure based schemes, these have been exceptionally popular, despite resistance by traders, but fail to address the wider issue of traffic restraint throughout destinations.

Of the non-motorised modes of transport, walking and cycling are the most significant at most destinations but other forms are popular at specific destinations throughout the world, for example, the use of the kayak or snow boarding in Canada or the rickshaw in Asian cities. In tourism transport it is useful to sub-divide the analysis, as discussed by Lumsdon and Page in Chapter 1, into transport for tourism and transport as a tourism experience. Firstly, non-motorised forms of transport are an important part of a journey chain, i.e. the visitor walks between the airport railway station and the flight terminal or on arrival at a destination the visitor walks from their hotel to a nearby restaurant. It is an integrating form of transport, often described as the glue which binds other forms of transport together.

The other dimension is non-motorised transport as a form of tourism experience. The mode of transport, in this case, is not only the main motivational factor for the visit but is also a core element of the tourism experience. There has been some discussion as to whether or not non-motorised transport is more appropriately defined as a special interest, i.e. it is not a form of transport but more appropriately it should be regarded as a holiday activity. An alternative perspective is that whilst it is an activity, it is also often the core transport element enabling the visitor to travel from one point to another or to tour, calling at destinations on a circuit or along a linear route. Thus, it is an amalgam of both. It is a form of activity which requires varying levels skill, motivation and stamina depending on the location and a means of transport which seeks to enhance the enjoyment of the experience. In this respect, it can be referred to as a tourism transport experience.

Cycle Tourism

In order to explain this in more detail, it is necessary to determine the key factors and processes which constitute the tourism transport experience. This is discussed in relation to a fast emerging tourism transport experience, cycling. Cycling is an appropriate form of transport in this context as it offers considerable potential in terms of sustainable development in tourism (Lumsdon 1997, 2001b). Recreational cycling has a number of core appeals; it allows a visitor to enjoy at a slower pace a closeness to nature, the physical environment, nearby sights and human settlements (Simonsen *et al*. 1998). Cycling (and walking) have therefore been presented as a more rewarding way of travelling at the destination than other faster forms of transport; the element of travel itself brings a high positive value or benefit (Gardner 1998).

The Cycle Tourist

Cycle tourism is defined by Sustrans (1999) as "recreational visits, either overnight or day visits away from home, which involve leisure cycling as a fundamental and significant part of the visit." This definition encompasses both the more casual recreational cyclist, such as the day excursionist and the cycle tourist travelling on bicycle for several days. In either case, cycling is perceived by the visitor as a key element of an excursion or holiday, i.e. a positive way to enhance leisure time at a destination involving a cycle, a route and a range of support facilities.

Research into travel mode selection has for the most part drawn on the earlier psychological model of consumer choice, for example, as developed by Howard & Sheth (1969). The work brings together the following factors modelled by transport planners: mode availability, design, mode operations and marketing on the supply side and demographics, life styles, prior use, trip purpose and level of satisfaction on the demand side. A number of tourism researchers have explained modal choice as a subset of destination selection (Goodall 1988; Oppermann 1997) and have extended the nature of the analysis to identify links between motivations and destination choice through activities. However, few other studies have investigated the choice of travel mode while at the destination (Cullinane 1997). In the cycle tourism literature several authors report findings from empirically-based studies of cycle tourists. The main desire of cycle tourists is to recreate and restore a feeling of well-being (Cope & Doxford 1998; Froitzheim 1995; Lumsdon & Smith 1997). Several other core motivational factors have been identified, namely, physical challenge, relaxation, social escapism, peace and quiet (Lumsdon 2000). The strength of each factor in the decision-making process varies for each different market segment (Hundt 1998; Ritchie 1998; Simonsen *et al.* 1998). There is also increasing recognition that there are motivational links between health and recreational cycling which also have an impact on the demand for cycling (and walking) within the tourism sector (Lumsdon & Mitchell 1999; Owen 1998).One final point relates to the barriers to cycle tourism which affect the perceptions of potential visitors and hence the level of demand at any given destination, which are a universal fear of traffic, and to a lesser extent a resistance to cycling where there are hill climbs or in inclement weather(Countryside Commission 1995).

There is another dimension. The nature of motivation and use that a tourist makes of any given tourism transport system will not be uniform; the market is not homogeneous. It is fragmented into a range of segments, each one portraying a cluster of similar characteristics or wants. For example, there is a marked variation between the needs of occasional or casual cyclists and enthusiast cyclists. The former will cycle infrequently and possibly only for leisure or social reasons; they tend to need assurance that there will be traffic-free cycling. The latter is a lifestyle cyclist, a person who cycles regularly and for all purposes. He or she is more likely to cycle longer distances and prefers "away from it all" destinations (Ritchie 1998). These market needs are not always reflected in the supply of facilities for cycle tourists. Cycle tourism relies on public sector investment at a destination in order to develop a tourism transport offering, which is often designed as a multi-purpose and multi-user facility; like other tourism places it is publicised and "sold" by a variety of public and private organisations (Goodall 1988).

Unlike visitor attractions which are site specific, the cycle tourism offering includes meeting local residents, suppliers in the villages and towns through which the cyclist passes and accommodation providers. Whilst there are numerous studies reporting the impacts of visitation on residents (Gitelson 1998; Jurowski *et al.* 1997; Pearce 1994; Smith & Krannich 1998) little attention has been paid to social impacts of tourism transport such as cycle tourism (Cope *et al.* 1998). This is surprising given that many greenways, cycle routes and networks developed during the past decade now attract high levels of use. For example, the provision of multi-user routes in the USA has led to a substantial demand for cycle tourism with popular trails generating between 1 and 2 million users per annum, although not all of these trips will be for tourism purposes (Rails to Trails Conservancy 1998). In a micro context, a recent study of cycle tourists on the Danish island of Bornholm suggests that there are likely to be some negative as well as beneficial social impacts but the balance between the two is not clear. It is an area which requires further research (Simonsen *et al.* 1998).

Furthermore, when trails become heavily used there is a likelihood that there will be negative impacts on flora and fauna. Very few studies have addressed this factor and the overall opinion is that impacts are minimal. However, there have been calls for more studies in this field in order to inform route planners.

Cycle Tourism Infrastructure

Route design for cyclists tends to be either in the form of a network, i.e. links and loops across a destination or a region, or in the shape of a long distance linear route or circuit.

Studies in cycle tourism have defined this core element, the route, according to physical or environmental features, which are often referred to in transport studies as the "hardware." However, this is too narrow a description for the cycle tourism offering; a full analysis would include natural attributes, socio-cultural aspects, the built environment, or thematic emphasis (Lew 1987; Murray & Graham 1997).

An example is La Route verte currently being developed in Québec, a 3,400 km network across Québec and with proposed links to New England in the USA (Pronovost & Joly 1998). In 1996, the Urbanisation National Research Institute undertook a preliminary study of the potential tourism impacts of La Route verte. It defined the key offering as a route network of segregated cycle paths, which pass through generating urban areas, and variety of countryside landscapes. The route comprises infrastructure such as the trail or path surface, curves, slopes and sight distances, bridges, tunnels and culverts, directions and interpretation, route furniture such as picnic areas, water fountains, surrounding flora and fauna, and places to view and visit (Ryan 1993; Tripp & Higginbotham 1998). A return on this investment is expected from the user. Public and private sector providers, often in partnership, look to visitor expenditure as a measure of success; it relates mainly to accommodation, refreshment stops and to a lesser extent monies spent at other retail outlets en route. Thus, the projected level of demand for La Route verte in terms of recreational and cycle tourism trips was estimated at the initial stages of development to be 2.7 million cycle trips per annum. (Archambault *et al.* 1997). The study also estimated that La Route verte, when complete, would generate expenditure within the range of $25,894,000 and $31,267,000 (Canadian $) of which approximately 10% would be new visitors attracted by the facility. Retention of existing domestic tourism is expected to generate a further 13%.

An interim report suggests that the predicted 25% of the additional cyclists' spending in the Québec economy can be attributed to the overall appeal of La Route verte as a tourism attraction in its own right, rather than being simply a transport network (Couture *et al.* 1998). The design of network of routes is based on the assumption that visitor spending forms an intrinsic part of the cycle tourism experience.

The other major form of cycle tourism provision is the linear route, which often makes best use of a geographical feature at a destination. For example, the North Sea Cycle Route, launched in Northern Europe in 2001, combines the appeal of a coastal route with ferry crossings within or between countries bordering the North Sea. Others routes feature old pilgrimage trails or riverside paths, as in the case of the Donauradweg (Danube Cycle Route), a 220 mile route from Passau to Vienna in Austria. It was developed as a linear tourism route, primarily for cyclists but also for walkers, along the banks of the River Danube in 1983, to accommodate an increasing demand for cycling experienced by tourism authorities in the early 1980s. The core infrastructure is a cycle path alongside the Danube but this enables the visitor to pass through changing scenery which has been described in the case of cycling as the "travelling landscape" (Grimshaw 1998). In the case of the Danube the appeal is the story of the river, its natural setting and its heritage as a transport artery over the ages. Between 1987 and 1991 the number of cycle trips recorded per annum rose from 738,000 to 1,527,000 per annum, an increase of 48%. In 1994, it was estimated that between Passau and Vienna the route generated 80,000 overnight stays per annum, an increase of 27.33% in ten years Landesverband für Tourismus (1996). Several towns on the route now depend on cycle tourism; bednights from cycling visitors accounting for between 60 and 80% of all stays. Thus, the Danube, particularly in Upper Austria has become Europe's main cycle tourism destination; it is dependent on cycle tourism although visitor use of boats, trains and tourism buses in association with the cycle route is also important.

Another dimension of development is the route or network image. This includes three dimensions — branding, publicity and thematic interpretation. Within the context of a tourism transport system this could well be referred to as software, which includes the processes of devising images, messages and information which both attracts and informs the potential and existing visitor prior to and during the tourism experience. For example, EuroVelo, the cycle network spanning Europe includes a Wine and Gourmet, Atlantic Coast and Capitals routes. On EuroVelo routes, contiguous signage is an integral element of design, not only in terms of the provision of directions but also in terms of interpretation and branding as the medium to convey a standard or quality of route which introduces the visitor to each destination's local distinctiveness (EuroVelo 1999). The wider publicity represents an overall imagery which appeals to the expectations or perceived benefits a visitor might receive if they chose to cycle a particular route; recurring themes are nature, culture and well being. However, given the need for the cycle tourist to negotiate a route, maps and guides are also of significance to the visitor as are way-marks (Bloy 1999; Cope 2000). There has been little research on the development and design features of routes in relation to satisfying user needs, most non-motorised facilities are design led (Lumsdon 2001a).

Tourism Transport as an Attraction

Regardless of the growing imperatives of sustainable development highlighted in the literature, tourism planners and funding agencies continue to invest in motorised transport for tourism, for example, the proliferation of fly drive holiday packages and increased highway capacity at the destination. However, the role that walking in particular, but also cycling and other forms of non-motorised transport, have in terms of enhancing inter-modality and raising the quality of the destination requires further examination. There is also a need to evaluate the interconnectivity of transport elements, and to investigate the factors and processes at work within the system which lead to unacceptable levels of externalities and those which enhance the overall appeal of a destination. The concept of transport as a tourism attraction, for example, enables the researcher to explore the integration between different layers of the tourism system. This initial analysis of cycle tourism provides a basis on which to examine the linkages between transport as a tourism experience and the wider transport system. The analysis suggests that the tourism transport experience might well bridge the tourism attractions system as defined by Leiper (1990a) and the tourism transport system.

However, there are also several distinctive aspects which set them apart. Tourism as transport in the main uses a transport system, which is designed on a multi-functional basis to enable people to travel from one place to another regardless of purpose. The greenway between city and countryside, or the riverside cycle route might well be positioned to attract visitors but these pieces of infrastructure are often designed to meet the transport needs of local resident trips too. In a spatial dimension the static visitor attractions do not serve resident communities in a similar way.

Secondly, the nature of the travel itself is important. Whilst non-motorised forms of transport are characterised as short trips this is not necessarily the case in relation to tourism transport. On the supply side, routes or networks are often extensive or lengthy. For example, the Velo verte network in Canada spans 3,400 km, and EuroVelo in Europe which will offer, when complete, 61,709 km of cycleways across Europe. Most of the National Trails in the USA, which are designed primarily for tourism and recreational use, each offer between 1,600 and 4,800 km of continuous linear recreational route (Elkington 1997). Surveys of cycle tourists indicate that the distances covered are lengthier than utilitarian trips (Cope 2003). Richardson (1999), for example, indicates that cycle tourists on a long stay holiday using the Veloland Schweiz network in Switzerland travel an average distance of 303 km per trip in comparison to those on short breaks who cycle 232 km per trip. Day excursionists travel using Veloland Schweiz, the Swiss national cycle tourism network, cycle an average distance of 42 km. This suggests a major difference between the tourism transport and tourism attractions system; the latter assumes that visitors will travel short distances to a particular site in line with the principles of the travel cost decay model. In contrast, tourism transport is designed to encourage visitors to traverse a destination area or region as an attraction. Hence, the aim is to disperse visitor demand spatially, albeit on a linear basis, and to regard travel as a consumer benefit.

Another important distinction between the two systems is the nature of visitor motivation and degree of satisfaction which is derived from an element of tourism transport. Cycle tourism requires a degree of physical activity and the degree of intrinsic satisfaction in visiting a destination is enjoyed in this particular way. The extent to which cycle tourism brings about a new state of "creative leisure" (Leiper 1990b: 372) has not as yet been explored in the literature. The concept of flow as developed by Csikzentmihalyi & Csikzentmihalyi (1988) and discussed within the context of tourism by Ryan (1995) could be a useful tool of analysis in developing this line of research enquiry. The concept would measure the extent to which different types of cycle tourists become absorbed in the process, i.e. by forgetting of self and developing feelings of freedom from the cycling experience. It would be an equally useful addition to research in other forms of non-motorised tourism transport. Transport *as* tourism warrants investigation as part of the tourism attractions system, both at a destination region and resort level, but bearing in mind that it is also as a part of the overall transport system.

Conclusion

In the case of non-motorised forms of transport, there has always been an interest to market transport *as* tourism from the days of the pilgrimages through to early decades of the 20th century. Witness the rich iconography of the bus and railway companies, at the time, extolling the virtues of walking and cycling. Given the growth of tourism, the extent to which cycle tourism, walking and surface passenger transport, can be integrated into the process of sustainable tourism development is likely to be one of the fundamental challenges of the

21st century. This will extend the multi-disciplinary research agenda to the analysis of space for non-motorised modes and increased demands for car free spaces in cities (Inayatullah 2003). There is also a growing interest in what happens when visitors pause from their travel, in how they spend their time and disposable income when visiting a destination (Downward & Lumsdon 2000). Perhaps, there is also a need for additional research to examine, at a destination rather than a specific route level, the value of non-motorised transport in order to establish its position within the tourism sector. It is an area which deserves far greater attention in tourism and transport research than currently afforded.

References

Archambault, M., Giguére, N., & Joly, P. (1997). *Les retombées de la Route verte*. Montréal, Université du Québec à Montréal.

Barwell, I. (1996). *Transport and the village: Findings from African village-level travel and transport surveys and related studies*. World Bank Paper 344, Washington, DC: World Bank.

Becken, S., Simmons, D. G., & Frampton, C. (2003). Energy use associated with different travel choices. *Tourism Management, 24*, 267–277.

Bloy, D. (1999). *Cycle route survey, interim findings* (2nd ed.). Leisure Industries Research Centre, Sheffield Hallam University.

Cope, A. (2000). Monitoring cycle tourism on the C2C cycle route during 1999. University of Sunderland.

Cope, A. M., Doxford, D., & Hill, A. I. (1998). Monitoring tourism on the U.K.'s first long-distance cycle route. *Journal of Sustainable Tourism, 6*(3), 210–223.

Countryside Commission (1995). *The market for recreational cycling*. Cheltenham: Countryside Commission.

Couture, D., Jollicoeur, M., & Pronovost, J.-F. (1998). *Bicycling in Québec in 1995 and 1996* (Vol. 1, pp. 25–27). Ministère des Transports, Gouvernement du Québec.

Csikzentmihalyi, M., & Csikzentmihalyi, I. S. (1988). *Optimal experience*. New York: Cambridge University Press.

Cullinane, S. (1997). Traffic management in Britain's national parks. *Transport Reviews, 17*(3), 267–279.

Downward, P. M., & Lumsdon, L. (2000). The demand for day visits, an analysis of visitor spending. *Tourism Economics, 6*(3), 251–261.

Elkington, S. (1997). CRM and the national trails system. *Conservation and Recreational Management, 1*, 3–5.

EuroVelo (1999). *The market for cycle tourism*. Brussels: EuroVelo.

Feldt, A. G. (1996). An index of societal well-being. *Urban Quality Indicators, 1*(3), 8–20.

Forward, S. (2000). *Walking at the beginning of the 21st century, attitudes and motivations*. Walk 21 Taking walking forwards in the 21st century. London, February 21–22.

Froitzheim, T. (1995). *Radwandern als Wirtschaftsfaktor*. Bremen: ADFC.

Gardner, G. (1998). *Transport implications of leisure cycling*. Transport Research Laboratory, Report 339, Crowthorne.

Gitelson, R. (1998). Determining the benefactors of tourism: A case study of a small rural Pennsylvania community. *Tourism Analysis, 3*, 209–214.

Goodall, B. (1988). How tourists choose their holidays: An analytical framework. In: B. Goodwin, P. Hallett, S. Kenny, & G. Stokes (Eds) (1991), *Transport: The New Realism*. Oxford: Transport Studies Unit.

Grimshaw, J. (1998). Quotation cited. In: M. J. Woods (Ed.), *A Strategic Environmental Assessment of the National Cycle Network* (p. 28). Cheddar.

Howard, J. A., & Sheth, J. N. (1969). *The theory of buyer behaviour*. New York: Wiley.

Hundt, G. (1998). Touristische Faahrraadrouten in NRW-Thesen zu einen Maarkenkonzept für Nordrhein-Westfalen, Qualitätssoffensive für den fahrraadtourismus in Nordrhein-Westfalen (p. 29). Düsseldorf: Allgemeiner Deutscher Faahrraad-Club.

Inayatullah, S. (2003). Alternative futures of transport. *Foresight, 5*(1), 34–43.

Jurowski, C., Uysal, M., & Williams, D. R. (1997). A theoretical analysis of host community resident reactions to tourism. *Journal of Travel Research, xxxxvi*(2), 3–12.

Landesverband für Tourismus (1996). Die Radreisenden auf dem Donauradweg, Linz, 3–4.

Leiper, N. (1990a). Tourist attractions systems. *Annals of Tourism, 17*, 384–387.

Leiper, N. (1990b). Tourist attractions systems. *Annals of Tourism, 17*, 372.

Lew, A. (1987). A framework for tourist attraction research. *Annals of Tourism Research, 14*, 533–575.

Lumsdon, L. (2000). Investigating the needs of the recreational cyclist: The experience of the Peak District National Park. *Transport Planning Review, 71*(3), 379–389.

Lumsdon, L. (2001a). Transport and tourism: A sustainable tourism development model. *Journal of Sustainable Tourism, 8*(4), 1–17.

Lumsdon, L. (2001b). Cycling tourism. In: L. Roberts & D. Hall (Eds), *Rural Tourism and Recreation I* (pp. 173–174). Wallingford: CABI.

Lumsdon, L., & Swift, J. S. (2001). *Latin American tourism*. New York: Continuum.

Lumsdon, L. M. (1997). Recreational cycling: Is this the way to stimulate interest I everyday cycling? In: R. Tolley (Ed.), *The Greening of Urban Transport*. Chichester: Wiley.

Lumsdon, L. M. (1999) *EuroVelo the market for cycle tourism*. Brussels: EuroVelo.

Lumsdon, L. M., & Mitchell, J. (1999). Walking, transport and health: Do we have the right prescription? *Health Promotion International, 14*(3), 271–279.

Lumsdon, L. M., & Smith, M. W. (1997). Developing the potential of recreational cycling in the Peak National Park, Velo City 1997 conference proceedings, Barcelona, September 15–19, pp. 511–514.

Lumsdon, L. M., & Tolley, R. S. (1999). Techniques for planning local networks: Developing a walking strategy. *World Transport Policy and Practice, 5*(1), 38–49.

Murray, M., & Graham, B. (1997). Exploring the dialectics of route-based tourism: The Camino de Santiago. *Tourism Management, 18*(8), 513–524.

Oppermann, M. (1997). Predicting destination choice — A discussion of destination loyalty. *Journal of Vacation Marketing, 5*(1), 51–65.

Ortúzar, J. d e D., Iacobelli, A., & Valeze, C. (2000). Estimating demand for a cycleway. *Transportation Research Part A, 34*, 353–373.

Owen, H. (1998). Visions of the future: Cycling and the health of nations, Conference Proceedings Velo Borealis, International Bicycle Conference, Trondheim, June 23–26.

Pearce, P. L. (1994). Tourist-resident impacts: Examples, explanations and emerging solutions. In: W. Theobold (Ed.), *Global Tourism: The Next Decade* (pp. 103–123). Butterworth-Heinemann.

Pronovost, J.-F., & Joly, P. (1998). Economic of a National Bike Route: La Route verte. In: *Pro Bike Pro walk 98 Creating Bicycle Friendly and Walkable Communities: Building for the Next Generation*, Santa Barbara, September 8–11, pp. 249–253.

Rails to Trails Conservancy (1998). RTC White Paper Report: The local economic benefits of rail-trails, Washington.

Richardson (1999). *The 1998 survey of the Veloland Schweiz National Cycling Network*. Veloland Schweiz, Bern.

Ritchie, B. W. (1998). Bicycle Tourism in the South Island of New Zealand: Planning and management issues. *Tourism Management, 19*(6), 567–582.

Ryan, C. (1995). *Researching tourism satisfaction*. London: Routledge.

Ryan, K. (1993). *Trails for the twenty-first century*. Rails to Trails Conservancy. Washington, DC: Island Press.

Seekings, J. (1989). Components of tourism. In: S. Witt, & L. Moutinho (Eds), *Tourism Marketing and Management Handbook* (pp. 57–62). Hemel Hempstead: Prentice-Hall.

Simonsen, P. S., Jørgensen, B., & Robbins, D. (1998). *Cycling tourism* (p. 92). Unit of Tourism Research, Bornholm.

Smith, M. D., & Krannich, R. S. (1998). Tourism dependence and resident attitudes. *Annals of Tourism Research*, *25*(4), 783–802.

Sustrans (1999). Cycle tourism, Sustrans, TT21, Bristol: 1.

Tolley, R. S. (1997). Obstacles to walking and cycling. In: R. S. Tolley (Ed.), *The Greening of Urban Transport* (pp. 3–20). Chichester: Wiley.

Tolley, R. S., Lumsdon, L., & Bickerstaff, K. (2001). The future of walking: A delphi exercise. *Transport Policy*, *4*(1), 301–315.

Tripp, T., & Higginbotham, J. (1998). Developing successful trails, conference proceedings, Pro-Bike, Pro-Walk 98, Santa Barbara, September 8–11, pp. 263–266.

Whitelegg, J. (1993). *Transport for a sustainable future: The case for Europe*. London: Belhaven.

Chapter 12

Tourism Transport: The Green Key Initiative

Les Lumsdon and Elwyn Owen

Introduction

Not only is transport a necessary condition for tourism to exist; it often forms a key part of the tourist experience at the destination (Page 1999). However, whilst this essential element, i.e. the provision of transport infrastructure and operational services, facilitates tourism development, it can also detract from a destination's overall appeal. Therein lies the dilemma. There's a fine balance between increasing access and convenience for the visitor and the degree of attractiveness of a destination in the long term. This is especially the case with rural tourism destinations where scenic quality and peace and quiet are often the key motivations for travel. In this context, the challenge for tourism and transport planners is seemingly straightforward. There is a need to stimulate tourism without generating transport modes which have a heavier environmental impact. In some cases, the discussion might relate primarily to air or sea travel, but for the most part, it is the motor car which presents the greatest challenge for destinations in the 21st century.

However, planning sustainable transport at a destination is not always a universally welcome approach in tourism development. A fundamental tenet of sustainable tourism relates to the need to take into account the views of stakeholders in the community as well as visitors' opinion. The case study presented in this chapter focuses on one recent attempt to do this; it evaluates several of the key issues arising from an attempt to redress the current tourism transport imbalance in the Snowdonia National Park situated in North Wales.

The Dominance of the Car

In North America and most European countries the car remains the major form of transport for tourism. However, there has been a growing recognition of the impacts associated with the car-based tourism, for example, emissions of carbon dioxide, other pollutants, noise, congestion and illicit parking which reduce the quality of the visitor environment (Whitelegg 1993). Whilst much of the debate has focused on the improvement of urban central zones and especially historic quarters (see, for example, the chapter by Orbaşlı & Shaw) there is

Tourism and Transport: Issues and Agenda for the New Millennium
Copyright © 2004 Published by Elsevier Ltd.
ISBN: 0-08-044172-6

an increasing literature which discusses the problems associated with tourist traffic at rural destinations. Within the context of areas of natural beauty, such as national parks in the U.K., the discussion as to which measures are more appropriate and effective have been well rehearsed (Holding & Kreutner 1998). In the main, the response has been to increase the level of public transport provision as an alternative to the car. These measures have enjoyed only moderate success in the U.K. partly because the lack of investment, and in some cases because they have been inadequately marketed (Cullinane *et al.* 1996).

On the other hand, the use of traffic management schemes to restrain traffic by pricing, regulatory or physical means have been less prevalent (Cullinane 1997). While the legislative framework in the U.K. enables traffic reduction or road user charging, there have been few examples of national parks selecting this option. This is despite research findings which suggest that most visitors would be willing to accept rural road pricing, for example, in relation to park and ride schemes in national parks (Harcup 1996; Steiner & Bristow 1999).

Thus, in the U.K., it is argued that the difficulty in attracting car-borne visitors to use other modes of transport is almost insurmountable given the levels of those who are car dependent (RAC 1995). Consequently, several transport studies have investigated the extent to which current attitudes and behavioural patterns can be modified. The findings indicate that different segments of the market can be persuaded to switch modes if acceptable alternatives are provided (Curtis & Headicar 1997). They are clearly applicable to tourism transport, particularly if the transport element adds value to the overall tourism experience.

Perhaps of greater importance is the reluctance of the tourism supply sector to support change. Many recent case studies report a resistance by some stakeholders to change the current pattern of travel at destinations despite the pressing nature of the problems associated with the accommodation of more car-borne travel. In some cases, opposition to innovative transport schemes has come from resident or visitors themselves (such as outdoor pursuits groups), but in many instances, it is the business sector which has been at the forefront of resisting any reduction in car-borne activity on the grounds that it would be detrimental to trade (Dilley 1993; Eaton & Holding 1996).

Wales is no exception to this general rule. It has witnessed a sustained increase in visitation by car in recent decades and given its essentially rural nature there are major issues to address with regard to future transport provision. Thus, over 90% of Wales' domestic holiday staying visitors arrive by car or camper van (Wales Tourist Board 2000). The problems associated with this level of car-borne tourism are now clearly recognised;

> The scale of tourist pressure, and especially its geographical concentration, poses a serious threat to the fabric of historic towns, leisure facilities and countryside which attract visitors in the greatest numbers. If these special areas are to be conserved, greater encouragement must be given to the provision of efficient and co-ordinated public transport for visitors and the promotion of alternative modes of transport. Innovative thinking on ways to increase access in the countryside, allied where necessary to management of non-essential traffic is needed.
>
> (Welsh Office 1998, para 8.11)

Key Issues

It is in this context that organisations entrusted with tourism development are re-appraising approaches to the provision of tourism transport. General policy guidance is to encourage sustainable tourism transport initiatives that seek to assuage current problems, which are otherwise expected to worsen. For example, *Achieving Our Potential — A Tourism Strategy for Wales* recognises that:

> ...the issue of transport's impact on the environment, and particularly the high density use of private cars, will grow in importance. It will be necessary, therefore, to identify opportunities to promote acceptable transport alternatives for visitors to Wales by providing greater choice and information to the visitor.
>
> (Wales Tourist Board 1999: 58)

This paper refers to the development of a sustainable tourism transport initiative in the Snowdonia National Park and specifically pays attention to the way in which community participation in the process can be evaluated. The chapter considers the issues that can arise in managing multi-agency projects, where the interests of stakeholders do not always coincide and it concludes by considering the lessons arising from the *Snowdonia Green Key Initiative* for future schemes to reduce car dependency among visitors to vulnerable areas.

Of the three national parks in Wales, the Snowdonia National Park is the busiest. It features a range of magnificent mountains truncated by wide valleys and narrow passes. These give way to wooded foothills and a narrow coastal strip. The Park features a diversity of landscapes and wildlife habitats which hold strong appeal to the visitor. The thinly populated area comprises mainly isolated farming communities with most residents living in the old slate mining communities or coastal towns such as Bangor and Caernarvon. One estimate is that 6.6 million visitor days are spent in the Park each year; approximately 92% of these visits are made by car (Coalter *et al.* 1996). A major issue, which had been discussed in recent years, has been the trade off between the environmental impact of the car, especially by day visitors, in relation to economic gain brought by visitor expenditure in the locality. For example, the 1994 All Parks Survey in Snowdonia indicated that over 10% of visitors in cars did not spend any money in the Park during their visit (Centre for Leisure and JMP Consultants Ltd., 1995). There has also been concern that the benefits are not spread evenly across the communities situated in the Park;

> Despite 500,000 people reaching the summit of Snowdon each year, certain communities within the shadow of the mountain are now some of the most economically deprived parts of Wales. GDP per head in parts of Northern Snowdonia is nearly 30% below the U.K. and EU averages.
>
> (Ogden 2001: 1)

Forecasts of demand suggest that flows of traffic will increase between 15 and 20% during the next 20 years and that this will have a serious effect on both the natural attraction of the Park but also increase impacts such as illicit parking, congestion at "honeypot" locations, noise and additional pollution. Within this context attention has focused on how car-borne tourism can be managed to minimise environmental damage and to maximise social and economic impacts?

In response to this question a consortium of statutory agencies, local authorities[1] and other bodies proposed a pioneering and innovative scheme aimed at achieving sustainable rural development whilst seeking to manage car-borne tourism, a scheme which was entitled *The Snowdonia Green Key Initiative* (GKI). Its aim is to stimulate new business and tourism opportunities, coupled with improved environmental management, through developing a network of efficient, flexible and integrated transport alternatives to car travel in Northern Snowdonia. Much of the research and strategic framework which forms the basis of this initiative had been the subject of a detailed analysis in a report published in 1988, known as The Northern Snowdonia Study. It is important to note, in this context, that GKI is primarily about sustainable development and is not simply a scheme to reduce the excesses of traffic in sensitive areas within the Snowdonia National Park. In this respect, The Northern Snowdonia Study described the vision which inspired GKI;

> Our vision for the future of North Snowdonia is of an area of high landscape value where tourism makes a major contribution to the economic, social and cultural wellbeing of host communities, without placing in jeopardy the very resources and assets upon which its appeal is founded. In short, we see it as an area which has grasped the principles of sustainable development, seeing them as aids rather than barriers to progress.
>
> (Northern Snowdonia Study, 1998: 49)

The core elements identified in the Northern Snowdonia strategy, however, referred primarily to the way in which transport can be managed in order to enhance the overall tourism experience, i.e. it embraced the assumption that the cornerstone of sustainable development is dependent on car reduction. Thus, the strategy was advanced in terms of five main strands which would seek to reduce traffic while at the same time improve the social and economic fabric of tourism areas. They were to:

(1) Create a zone of controlled parking with rural clearways on the main highways. This would severely restrict linear roadside parking throughout the area;
(2) Devise a bus network which is integrated with rail connections and walking and cycling opportunities in order to encourage modal switch;
(3) Develop several park and ride "gateways" and public transport "gateways" where interchange is encouraged. The gateways would offer enhanced facilities and opportunities to encourage visitor spending;
(4) Introduce a "positive parking" scheme to manage car parking provision more effectively. There would be clearly signed official parking areas which are integrated with the public transport network. It was envisaged that the scheme could be marketed as a package;
(5) Enhance promotional activity with a "Pass Snowdonia" which would include a long stay parking fee and an all-system bus ticket entitling a visitor(s) to unlimited travel.

The study team recognised that whilst many of the technical aspects of the strategy had been tried and tested elsewhere, such a combination of initiatives within a tourism zone in a national park would be considered radical within the context of the U.K. Similar schemes in the continental Europe and in North America had been implemented with a degree of success but a development of this scale had not been envisaged in any of the national parks of England and Wales. The consultants also indicated that there would be mixed reactions from different sections of the community to the strategy depending on such factors as proximity to the scheme, involvement in tourism, etc. It was therefore expected that the introduction would be gradual and in stages; it would be a long term implementation process. The report also provided details of how tourism-orientated businesses could gain from the process and a number of indicative sustainable tourism projects which could be developed in parallel to the main framework. In order to verify the level economic impact estimated in this first study, the consortium engaged another consultancy to re-appraise the proposals. Newidiem (2000) duly re-affirmed the benefits likely to accrue from a sustainable tourism strategy which addressed the management of car travel through the area.

The core elements of these two studies formed the basis on which the Green Key Initiative was prepared for a second wave of public consultation. The overall goal of GKI remained the prospect of sustainable rural development;

> that is to ensure that tourism helps to sustain thriving local communities and economies without compromising the area's unique environmental and cultural characteristics. Such a goal will only be achieved if economic and in particular future tourism development is linked to management of the environment.

The key elements were outlined in discussion documents explaining the following five approaches:

(1) To develop new tourist facilities of high quality at a series of inner gateway towns, namely Llanberis, Bethesda, Llanrwst, Betws-y-coed and Porthmadog. In addition, improved services would be provided at communities such as Capel Curig, Beddgelert, Rhyd Ddu and Waunfawr.
(2) Re-vitalise and extend the bus system linking attractions and mountain walking areas to the larger towns and railheads.
(3) Establish improved public transport interchanges at outer gateway centres such as Bangor and Caernarfon as well as those at the inner gateway towns at the same time as other facilities are advanced.
(4) Development a strategic cycle route network linking settlements and transport interchanges to attractions.
(5) Reorganise in a progressive manner existing car parking in the core mountainous areas of the Park and gateways in line with seasonal variations and the needs of different type of visitors.

The initiative was therefore subjected to a more lengthy and wider public consultation exercise in August 2001. A detailed proposal was made available on the internet and in leaflet and booklet form throughout public locations in the area. It was soon to evoke polarised and very strongly expressed views. Proponents viewed it as a bold and imaginative scheme which would benefit the visitor, the host community and the environment. Several local businesses and user groups, on the other hand, were extremely concerned about the proposals, believing that they would severely restrict the freedom of visitors and that they would damage rather than enhance the economic well being of the area.

Faced with mounting opposition, the promoters of *the Snowdonia Green Key Initiative* decided that the scheme would have to be fundamentally reassessed. It therefore commissioned a third report by RPS Planning, Transport and Environment in January 2002 which provided a critical appraisal of the previous studies. The RPS report recommended the retention of GKI but not in its existing format. RPS also concurred with the view of the previous studies that the development of sustainable tourism could make a significant contribution to the local economy. However, the revised strategy in the RPS report effectively dismantled the core elements of GKI. Instead it recommended a set of measures which:

(a) excludes park and ride;
(b) advocates the retention of existing car parking with improved landscaping;
(c) suggests that increased car parking provision might be appropriate, especially in some of the towns and near the start of popular walks;
(d) recommends the rejuvenation of a dedicated but limited "Sherpa" bus service rather than the wider system of integration envisaged previously;
(e) suggests improved walking and cycling routes which is the only dimension of GKI which seems to have enjoyed universal approval by consultants and opponents of the scheme.

The report, in effect, advocates a collection of approaches favoured by a small group of lobbyists who have combined forces to see the reversal of the proposals presented in the *Snowdonia Green Key Initiative*.

What lessons can be learned by this review of the approach to date? The *Snowdonia Green Key Initiative* has to date involved at least three studies by independent consultants. These are helpful in charting the history of the initiative. They also provide a valuable insight of the techniques used to ascertain the views of key stakeholders at the initial research stage and subsequently to consult members of the community on the draft strategy proposed by the *Green Key Partnership*. The final section of the paper refers to these approaches to participation and in particular in relation to the efficacy of focus groups in the context of this type of study.

Indicative Findings

The literature suggests that residents of communities that attract visitors have a wide range of opinions about proposed developments in their area (Mason & Cheyne 2000). The studies reported on in this case used a variety of techniques to elicit stakeholder opinions. They included focus groups, public meetings and face-to-face interviews with key personnel. Of all of the approaches, the focus group technique is perhaps the most widely used of the qualitative research techniques and was used in the Northern Snowdonia study and in the subsequent RPS study. In tourism studies such as these, this is an appropriate technique to utilise as it involves open discussion and reflection on issues of mutual concern (Goss 1996). The benefits associated with the focus group approach are well documented in the literature (Frey & Fontana 1993; Kreuger 1988). These include the potential to encourage a sharing of insights, the stimulation of discussion which leads to either consensus or clearly defined disagreement, and the generation of knowledge from participants with detailed experience of the tourism area and its particular problems. Thus, the researchers in the Northern Snowdonia study held a view that the focus group would help to build a more accurate picture of the social reality of local people rather than a series of individual interviews or an empirical survey of a sample of resident population.

According to the study team's interim report, the aim of the focus group programme was as follows:

> The principal aim of these meetings was to inform and advise the study process by eliciting the views of individuals living or working within the study area or having some other interest in the study, thereby supplementing other forms of information gathering. It was further hoped that the meetings would help create a greater awareness of the issues being considered within the study, coupled with a sense of ownership of the conclusions and recommendations that might emerge from it. These were not public consultation meeting in the sense that were consulting on specific recommendations.
> (Northen Snowdonia Study, Report of Local Forum Meetings, 1998)

It is well recognised that selection of the focus panel is the key to success, certainly in terms of the quality of the material gathered during the process. In this case, the groups were selected with considerable care The aim was to encourage participation by a wide range of organisations including the community councils, community, voluntary and trader interests. Meetings were held in six communities: Beddgelert, Capel Curig, Betws-y-Coed, Bethesda, Llanberis and Waunfawr. These were chosen because they suffer from traffic-related impacts. A bilingual Issues Report was given to the 80 attendees prior to each meeting so that they could consider the issues and potential solutions. Participants were encouraged to express their views in the language of their choice and with minimum intervention by the moderator. The discussion at each meeting was recorded and the transcripts analysed in due course.

The moderator recorded a diversity of opinion but felt that it was possible to categorise the opinions expressed into three groups — the rejectors, the unconvinced and the open minded. The rejectors were a small minority who were opposed to the notion of developing new park and ride schemes primarily because they restrict freedom, as reflected in the view of one respondent;

> You have to be careful not to penalise visitors. Tourism is going to be a bigger factor in the future. People want to escape from the cities, to do as they please

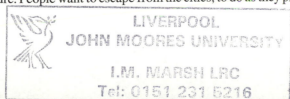

and they are very reluctant to be organised. Some may feel intimidated and
decide that Snowdonia is not a place they want to visit.

[Focus group-Betws-y-Coed]

The second group accounted for about half of the participants involved in the groups. Whilst
they appreciated the need for visitor management they felt that park and rides or restriction
of car access would not lead to a transfer from cars to other forms of transport as the
motorists would be reluctant to switch to what was in reality a less convenient alternative.
Furthermore, this group felt that such a scheme would be costly for local communities. The
feeling was expressed as follows:

People want to get to more remote areas. A bus service won't solve the
problem. You will not get people leaving their car in order to take the bus,
say, to the foot of Moel Hebog, knowing that they've got to get back at
exactly 3.30 pm to catch the bus back. It is a nice thought — but you won't
get people doing it.

[A comment from the Beddgelert group]

The third group was smaller but recognised that something had to be done to improve traffic
management in Snowdonia as otherwise matters were likely to get worse. They were of the
opinion that park and ride or something similar would be attractive to the visitor:

It's got to happen, hasn't it? Common sense tells us that something has to be
done. But it has to be done in a way that doesn't antagonise people. If you
have to drive around for hours finding a car park, then stand in the rain for
hours waiting for a full bus to arrive, with all the windows steamed up and
chewing gum on the seats, then it is never going to work.

[Comment from the group member at Bethesda]

A number of important themes emerged from the groups. Firstly, the participants did not
feel there was a problem of widespread congestion. They considered that the issue of traffic
congestion prevails only in relation to a number of localities and during peak times only.
However, indiscriminate parking was perceived as a major problem. The combined solutions
of gateway communities and park and ride achieved some degree of support but this was
tinged by scepticism about its prospect of success and the level of public funding that might
be necessary.

This approach was complemented by other forms of feedback including an invitation
for organisations and individuals to respond to the Issues Report which was widely
circulated via community facilities and local media. This elicited 31 written responses,
21 from individuals and 10 from organisations. Furthermore, face-to-face interviews
were conducted with local authorities and a wide range of stakeholder organisations. The
limitations of the method are discussed.

The RPS study team undertook a similar exercise in 2002 with public meetings held in
Beddgelert, Bethesda, Betws-y-Coed, Capel Curig, Llanberis, Llanwrst and Porthmadog
followed by focus groups. These were augmented by discussions with activity user groups

and trader-based organisations such as "Freedom to Choose" and "Snowdonia Active." The conclusions drawn from these group discussions were very different. The participants opposed GKI on the basis of the park and ride and rural clearway proposals primarily. Other elements such as the overall environmental and economic objectives enjoyed general support. The entire direction of consultation had changed in scale, content and direction.

It is worthwhile, at this stage of the analysis to reflect on why this might be the case.

One first observation is that the reaction against the strategy was to be expected as given the pressure applied by a number of groups. What is interesting is that in Snowdonia there had been a reversal of the roles of the identified stakeholders. Earlier tourism studies invariably reported that residents have concerns about institutions imposing a "tourism advocacy platform" (Jafari 1990). In this respect, parking and traffic congestion are often cited as key problems in studies of residents in national parks. For example, in a study of Bakewell in the Peak District National Park residents were supportive of tourism in general. However, traffic congestion was highlighted as one of two main negative factors (Ryan & Montgomery 1994). In this case, user groups and trading concerns are arguing the opposite, i.e. that there needs to be greater access for car-borne visitors:

> There are only four main roads in this scheme, all trunk roads, and almost all their length is clearway, either in fact or in safe practice. Provision for the tourist is minimal, much of it in the form of cut-offs from road improvements not planned in response to tourism. To confiscate this access is to rob us of what little remains. The reverse policy is the solution, opening up whole new areas.
>
> (Freedom to Choose 2002: 1)

There may well be particular circumstances in this case which explain the position. This follows the lean times for tourism after the impacts of the Foot and Mouth crisis. At another level, the positions held by some organisations and the national park may have led to this unusual situation. For whatever reason, there is a degree of irony in the situation. Elsewhere in Wales similar combinations of residents have been campaigning to stop the development of "sustainable" recreational routes such as in the Vale of Clwyd and the lower Wye Valley on the grounds that such routes will encourage more cars, illicit car parking and disturb sensitive habitats and quiet local communities.

A second major implication is that while focus groups provide a broad canvas of opinion across different communities this balanced feedback can be over-ridden when the particular views of user groups or resident action groups are well articulated at public meetings, through electronic media and the local media. In the case of GKI, one organisation was established "Freedom to Choose-Snowdonia Group" to oppose the strategy. "Freedom to Choose" describes itself as:

> a body comprised of both local residents and people from outside Snowdonia representing a wide range of interests who are bound together by deep concern for the future of Snowdonia and the quality of experience that it can provide.
>
> (Freedom to Choose 2002: 1)

The group's policy statement comments that there is no traffic movement problem in Northern Snowdonia and that roadside parking is essential to the freedom of the individual. The statement also emphasises that a compulsory park and ride scheme is:

> ill conceived and unworkable because most mountaineers, hill walkers, etc. wish to be at their start point e.g. Pen y Pass or Ogwen at the same time, i.e. between 8 am and 9.30 am and to be picked up around dusk . . . In addition, the scheme also ignores the needs of the huge numbers of visitors who neither climb or hike and simply wish to enjoy the scenery, picnic, take photographs, etc. These people would never use a park and ride scheme.
>
> (Freedom to Choose 2002: 1)

Many other individuals and users groups such as mountaineering clubs have since posted similar messages on websites and there has been a deluge in letters and e-mails to the national park offices during the early months of 2002. The main issue has become the park and ride scheme and comments in relation to other aspects have been minimal. There has been a lack of familiarity, interest or both in relation to the other elements of the strategy. In effect, the entire consultation phase has centred on one issue as a result of a well-orchestrated campaign by a small number of groups.

Implications

The case of the *Snowdonia Green Key Initiative* focuses on the practical problems that can arise when techniques such as focus groups are used to provide information and policy guidance on controversial subjects. The representation of the attitudes and opinions of the six communities involved in the preparation of the northern Snowdonia study suggested a scenario of mixed opinion with some degree of scepticism and even antipathy toward the National Park Authority. Nevertheless, the groups signalled a broad consensus that there was a need to address problems such as parking that some form of public transport scheme could be progressed over a medium to long-term time scale.

However, where there is significant media interest and deep concern within some sections of the community about the consequences of seeking to change established patterns of user behaviour, focus group feedback can be overshadowed. There are a number of implications for those involved in the design and planning or tourism schemes which seek to include some form of car reduction. Firstly, it is important that residents, user groups and traders are well informed from an early stage. Recent discussions with practitioners suggest that those who are reactionary to such schemes are faster responders than supporters or proponents. The lack of understanding of the key elements of such strategies and how they relate can clearly lead to an adverse reaction among residents but in particular by clusters of interest groups such as traders or users. It is significant that throughout its evolution the Snowdonia Green Key Initiative was seen as being driven solely by the National Park Authority for narrow conservation reasons, despite the fact that it had been devised by a partnership comprising two local authorities and two economic development agencies.

The critical role of public consultation needs to involve a range of qualitative research techniques, especially focus groups or panels which can identify community issues and provide insights which would otherwise not be forthcoming. They also serve the purpose to provide information and generate levels of interest or commitment. However, in "controversial" projects, it might be best to undertake empirical survey work, based on the establishment for example of a panel of residents selected at random prior to the commencement of a major consultation exercise. The panel could be surveyed on a continuous basis throughout the process to assess the extent to which opinions change throughout the process. In this way, it would be possible to evaluate opinions from different sections of the community which can form a benchmark by which views of interested parties can be measured.

There are several other research implications which this initial study highlights. There is clearly a need to identify and measure the level of impacts associated with different modes of transport in relation to levels of spending in the locality. Furthermore, it would also be useful for policy makers to understand better the complexities of stakeholder participation in the tourism development process in the case of larger scale initiatives. The collection of a range of case studies, which can be evaluated within the context of tourism transport schemes, might allow lessons to be learned for future development (Baum 1999).

Conclusion

The Snowdonia Green Key Initiative is one of several innovative tourism transport schemes proposed in Wales in recent years. It is important that such schemes are subject to public consultation in order that different groups of stakeholders can make an input to the process. However, the extent to which tried and tested research approaches such as the use of focus groups are sufficiently robust in circumstances when intense lobbying activity distorts the process is questionable. The process of consultation in Snowdonia continues; it was announced by the Chairman of the Snowdonia Green Key Executive Group in April 2002;

> From now on, this Initiative, if it is to succeed in its purpose must be developed with the co-operation and active support of the local community and in close consultation with all interested parties.
> (Snowdonia Green Key Partnership Press 2002: 1)

Whether or not this will reflect feedback from all sections of the community remains to be seen but the prospects for a sustainable transport tourism experience in Snowdonia do not augur well at this stage.

Note

1. The Executive Members of the Snowdonia Green Key Initiative Consortium comprised: Conwy County Borough Council, Countryside Council for Wales, Gwynedd Council, Snowdonia National Park Authority, Wales Tourist Board and Welsh Development Agency.

References

Baum, T. (1999). Human resource concerns in European tourism: Strategic response and the EC. *International Journal of Hospitality Management, 12*(1), 18–31.

Bishop, K., Owen, R. Elwyn, Speakman, C., & Wilde P. (1998). *Northern Snowdonia Study – developing local economic opportunities through the management of visitor traffic.* Environmental Planning Research Unit, Cardiff University.

Centre for Leisure Research and JMP Consultants Ltd. (1995). *The 1994 all parks visitor survey: Report of the survey in Snowdonia National Park* (Vol. 11). Edinburgh: Centre for Leisure Research.

Coalter, F., MacGregor, C., & Denman, R. (1996). *Visitors to national parks.* Cheltenham: Countryside Commission and Countryside Council for Wales, CCP 503.

Cullinane, S. (1997). Traffic management in Britain's national parks. *Transport Reviews, 17*(3), 267–279.

Cullinane, S., Cullinane, K., & Fewings, J. (1996). Traffic management in Dartmoor National Park: Lessons to be learned. *Traffic Engineering and Control, 39*(10), 572–576.

Curtis, C., & Headicar, P. (1997). Targeting travel awareness campaigns. *Transport Policy, 4*(1), 57–65.

Dilley, R. S. (1993). Roads and traffic in the English Lake District National Park, problems and planning options. *Tourism Recreation Research, 18*(1), 33–37.

Eaton, B., & Holding, D. M. (1996). The evaluation of public transport alternatives to the car in British National Parks. *Journal of Transport Geography, 4*(1), 55–65.

Freedom to Choose (2002). Freedom to Choose — Snowdonia Group: Policy statement. http://www.snowdonia2002.fsnet.co.uk/English/ftc-s-policy.htm, 1 (accessed 18/08/02).

Freedom to Choose (2002). Freedom to Choose — Snowdonia Group: Policy statement. http://www.snowdonia2002.fsnet.co.uk/English/observation2.htm, 1 (accessed 18/08/02).

Frey, J. H., & Fontana, A. (1993). The group interview in social research. In: D. L. Morgan (Ed.), *Successful Focus Groups: Advancing the State of the Art* (pp. 20–34). Newbury Park: Sage.

Goss, J. D. (1996). Focus groups as alternative research practice: Experience with transmigrants in Indonesia. *Area, 28*(2), 115–123.

Harcup, A. (1996). National car parks. *The Surveyor*, January 18, 26–27.

Holding, D. M., & Kreutner, M. (1998). Achieving a balance between carrots and sticks for traffic in National Parks: The Bayerischer Wald Project. *Transport Policy, 5,* 175–183.

Jafari, J. (1990). Research and scholarship: The basis of education. *Journal of Tourism Studies, 1*(1), 33–41.

Kreuger, R. A. (1988). *Focus groups: A practical guide for applied research.* London: Sage.

Mason, P., & Cheyne, J. (2000). Residents' attitudes to proposed tourism development. *Annals of Tourism Research, 27*(2), 391–411.

Newidiem (2000). *Economic Impact Analysis of Northern Snowdonia Study.* Unpublished consultancy report. Newidiem, Cardiff.

Northern Snowdonia Study Team (1998). *Northern Snowdonia Study: Report of Local Forum Meetings.* Environmental Planning Research Unit, Cardiff University.

Ogden, P. (2001). *Access to Snowdonia — The Snowdonia Green Key Initiative.* Tourism without Traffic, Birmingham, September 13th, 1–8.

Page, S. (1999). *Transport for tourism.* London: Routledge.

RAC (1995). Foundation for motoring and the environment. In: *Car Dependence* (p. 15). Basingstoke: Royal Automobile Association.

RPS Planning, Transport and Environment (2002). *Snowdonia Green Key Initiative Re-appraisal Report.* Unpublished consultancy report.

Ryan, C., & Montgomery (1994). The attitudes of Bakewell residents to tourism development. *Tourism Management, 15,* 358–369.

Snowdonia Green Key Partnership Press Statement (2002). http://www.snowdonia2002.fsnet.co.uk/English/SGK_Partnership_Press_Statement1.h (accessed 18/08/02).

Steiner, T. J., & Bristow, A. L. (1999). Road pricing in national parks: A case study in the Yorkshire Dales National Park. *Transport Policy*, 93–103.

Wales Tourist Board (1999). *Achieving our potential, a tourism strategy for Wales*. Cardiff: Wales Tourist Board.

Wales Tourist Board (2000). *Summary of statistics*. Cardiff: Wales Tourist Board.

Welsh Office (1998). *Transporting Wales into the future*. Cardiff: Welsh Office.

Whitelegg, J. (1993). *Transport for a sustainable future: The case for Europe*. London: Belhaven.

Author Index

Subject Index